PMP Exam Prep Made Simple

The Comprehensive Guide to Passing the Exam on Your First Try

Alex Westwood

Contents

Introduction-The Exam

WHAT THE EXAM TESTS:

Before we get into what the PMP certification exam really tests, let me clear up some common misunderstandings regarding the exam.

The PMP certification exam does not cover the following topics:

- Your project management knowledge or expertise

- Your good judgment

- Your understanding of industry procedures

- Your understanding of software tools

- What you learnt in business school

- Your intellect

The PMP certification exam includes the following questions:

- Your understanding of PMI's methods

- Your comprehension of the many words used to describe the processes

- Your capacity to put such procedures to use in a range of scenarios

- Your ability to apply important formulae to issues like as scheduling, costing, estimating, and others.

A PASSING GRADE:

Not to terrify you, but the cold, hard reality is that many people who take the PMP Exam fail. Those who do not pass represent a diverse group of people, ranging from those who approached the test with substantial study, including books and training programs, to those who put in little effort. You are tipping the balance in your favor by utilizing this book!

Although PMI no longer provides the precise pass score, it is expected that you must properly answer at least 106 of the 175 graded questions on the exam (more on graded questions later). That amounts to 61 percent, and if you think that 61 percent is not very outstanding, realize that this test revision is more difficult. 61 percent is an excellent result, although tens of thousands of project managers fail the exam each year.

Some individuals struggle to comprehend why they can not study and get a flawless score on the PMP. It is natural to want to perform well on the test, but given the massive amount of content, even passing it is a huge achievement! Experts differ on some of the questions, and you will undoubtedly miss several that you are positive you answered correctly. This has less to do with your study effort, intellectual aptitude, or test-taking talents and more to do with how the questions are created and presented.

When taking the PMP, your objective should be to perform your very best while staying within PMI's passing score boundaries.

THE EXAM MATERIAL:

Your PMP Exam will have more than 175 questions spanning a wide range of topics, but only 175 of them will contribute toward your score. The remaining 25 questions are considered experimental questions that PMI is testing for future tests. The good news is that these 25 questions will not affect your grade. The bad news is that since the questions are distributed randomly throughout the test, you will never know which ones count and which do not.

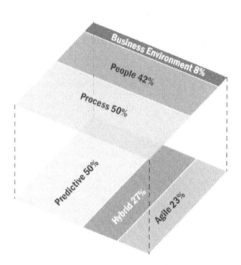

PMI does provide some rules for how the content should be delivered. On January 2, 2021, the test was extensively revised. The test contains approach questions regarding predictive, or classic waterfall, projects, agile projects, and hybrid projects, which combine predictive and agile techniques. The test is likewise divided into three sections: process, people, and business environment. The graphic above depicts the test coverage ratios for these two thematic viewpoints of the question kinds. The tables below indicate the numerical split of questions.

Category	# of Questions	% of Exam
Process	87	50%
People	74	42%
Business Environment	14	8%
Total:	175	100%
Category	# of Questions	% of Exam
Predictive	87	50%
Hybrid	47	27%
Agile	41	23%
Total:	175	100%

The methodologies shown (predictive, agile, and hybrid) will be used throughout the test in the domains demonstrated (process, people, and business environment). The questions posed by approach will not be limited to a single area.

Many test candidates are taken aback by this fact:

The PMBOK® Guide (pronounced "pim'-bock") is not a single study resource for the PMP® exam.

The current PMBOK® Guide does not provide information for the test question breakdown in the thematic perspectives indicated above. Although the information supplied is a great description and presentation of the project management processes, knowledge domains, and related process groups, it does not provide much assistance in determining how that content will convert to the test. Many people who failed the PMP® Exam attempted to utilize the PMBOK® Tool as a study guide and were astonished to find questions, phrases, and concepts on the exam that were not in the PMBOK® Guide. Furthermore, agile and hybrid ideas, which account for 50% of the new test, are treated relatively sparsely in the current PMBOK® Guide.

The book's chapters are divided according to the process framework—knowledge areas and process groups. Initiating, planning, executing, monitoring and regulating, and closing are the process group words. To emphasize differences for test preparation, information regarding agile projects and methodologies is interwoven throughout the text. Each knowledge area chapter also finishes with a section on agile perspectives.

GETTING TO THE TEST (APPLICATION)

It is strongly advised that you join the Project Management Institute before signing up for the exam. The new member charge was $139.00 at the time of publishing ($129.00 membership + $10.00 new member activation fee). You may apply online at www.pmi.org, or you can get an application from PMI by calling (610) 356-4600.

You will obtain a membership number after joining PMI, which you may use to earn a $150.00 reduction on the exam's non-member charge, so you can save money right away by enrolling. For a member in good standing, the examination fee will be $405.00. If you do not want to join PMI, applying to take the exam will cost $555.00.

Aside from the financial gain, there are several additional advantages to joining PMI, such as a subscription to PMI's magazines, PM Network and PM Today; discounts on books and PMI-sponsored events; and access to a plethora of project management material.

When you are ready to apply for PMP certification eligibility, you may do it online or on paper. You should apply online if at all feasible. Wait periods for printed applications via the mail have been known to extend out for weeks depending on the time of year, but online candidates often report response times of one to two weeks. The amount of time might vary based on the number of applications processed by PMI. To sit for the PMP certification test, you must receive a letter of eligibility from PMI.

You must show that you satisfy certain basic requirements to be eligible for PMP certification. The current credentials required by PMI are given here.

In brief, if you have a university degree, apply in the first category. If not, apply under the second option. More information on this topic may be found in PMI's official handbook, which is accessible online at www.pmi.org.

Minimum Requirements to Apply with a College Diploma

- A University Degree

- 36 months (3 years) of project management experience

- Project management education for 35 hours (note that the online class included on the key card in the back of this book can provide you with eight of those contact hours)

Minimum Requirements to Apply without a College Diploma

- A High school diploma or equivalent

- 60 months (5 years) of project management experience

- 35 hours of project management education

ONGOING EDUCATION

PMPs must show not just their knowledge and expertise, but also their continued dedication to the profession of project management. To encourage such dedication, PMI mandates all PMPs to renew their certification every 36 months by completing at least 60 Professional Development Units (PDUs). The standards for PDUs are outlined in further depth in the PMI Continuing Certification Requirements Program Handbook, which is distributed to all PMPs, and these requirements are similar in nature to those imposed by the legal, medical, and other professions. To keep this certification valuable, PMI expects PMPs to have a project management concentration and a continuing dedication to the profession of project management.

THE TESTING ENVIRONMENT

The PMP certification test is given in a formal setting. There is no talking allowed during the test, and you are not permitted to bring notes, books, paper, mobile phones, PDAs, or calculators inside the examination room. The PMP is a "high-stakes" or "high-security" test that is closely monitored. The test proctor is continually watching and recording video and audio of the exam takers. This may be both distracting and unsettling, so it is important to be psychologically prepared before you enter the test.

The test is done on a Windows-based PC that is running a secure, proprietary testing program. The computer setup is quite basic, consisting just a mouse and keyboard, as well as a minimal graphical user interface to show the exam. PMI may make special arrangements for test-takers with certain physical requirements. Though PMI has given a paper version of the exam for test-takers who do not reside near a testing location, they have also supplied an online version of the computerized exam to be conducted under strict security limits. The exam topic is the same in each situation, and your preparation should be the same. More information about test possibilities is available at www.pmi.org.

The test concludes when the 4-hour time restriction is met (more on this later) or when you want to terminate it. A 10-minute break is offered around halfway through the online test option. It is not authorized to return after the break to examine or amend the first-half questions. After the test, you will know your score in a matter of seconds, and the results will be instantly transferred to PMI. If you passed, you are now a "PMP," and you may begin using that title after your name. Within a few weeks, PMI will send you all of the official material, including your PMP lapel pin and certificate. If you do not pass the test the first time, you may retake it up to three times in a calendar year. If you do not pass on your third try, you must wait one year before reapplying.

THE TIME LIMIT

Taking an exam with the time ticking may be nerve-racking. The PMP Exam is a lengthy exam, but you are given plenty of time to finish it. You will have 240 minutes (4 hours) to complete the test from the moment you begin it. This is sufficient time for most individuals to complete the exam and evaluate the answers. If no breaks are taken, the allotment comes out to 72 seconds per question. While some of the more difficult questions will undoubtedly take more than 72 seconds, the majority will take significantly less time.

QUESTION FORMATS

The majority of the questions are in multiple choice style, with four potential responses labeled A, B, C, and D, and only one of those four choices is right. New question types, such as multiple-select (choose all 4-6 answers that apply), matching, and choosing the proper location or region on an image, have been added. Because there is no penalty for guessing on the PMP Exam, it is in your best interest to answer every question and leave no blanks.

The style of many of the questions is very brief; nonetheless, the PMP Exam is renowned (or notorious) for its lengthy, twisting questions that are difficult to comprehend. This book contains examples of various question formats to help you prepare. Going through all of the example questions in this book is a great approach to be ready for the sorts of questions you will see on the real test.

Success Secrets

1. PROVEN STRATEGIES TO correctly answer the PMP® exam questions

After spending months preparing for the PMP® exam with courses and books, your next logical step is to tackle the PMP® exam yourself! Whether you are confident you can pass the exam or you feel you need more exam preparation, it is always helpful to consider the following tips from many successful exam takers that have helped them pass the exam with ease:

Remember that the PMP® exam is as much about your knowledge as it is about your psychological preparation - the 4-hour exam time is a test of your stamina and psychological quality, in addition to your project management knowledge. Do not underestimate how exhausting it is to sit continuously in front of a computer screen and solve 200 questions of varying difficulty (you can, of course, take bathroom breaks, but that would count against your exam time).

We recommend that you visit the Prometric exam center before your actual exam date to estimate traffic times and familiarize yourself with the center's surroundings.

Understand the different types of questions that will appear on the exam so that you can use the most effective strategies to solve these exam questions. Although all PMP® exam questions are multiple-choice, they can be broadly categorized into specific genres that require different skills. Below is a detailed description of the different types of questions you will face in the real exam.

Tip 1 - Understand the question types

The exam contains many different question types to test your project management knowledge and exam question skills. The questions include:

- short and direct questions

- longer questions, which extend over 3 or more lines

- situational or scenario-based questions that give you a description of the current situation and ask you what the next step should be

- formula-based questions that require you to select and recall the most appropriate formula to calculate the answer (formulas must be memorized)

- ITTO questions that ask you about the inputs, tools and techniques, and outputs of project management processes

Tip 2 - Read the questions Carefully

This is especially true for long questions. You need to read the questions carefully to look up what is critical to the correct answer at KEYWORDS. Just look at the following list of keywords and you will know what I mean:

- Most likely

- Most unlikely

- Best

- Not

- Except

Pay attention to these key words (they are not highlighted or italicized in the real exam paper!) by reading the questions at least twice during the exam, especially toward the end of the exam when your mind is a little tired and your attention span exhausted.

Below is an example of such a tricky question:

Question: All of the following statements about the Perform Qualitative Risk Analysis process are false except:

    1. Project risks are evaluated in numerical values.

    2. Project risks are prioritized.

    3. Project risks are identified in this process.

    4. The risk register does not need to be updated.

The correct answer is 2. The question aims to determine which statement is necessarily "true" after the double negative - false + except.

1 is false: Since the process is about "Perform Qualitative Risk Analysis", risks are not quantitatively assessed in this process.

3 is false: risks are identified in the process "Identify risks".

4 is false: the risk register would record the assessment of the qualitative risk analysis.

Tip 3 - For longer questions, read the last sentence of the question and answer choices first.

One of the characteristics of many exam questions is their length - more than half of the questions span several lines. Just reading these long questions would take a lot of time, not to mention the time you need to find and understand the most important information so that you can answer the questions correctly.

A very useful technique for answering these long questions intelligently is to read the last sentence of the question and the answer choices - this will give you all the clues about what to look for in the long description before the question.

Question: Josephine is the designated project manager for a project to provide a secure messaging solution for various departments in the company. The project includes requirements gathering, design, contract negotiations with an external vendor, user testing, integration testing, deployment on the company's infrastructure IT, and employee training. With employees working in 5 different locations around the globe, access control and security are also paramount. The project is now falling behind schedule as some employees Josephine met for the first time want changes. One of the main criticisms is that the product delivered so far does not really address the needs of the employees. Which of the following project management processes was more likely to be overlooked by Josephine?

A - Identify stakeholders

B - Control schedule

C - Project Stakeholder Management

D - Control stakeholder engagement

The correct answer is A. The key word for the question is "whom Josephine first met and got to know" - this means that these collaborators have the power to influence the project, but Josephine has not identified them before. During the "Identify Stakeholders" process", the project manager is responsible for identifying all individuals and groups that are "potentially affected by the project or may positively or negatively affect the outcome of the project."

B is related to the project but is not the primary cause of delay to the project schedule.

C is not a project management process, but rather a knowledge area.

D is about controlling stakeholders that have been previously identified, not someone who suddenly shows up.

Tip 4 - For situational questions, select BEST from among several correct answers

Situational questions are usually lengthy in themselves, but also trickier. These questions describe a (usually problematic) situation and ask you how best to handle it. There is usually no black and white distinction for the "right" answer, as usual 2 to 3 answer choices are logical or reasonable. For situational questions, you will usually be asked to determine:

- the best next course of action

- what to do first

- the best answer

Do not make the common mistake of reading the answer choices from A to D and selecting the first option that seems okay - there are usually 2to 3 options for situational questions that seem okay. Your job is to find the BEST among them that matches the PMI's point of view.

Since the PMP expects project management to exercise responsibility and autonomy, it is usually wrong to ignore the problem, refer it to management, or interrupt the project to ask others for advice... Be careful here because this is a general statement NOT a law.

Question: Sally is a project manager of two related projects (Project A and B - Project A is more important) that run concurrently and share resources. Given the changing business scenario, management has just decided to reprioritize the projects and focus on Project B with more resources. Some members of the project team have been assigned to Project B. However, the remaining team members of Project A have found that the project milestones cannot be met with the reduced headcount. Morale among them is low because this project looked promising. They have no understanding of management's decisions. What is your best next course of action?

A- Brainstorm conflict resolution with team members to find a way to restore their morale and commitment to the project.

B - Ask employees to work overtime on weekends for Project A to stay on schedule. This way, you can ensure that both projects stay on schedule without asking for more resources from management.

C - Escalate the issue to management in hopes that they will allocate more resources to Project A by reallocating some of Project B's resources.

D - Review resource allocation and project data for both projects to find ways to better utilize available resources by sharing them.

At first glance, all 4 possible answers are conceivable. Before we give the answer, we would like to explain one possible solution to this type of question in a little more detail. We recommend that you follow the steps below:

1. Select the most important and relevant information from the description of the situation.

2. Read all answer choices carefully at least twice (it may be helpful to read the options in reverse order, i.e., from D - > C - > B - > A for the second time).

3. Cross out the obviously wrong answer(s) - usually only 1 to 2 options are obviously wrong.

4. Carefully re-read the remaining options to understand the implications/reasons and determine the best answer according to the principles outlined in the PMBOK® Guide. Pay attention to the consequences of the actions.

The correct answer is D. Let us explain how the answer is arrived at using the strategy described above.

1. Choose the info: Due to the changing environment, management has made the important decision to focus on Project B, which is now seen as more beneficial to the company.

2. Read and repeat the choices: from A to D and from D to A

3. Cross out the wrong ones:

B is obviously wrong because overtime is not recommended by PMI;

C is obviously wrong because management should have considered all possible scenarios and still believes that shifting the focus to project B is beneficial to the company.

1. We now have answer choices A and D to think more carefully about which is the BEST:

A is a possible solution, but it is also likely that brainstorming will lead to false hopes, as team members actually have little to contribute in this case.

TIP 5 - FORMULA QUESTIONS: USE THE CORRECT FORMULAS

The most important tip for answering formula questions correctly is to remember the correct formulas and use them. Since the exam is a closed-book exam, aspirants must memorize all PMP® formulas. Most PMP® sneakers and exam takers recommend using the first 10 minutes of the exam (since writing is no longer allowed during practice time) to write down all the formulas on the paper provided at the exam center (a.k.a. PMP® Exam brain dump).

Although some PMP® aspirants consider the formula questions to be the most difficult questions on the exam, there are several types of formula-based questions on the PMP® exam, ranging from very easy to very difficult:

- EVM Graph Questions

- Definition of EVM Metrics

- Simple EVM Calculation Questions

- EVM Estimate At Completion (EAC) Questions

- Wordy Calculation Questions

- Complicated EVM Calculation Questions

Again, the technique is to read the questions carefully to extract the important parts and use the correct formula to replace the values in them.

Question: you are currently managing a construction project in which 20 houses are to be built in 20 months (i.e. 1 house per month). The budget allocated for the project is $2,000,000. At the end of the 12th month, 10 houses have been built and $1,000,000 has been spent. There was a labor strike for one month that affected the project. What is the Cost Performance Index (CPI) of the project at this point?

1. 1.0

2. 0.9

3. 1.1

4. 1.2

The answer is 1. The formula to be used to calculate CPI is:
CPI = EV / AC
CPI = $1,000,000 / $1,000,000 = 1.0

TIP 6 — CORRECT ITTO QUESTIONS BY LOGICAL ANALYSIS.

There are over 600 Inputs, Tools & Techniques and Outputs (ITTO) for the project management processes described in the PMBOK® Guide. Many aspirants question whether they need to memorize all ITTOs for the exam.

Since the PMP exam is not about your ability to memorize many facts (it is a test of your expertise in project management), aspirants are not expected to memorize all ITTOs.

After careful study, you should be able to understand the logical relationship of ITTO to project management processes. And you should be able to recall these relationships when answering the ITTO questions - i.e., you do not have to memorize them. Your time can be better spent on PMP® mock exams and memorizing PMP® formulas.

2. Practicing PMP® Preparation the Right way

1. The single most important content to remember for the Exam:

The most important thing to remember for the PMP® exam is the overall view of all project management process groups and knowledge areas and how they relate to each other. The table presents the complex relationships between the project management processes, the process groups, and the knowledge area (which are the core topics of the Project Management Body of Knowledge and the Project Management Framework of the PMBOK® Guide) in a simple and very visual way. If you remember this chart, you will be able to answer the exam questions more easily.

Many PMP® aspirants have made this table a must for their brain dumps, so they try to reconstruct the entire table from their memory every day before the exam and transfer it to the provided paper during the exam so that they can refer to it again and again when answering the questions.

2. What formulas do I need to understand and remember for the exam?

The PMBOK® Guide mentions many project management formulas (more than 20 or 30). In practice, only about 15 formulas are needed for real testing. The bad news is that the aspirants have to memorize the formulas as the exam is a closed book exam. For this reason, formulas are another important point for the brain dump.

The good news is that the exam will test your project management concepts rather than your math skills. The math questions that appear on the exam paper are usually quite simple. All you have to do is select the correct PMP® formula to use and enter the variables to get the answers. An on-screen calculator (for computer-based tests) will also be provided to help you solve the math problems. Do not worry if you do not come from a science background. All you need to do is memorize the formulas and work through more practice questions to understand when to use which formula.

3. What are ITTOs (inputs, outputs, tools, and techniques) and do I need to memorize them all?

Many aspirants are quite concerned about ITTOs. After all, there are more than 600 ITTOs for all project management processes described in the PMBOK® Guide. How to remember all these ITTOs for the exam?

Again, the good news is that the exam is not a test of your memory or how well you can recite things. From random surveys of exam takers, there are usually about 5 or fewer questions directly on the ITTOs. Remember, the exam is a test on your ability to start as a project manager and NOT a test on your memory. PMI will not require you to recite all the ITTOs.

PMP® aspirants need to understand the key ITTOs and how and why they relate to each project management process. Many outputs of one process eventually become inputs of another process. Typically, after reading the PMBOK® Guide once or twice, PMP® aspirants are able to create a mental map of the relationship between the ITTOs and the project management framework. The knowledge acquired in this way should be sufficient to answer the exam questions correctly.

4. How do I answer the long scenario-based/situational exam questions?

The long situation questions are considered by many applicants to be the more difficult and 'tricky' questions on the paper. The questions usually contain a variety of facts and descriptions that are meant to serve as a red herring to test whether you can extract the most important information from the scenario. There are some tips to help you master such long scenario-based questions:

Read the last sentence of the question FIRST, to understand what you are being asked.

Read all the answers and cross out obviously unrelated or incorrect answers.

Use your brain dump sheet for the exam to highlight the important information in the question.

Practice more scenario-based sample questions.

5. How to manage the exam time for the exam?

The exam lasts 4 hours, which seems very long to you. However, PMP® aspirants have to answer 200 questions in the 4 hours and take the necessary breaks to use the restroom or rest. Some exam takers reported that they were just able to answer all the questions before the time ran out.

The most important tip to help you manage exam time is to take several full-length 4-hour PMP® practice exams before the actual exam. Try to understand your stamina, need for bathroom breaks, etc. during these practice exams and formulate your exam strategies.

Some candidates would try to write the first 100 questions continuously, take a toilet break of 10 minutes, do the remaining 100 questions, take another break and then review all the questions. It would take them about 4 hours to complete the entire process. And many of the exam takers (including me) found that the "performance" on the real exam was lower than on the simulated tests - you would need more time to answer the questions than planned. It is advisable to plan for this when scheduling your exam time.

6. What is the best way to study for the Exam?

The answer to this question is indeed very personal. It depends on what your learning style is:

- For those who learn best by reading on their own, reading the PMBOK® Guide as well as another exam preparation book would be a good idea. We also recommend that you purchase or create your own "flashcards" to refer to at any free time.

- For those who learn best in a visual way, purchasing podcast exam prep courses would be very helpful. You can listen to and watch the lessons on your smartphone wherever you want, subconsciously understanding/remembering the content for the exam. Also, if you find lessons difficult at first, you can repeat them an unlimited number of times. We also recommend that you read the diagrams in the PMBOK® Guide to familiarize yourself with the project management processes.

- For those who learn best with others, participating in a classroom bootcamp or learning group is best. If you encounter difficult topics, you can always ask others for clarification. Plus, the "peer pressure" (in a good way) will spur you to keep your learning on track.

Or you can adapt the above approaches and create your own learning plan based on your learning style.

7. How many practice exams should I take before the actual Exam?

Practice exams are a must for applicants. Practice exams give you many opportunities to take the exam in a realistic setting. This is NO penalty for failing the practice exams (note: if you fail the real exam, you must pay the retake fee). Most simulated practice exams will also give you detailed reports on your performance and suggestions on what to focus on.

There are NO a certain number of practice tests that you must take before your exam. However, there is a general recommendation that you should be ready for the real exam if you can score 80% or higher on more than one practice test that you are taking for the first time.

However, do not be discouraged if you only score 70%+, because many aspirants who score around 70% in their practice exams can also pass the PMP® exam on their first attempt. The "80% pass rate" is just a bet on the safe side. Again, the good news is that you will find several high-quality practice exam questions in this guide.

3. Vital Tips to be Psychologically Well Prepared and Have the Right Mindset

Just as a marathon runner runs a full marathon in his head every day to keep his body up, aspirants can practice taking the full-length exams (i.e., 200 questions for 4 hours) by simulating the exam interface and environment - it is recommended to use online exam simulators that have an interface very similar to the real exam, including the virtual calculator. It would be good to try the real exam if you can consistently score above 75% or higher on the mock exams that you are writing for the first time (i.e., you have not attempted the mock questions before).

Candidates are also advised to plan for brain dump (if needed) and breaks during the 4 hours to develop a strategy that they feel comfortable with.

It is our hope that after two or more attempts at full-length mock exams, candidates will be fully prepared, both psychologically and intellectually, to pass the PMP® exam on the first try!

- Make meaningful connections to the topic

- Relate the material to something you know or are interested in to make a real connection to the material.

- Stay healthy - healthy mind and healthy body

- Eating healthy before an exam can improve your concentration. Do something to relax the night before and get plenty of sleep. Before the test, imagine yourself doing well.

Do not cram

If possible, do not study on the day of the test (this can increase anxiety, leading to test anxiety and memory loss). Schedule several review sessions before the test - short but frequent sessions are better than one long cramming session. Go over the key points the night before.

Look at the entire test first

Breathe deeply, relax, and forget about the people around you. Be sure to read the instructions carefully. Determine what types of questions there are, how many points will be given for each question, if you have a choice of questions to answer, etc. Set a time budget for each type of question and allow extra time for review. Answer the easiest questions first and then move on to the more difficult questions.

Do not be frustrated if you get stuck

Read through the question again and make sure you understand what is being asked. Do not hesitate to skip over the question and mark it with a circle so you can come back to it later. If you get stuck and can only guess, choose an answer that makes the most sense to you.

Tip 1: **No Brain Dumps are allowed NOW**

You may be advised by your trainer or lessons you have read on the internet to do Brian Dumps during the practice time before the exam starts, so that you can always refer to it during the exam. This trick would give you an extra competitive edge for your performance. NO MORE NOW. Exam centers around the world prohibit this Exam Brain Dump tactic to ensure fairness. Do not get me wrong. You can still Brain Dump, but only after the PMP® exam has started (not during study time).

If Brain Dump is a useful technique for you, you should practice your Brain Dump on every mock exam you take during your exam preparation so that you can better manage the time to answer the 200 questions in 4 hours, including the 10+ minutes you spend Brain Dumping.

If your exam center still allows you to do a brain dump during the tutorial, it would boost your confidence by giving you 10+ more minutes to take the exam!

Tip 2: **The Washroom / Toilet may be very far away from your exam room**

Since each exam center is different, the location of the washroom/restroom may be quite far away and it may take you 5 minutes or more to walk to the washroom/restroom and back. Also, every time you need to take a break from the exam, you will need to wait for the exam center staff to help you complete all the administrative procedures and do the registrations and security checks when you get back.

So when you schedule breaks, they should never be shorter than 10 minutes (15+ minutes is better).

Also, try to walk from the door of the exam room to the restroom before the exam begins so that you do not waste time looking for the restroom during the exam, because the 4-hour exam will not be interrupted during your break!

Tip 3: **Security Checks**

Each time you enter the exam room (including the first time and after each break), you must sign in and undergo a security check. My security check consisted of rolling up my sleeves and showing all pockets (including pants pockets) in front of the proctor and a recording camera and being scanned with a metal detector. This took 5 - 10 minutes. So be prepared to arrive at the exam center at least 30 minutes before the scheduled exam time.

Tip 4: **Exam Room Environment**

You will probably be sitting in an exam room where different candidates are taking different exams. The different exams may have different start and end times, and the format may also be different. Some candidates may have to do a lot of typing, which can make annoying noises, while others may come and go frequently.

If you are easily disturbed by noise and commotion, you may ask to wear earplugs, which will be provided by the exam center. However, please note that some exam centers do not provide earplugs. It is recommended that you bring your own and ask permission before wearing an earplug.

The examination room may be cold or warm depending on the environment and weather conditions. We recommend that you bring your own coat/sweater to the exam center. However, please note that you will not be able to remove your sweaters while in the exam room. You can sign out and have your sweater stored in the locker if you feel too hot.

You may also want to know that the examination room is monitored by continuous audio and video recording.

Tip 5: **Beware of extremely difficult "Pre-test" questions**

Among the 200 questions you received in your PMP® exam paper, there are 25 pre-test questions. On your exam, some questions will be more difficult than the questions you were asked on the mock exam. And these are probably the "pre-test" questions.

Do not get discouraged. Just keep on going. There are some difficult and simple questions. It would be a shame if you spend too much time on the difficult questions and fail to score on the easier ones.

Tip 6: **No Immediate Exam Results after submitting your exam online**

After you submit your exam paper for grading by clicking the "Finish Exam" button, you will see the screen at NOT that tells you whether you passed or failed the PMP® exam.

You will first be greeted with a survey asking you about your exam experience. I am sure no aspirant is in the mood to answer the survey with gusto. Exam candidates can also skip the survey.

After submitting/skipping the survey, candidates will be presented with a blank screen for a few seconds before finally receiving the results of the exam. I hope you can read the message "Congratulations"!

4. PMP® Exam Time Management Tips

With a well-thought-out schedule for your PMP® exam, you have a much better chance of passing the exam than other aspirants who simply take the exam as it comes (after all, the PMP® exam is a measure of how well you do compared to other exam takers). Below are my personal, tried-and-true time management tips for writing the exam.

Tip 1: **You have much less than 1.2 minutes for each question**

Do the simple maths of 4 hours for 200 questions, 240 minutes / 200 questions = 1.2 minutes (72 seconds) for each question. But don't forget you would need to allow for time to take breaks (the stopwatch will not stop while you are taking breaks). Also, it is advisable to leave some time near the end of the exam for reviewing all the questions (preferably not just those marked for review) to spot any careless mistakes as each question carries the same weight on the exam paper and there are 15 pre-test questions (which are usually much harder or out of PMP® Exam syllabus), it is highly recommended to set a hard limit for the time to answer each question. After considering all the factors, Aspirants may have 50 - 60 seconds to answer each exam question as the hard limit

Tip 2: **Take at least 2 to 3 mock exams (each with 200 questions for 4 hours continuously) to understand your stamina and need for breaks**

- Some applicants can go through the exam for 4 hours without a break, while others need up to 3 breaks to go to the bathroom and clear their heads

- Aspirants are strongly encouraged to simulate real exam conditions (i.e., answer 200 practice questions for 4 hours each, preferably at the same time of day as the scheduled PMP® exam) to understand your own need for breaks

Tip 3: **Account for time to write the brain dumps**

In many PMP® exam centers nowadays it is not allowed to write during the practice time before the actual exam starts, you also need to allow extra time at the beginning of the exam to write your own brain dump, which can help you save a lot of time during the exam.

Tip 4: **Take 10 – 15 minutes for each break**

For each break, you will need to undergo all the security measures taken when you show up for the exam:

- present your ID

- leave all your belongings in the locker

- checking the pockets before a camera

- sign in

You may even have to wait for the exam invigilator to be ready to serve you as there are many other exam takers at the same center.

Also, the toilet may be quite far away from your exam room (mine was 2 floors away), this would take up considerable time to locate and get to the toilet.

Though it normally takes several minutes for a toilet break, after considering all the above factors, it is advisable to schedule at least 10 minutes for each break.

Tip 5: **People perform worse under pressure**

So be prepared that you may not do as well as you do on exam simulators or mock exams. From our own experience and from the experience of many others, we know that the first 10 or more exam questions are much more difficult than in the mock exams (and that is demoralizing) - but if you persevere and do not lose heart, you will find the later questions much easier. Also think about the pressure of the real exam. You may end up needing a break more than you did on the mock exams.

Tip 6: **In case you are not good at calculation questions, just guess an answer and move on ASAP**

It may be a good idea to guess all the calculation questions immediately without even reading the question, pick a random answer, mark it for review, and move on to the next one - this will give you more time to tackle the questions you are confident in, which in turn will boost your confidence for the exam (guessing answers will not be marked negatively if they are wrong). After you have worked through all the exam questions, you should return to the calculation questions. You may find it easier to solve them then, since you have already built up confidence.

(Only in theory) It is also advisable to guess the same answer choice for all these questions, as the chance of guessing the correct answer is higher

5. What Comes After the PMP® Certification

Receiving your PMP certification is a great accomplishment that you should be proud of. However, think of it as a stepping stone to your career, not an end goal.

From leveraging your new certification status to continuing education and more, there are many new opportunities available to you after becoming a PMP certification holder.

What to do After Earning Your PMP Certification

After you pass the PMP exam, there are a few steps you should follow to take full advantage of your new professional accreditation.

Receive your PMP Credential Certificate by mail

You are officially certified once you pass the PMP exam. You will immediately receive a digital badge via Credly, but it may take 6-8 weeks to receive the certificate in the mail. PMI will send you the following:

- Your PMP certificate

- A congratulatory letter

- Instructions on how to maintain your certificate

In the meantime, you can use your digital badge on social media, update your professional information, and show employers proof.

Update your professional information

PMP certification is the global standard for project management around the world and in every industry. Show current and potential employers and clients your qualifications with this checklist:

Update your resume, business card, LinkedIn profile, online bio, and more.

Include the PMP credential in your online name (e.g., first name last name, PMP).

Add the PMP logo to your personal business card.

Share your digital badge on social media, your website, or your company card.

Updating your professional information to showcase your success is a great way to demonstrate your project management skills and experience.

Request your PMP Lapel Pin

PMI will not automatically send you your PMP pin. You can request it for free by mail by logging into the PMI website, going to the Marketplace, and adding it to your cart.

Continuing Education

Learning does not stop after certification. Project management practices are constantly improving. Therefore, you must meet PMI's Continuing Certification Requirements (CCR) within a specific CCR cycle to maintain your certification status.

PMI's CCR program helps certificants continuously improve their project management skills. By staying up-to-date on relevant practices, you will be equipped for the complex and ever-changing modern business environment.

How to maintain the PMP Credential

For PMP certification, you have three years from the date you pass the PMP exam to earn a minimum of 60 Professional Development Units (PDUs). If you achieve more than this minimum, some of the PDUs you earn in the last 12 months of your CCR cycle may count toward your next cycle.

If you do not meet the minimum requirements during your CCR cycle, the following may occur:

- Suspension: If you do not earn 60 PDUs during your 3-year cycle, you will be suspended for one year or until you have earned the required PDUs and completed the renewal process. During this period, you may not use the certification designation. Suspension does not change the dates of your next CCR cycle.

- Forfeiture: If you do not acquire the required PDUs or complete the renewal process during the suspension, you will lose your certification status. To regain PMP certification, you must reapply, resubmit all fees, and retake the PMP exam.

- Retirement: If you have held certification for at least ten years but wish to retire and voluntarily end your active certification status, you may apply for retirement status. In retirement, you are not required to collect or report PDUs, but you can reapply for active status when you come out of retirement.

PMI makes some exceptions for life events such as military personnel called to active duty, incapacity due to illness, or maternity leave. If this applies to you, you can apply for an extension to meet your continuing certification requirements.

Guide to the acquisition of PDUs

PMI requires certification holders to participate in professional development activities to earn PDUs and gain further insight into the industry. These activities fall under two categories: Education and Professional Engagement.

Education PDUs include learning opportunities that teach or enhance your technical, leadership, or strategic and business skills. Of your 60 required PDUs per cycle, you will need at least 35 Education PDUs.

Education PDUs are aligned with the PMI Talent Triangle®, which describes ideal skills as a combination of technical, leadership and strategic skills. Of your 35 required Education PDUs per cycle, you will need at least 8 Technical PDUs, 8 Leadership PDUs, and 8 Strategic PDUs. The remaining 11+ PDUs can fall into any area of the Talent Triangle.

Giving Back PDUs include all activities that you use to contribute your knowledge and skills to building the project management industry. You can count a maximum of 25 Giving Back PDUs toward your continuing certification requirements.

Sharing your project management knowledge and skills can be valuable to the profession as well as to your own professional development. For this reason, Giving Back is included in PMI's CCR program. However, this is an optional method of earning PDUs.

As with contact hours, one hour of instruction or activity equals one PDU. Unlike contact hours, these PDUs must be earned during your CCR cycle. As you accumulate PDUs, you can submit the information to PMI through the CCR system. You can only earn credit for one PDU per course hour or activity.

Once PMI has verified that you have met your PDU requirements, you will receive further instructions on how to submit your renewal fee. After your fee has been processed, PMI will send you your updated certificate and new CCR cycle dates.

Job Opportunities After PMP Certification

After passing the PMP exam, you are likely to experience rapid career growth, especially if you are a PMI member. Learn more about why the job outlook is so good for PMP certificate holders anywhere in the world.

WHAT'S THE PROJECTED JOB OUTLOOK FOR CERTIFIED PMPs?

Use your PMP certification strategically to accelerate your career in many ways. Your certification paves the way for your personal and professional growth. Here are some ways a PMP certification can improve your job prospects.

- Increase your productivity

- Provide networking opportunities

- Show management that you are ready to advance professionally

- Provide leverage for a salary increase

- Prove your qualifications when you apply for new roles

Your local PMI chapter is a great place to network with other PMI members, learn more about global project management trends, and share resources, ideas, and experiences.

What do employers see in certified PMPs?

Even experienced project managers who are well versed in several areas of project management can learn a lot by studying for and passing the PMP exam. Therefore, employers view PMP certification holders as valuable assets to protect and grow the business.

PMP graduates have proven "soft" life skills in dealing with people and communication. Passing the PMP exam also requires "hard" skills such as monitoring and creating deliverables, calculating costs and other project elements, and using computer programs to manage projects more efficiently.

Having a certified project manager on your team opens up new opportunities for employers looking to take on new, large or complex projects.

Next Certification After PMP

If you are wondering what degree to pursue next, first take some time to consider two things:

- Where: Where do you live, work, or plan to move? If you plan to live or work in the United Kingdom or another Commonwealth country, consider PRINCE2 certification. However, if you live or work in the United States or elsewhere, PRINCE2 certification is rather redundant. Instead, focus on meeting your PMP CCR requirements.

- What: What is your main area of work? You may benefit from the PMI Risk Management Professional

(PMI-RMP)® certification, the PMI Agile Certified Practitioner (PMI-ACP)® certification, the Certified Scrum Masters (CSM) course, or other accreditations for specific industries.

Remember that you must maintain your PMP certification by earning Professional Development Units. Do not underestimate the time it will take you to earn the required PDUs during your CCR cycle! It may be best to focus on maintaining your certification status rather than pursuing additional certifications.

Management Framework

WHAT DO THE EIFFEL Tower, the Internet and this book have in common? Projects! All three are the result of projects. Even if you have the necessary materials and knowledge, how do you actually build huge and complex structures or systems like the Eiffel Tower of Paris, the Taj Mahal of Agra, or the Internet and the World Wide Web of the Information Age? The answer is again: projects. Through projects it is possible to build small and large, simple and complex things in an effective and efficient way. All projects need to be managed. A so-called unmanaged project is simply a poorly managed project that is doomed to fail. Therefore, the importance of project management cannot be overstated.

We all know from experience that every project has (or should have) a beginning and an end. Managing a project therefore means managing the lifecycle of the project, from the beginning (initiation) to the end (completion); this is done with the help of processes, which are so-called knowledge areas of project management. Although you use your knowledge in the form of processes to manage projects, management is highly influenced by the environment in which the project takes place, e.g., the structure and culture of the implementing organization. Projects also originate in their environment.

The goal of this chapter is to walk you through the framework of project management. To that end, we will explore three avenues: the project lifecycle, the project management knowledge areas, and the project in the context of programs, portfolios, and the organization's strategy. In the process of doing so, we will introduce some basic concepts of project management.

Basic Concepts of Project Management

Every discipline of knowledge, from physics to biology and from computer science to poetry, is built on some fundamental concepts. The terms that refer to or define these concepts form the language of that discipline. The basic concepts of project management are briefly described in the following list:

- **Project.** A project is an effort that takes place over a limited period of time and has a beginning and an end to create a unique product, service, or result. Because a project has a beginning and an end, it is also referred to as a time-limited effort or undertaking.

- **Project Phase.** A project phase is a series of logically related activities that typically complete one or more major deliverables of the project. Phases are usually completed sequentially; however, in some situations, overlap is possible. Depending on its size and complexity, a project may have one or more phases.

- **Project Lifecycle.** It is the total project duration from start to finish, including all project phases. A project has at least one phase. The life cycle of a single-phase project consists of five project phases: Initiation, Planning, Execution, Monitoring and Control, and Closure. If a project has multiple phases, all of these phases are repeated in each phase.

- **Process Groups.** These are the technical terms for the project phases: Initiate, Plan, Execute, Monitor and Control, and Close.

- **Organization.** An organization is a group of people organized for a specific purpose or task. Computer companies, energy companies (to which you pay your electric bills), and cable companies are examples of organizations. An organization may provide products, such as books or donuts, or services, such as Internet access or online banking.

• **Performing Organization.** The executing organization, also referred to as the project organization, is the organization that carries out the project.

• **Project Stakeholder.** A project stakeholder is an individual or an organization that can affect or be affected by the project execution. A project can have a wide spectrum of stakeholders, from the project sponsor to an environmental organization, to an ordinary citizen.

• **Process.** In the context of projects, a process is a set of related tasks performed to manage some aspect of a project, such as cost, scope, or risk. Each process belongs to a knowledge area and corresponds to a process group.

• **Knowledge Area.** A knowledge area in project management is defined by the knowledge requirements associated with managing a particular aspect of a project, such as cost, using a set of processes. PMI recognizes a total of ten knowledge areas, such as cost management and human resource management.

• **Tailoring.** Of course, you do not apply all project management skills to a project. For a given project, with the help of the project team, you select the appropriate lifecycle phases and the required deliverables, and to achieve those deliverables, you select the right processes, inputs, tools, and techniques. This method is called tailoring.

• **Project Management.** Project management is the use of knowledge, skills, and tools to manage a project from start to finish with the goal of meeting project requirements. This includes the application of appropriate processes.

• **Phase Gate.** This is a review at the end of each phase that leads to the decision to proceed with the next phase as planned, proceed with the next phase with a modified plan, or terminate the project.

This is a minimal set of terms you need to understand before you can begin your exploration of the world of project management. More terms will be introduced as you further explore the discipline of project management in this book. Now that you understand these basic terms, you can ask yourself a very basic question: What does it mean to manage a project? In other words: What is involved in managing a project?

Understanding Projects

Before diving into the details of project management, you need to understand what a project is, where it comes from, and why. In any organization, many activities are performed on a daily basis. Most of these activities are organized into groups of related activities. These groups fall into two categories: Projects and Activities. An activity is a continuous and repetitive set of tasks, while a project has a life cycle - a beginning and an end.

What Is a Project?

A project is a work effort performed over a finite period of time that has a beginning and an end to create a unique product, service, or result. Because a project has a beginning and an end, it is also referred to as a time-limited effort or undertaking. In other words, according to PMI's definition, "a project is a time-limited effort undertaken to create a unique product, service, or result" A project, then, has two defining characteristics: it is time-limited, and it creates a unique product. Let us take a closer look at these two defining terms: time-limited and unique.

Temporary. The temporary nature of projects refers to the fact that each project has a definite beginning and end. A project can come to an end in one of two ways:

The project has achieved its goals - that is, the planned unique product has been created.

The project was terminated for some reason before its successful completion.

Note that the temporary nature of a project does not mean that the project is short-lived, nor does it refer to the product it creates. Projects can create lasting products, such as the Taj Mahal, the Eiffel Tower, or the Internet.

The second defining characteristic of a project is that it must create a unique product.

Unique product. The outcome of a project must be a unique product, service, or result. How do a product, service, and result differ from each other?

Product. This is a tangible, quantifiable artifact that is either the final product or a component of it. The big screen TV in your living room, the Swiss watch on your wrist, and the bottle of wine on your table are some examples of products.

Service. When we say that a project can create a service, we actually mean the ability to deliver a service. For example, a project that creates a website for a bank to offer online banking has created the capability to offer online banking.

Result. This is usually the knowledge-related outcome of a project, such as the results of an analysis conducted as part of a research project.

In this book, we **will often refer** to a product, service, or result as just "product" or "project result" for brevity.

■ *Caution! Not only organizations undertake projects. A project can also be undertaken by a group of individuals or even a single individual.*

Projects are organized to accomplish a set of activities that cannot be accomplished as part of the organization's day-to-day operations. To clearly identify whether an undertaking is a project, you must understand the difference between a project and an activity.

Distinguishing Projects from Operations

An organization performs a variety of activities as part of its work to achieve its goals. Some of these activities are in support of projects, while others are in support of what are called operations. An operation is a set of tasks that do not qualify as a project. In other words, an operation is a function that performs ongoing tasks. It does not produce a unique (new) product and there is no pre-planned beginning or end. For example, building a data center is a project, but after you build it, keeping it running is an operation.

It is important to understand that projects and operations have some characteristics in common, such as the following:

- Both require resources, including human resources, i.e., people.

- Both are limited to limited, as opposed to unlimited, resources.

- Both are managed, i.e., planned, executed, and controlled.

- Both have objectives and contribute to achieving the strategic goals of the organization.

- Both can have and share stakeholders.

The distinction between projects and operations is possible if you stick to the definition of a project - that it is temporary and one-time.Operations are generally ongoing and repetitive. Although both projects and operations have goals, a project ends when its goals are achieved, while an operation continues to contribute to the goals-and possibly to a new set of goals if the organization's strategy changes.

Projects can be carried out at different levels of an organization; they vary in size and, accordingly, may involve only one person or a team. Table 1-1 provides some examples of projects.

Table 1-1. Examples of Projects

Project	Outcome (Product, Service, or Result)
Constructing Eiffel Tower	Product
Running presidential election campaign	Results: win or lose; Products: documents
Developing a website to offer online education	Service
Setting up a computer network in one building	Service
Moving a computer network from one building	Result: network is moved to another building
Study the genes of members of Congress	Results (of the research); Product: research paper
Book sold in a bookstore	Product
A software app like MS Word sold as CD and paid for once	Product
A software app integrated into the web and paid for monthly	Service
Human Genome Project	Result

Now that we have a clear idea of what a project is, we must wonder why an organization would launch a specific project. So, let's ask a fundamental question: Where do projects originally come from?

Origins of Projects: Where Do Projects Come From?

Projects are created by the leaders of an organization in response to one or more situations facing the organization. These situations or factors affecting the organization may fall into one of the following four categories:

1. Business/legal requirements. This category includes projects based on the need to meet legal, regulatory, or social requirements. For example, consider a building owner who approves a project to make the building accessible to the physically disabled to meet legal requirements for the use of the building for a particular business.

2. Stakeholder requests or needs. This category includes projects based on meeting the wants or needs of stakeholders. An example would be an environmental organization launching a project to educate politicians about the science behind global warming. Another example would be a company undertaking a project to reduce the negative impact of its operations or products on the environment.

3. Business or technological strategies. This category of factors would lead to projects based on the need to implement or change business or technological strategies. For example, a web design company approves a project to automate certain aspects of website maintenance in order to increase its efficiency and revenue. As another example, a cab company launches a project to introduce an automatic driving function in some of its cabs due to recent technological advances.

4. Products, processes, or services. This category of factors would lead to projects based on the need to create, improve, or repair products, processes, or services. For example, a biotechnology company approves a project to create and implement SOP (standard operating procedures) in all of its laboratories.

As an attentive reader will note, these four categories of factors mentioned by PMI are not mutually exclusive. For example, the last category is at least partially redundant; a project that responds to one of these categories may produce a product or service. For this reason, or because of the project's objectives, the project may fall into more than one of these categories. For example, an automaker's project to produce electric cars with advanced technology in response to the needs of environmentally conscious customers falls into all three of the last categories: 2, 3, and 4.

These categories of factors are collectively referred to as the context of project initiation. On the one hand, these factors are linked to the organization's strategic goals and influence its business strategy, and on the other hand, they are linked to the organization's business value through projects. In short, an organization with a certain business value, in response to one or more of these factors, undertakes a project that generates some business value and thus increases the previous business value of the organization. In this way, projects effect change by moving the organization from a state of lower business value to a state of higher business value, and in this way help the organization remain viable.

■ **Caution!** The factors discussed in this section influence not only the organization's current business strategies but also its current operations because operations are there to serve business strategies or objectives.

We will return to this topic in the next chapter to examine how, starting from the initiation context discussed here, a project is actually started in an organization.

Where there is a project, there is project management.

Understanding Project Management

In this book, we refer to project management as defined in the Project Management Institute (PMI) Project Management Standard: "Project management is the application of knowledge, skills, tools, and techniques to project activities to meet project requirements."

This standard, contained in the Project Management Body of Knowledge (PMBOK) Guide, represents, as PMI asserts, "a subset of project management knowledge that is generally accepted as good practice." By generally accepted, PMI means two things: 1) the knowledge presented is applicable to most projects, and 2) there is consensus on its value and usefulness. Good practice is the general consensus that applying the knowledge, skills, tools, and techniques presented to project management processes can increase the likelihood of project success.

■ *Note As a result of innovation and advances in science and technology, the body of knowledge in the project management profession is constantly changing, so the standard is updated accordingly every few years.*

In a poorly managed project, bad things happen, such as missed deadlines, cost overruns, and poor quality, resulting in dissatisfied project stakeholders. This leads to project failure and damages the reputation and viability of the company. However, effective project management helps in managing various aspects of the project such as cost, scope and stakeholders and makes the project more predictable during execution. This helps identify and resolve issues and problems in a timely manner, as well as identify and respond to risks, which increases the chances of project success. In addition, effective project management allows you to clearly link the project outcome to the organization's business objectives, enabling you to adapt project plans to a changing business environment. In this way, effective project management helps the business survive in a rapidly changing world by remaining relevant and viable. In this book, project management stands for effective project management unless otherwise stated.

Projects are inextricably linked to project management. At the time of initiation, a project is just being born, and it is brought to the top through a process called progressive elaboration through project management.

Understanding Progressive Elaboration

As the saying goes, Rome was not built in a day. But neither is the product of a project - even the project plan - built in a day. Usually, there is first a concept and a comprehensive vision for the final product, i.e., the outcome of the project. The clearer the vision you have of the unique product you expect from the project, the more accurate the project plan will be. So you approach the project plan incrementally, refining your vision of the final product and gradually getting more and more information about the requirements. This process of defining (or planning) a project is called progressive elaboration.

Here is an example of progressive elaboration. You wake up one morning with an idea to close the digital gap in your community. Now you have a concept for the end product (outcome) of your project: closing the digital gap in your community. But what do you really mean by that? This could include many things - building computers in an economical way and making them available at low prices to those who do not have them, raising awareness of the need for computer literacy, offering classes, and the like. Now you are really working on refining your vision of the final product. The second question is: How are you going to accomplish this? This is where you refer to the project plan. You can see that the project plan and its accuracy and details depend on how polished the end product idea is. The final product or goals and the plan to achieve them are elaborated in further steps.

■ **Tip** Uncontrolled changes that make it into the project without being properly processed are called scope creep. Do not confuse progressive elaboration with scope creep.

Progressive elaboration generally means developing something in small steps. The project plan is roughly defined at the beginning and then gradually becomes more precise, detailed, and explicit as the understanding of the project deliverables and objectives improves. These are successive iterations of the planning process that lead to a more accurate and complete plan.

Even after you have an approved final project plan and the project begins execution, incremental elaboration continues to some degree. For example, you will see later in this chapter that the execution and planning phases of the project interact with each other. Based on project performance and stakeholder desires, the project plan may change, even including the project scope.

The majority of project management is done through the execution of a series of processes.

Understanding a Process

Processes are at the heart of project management. In other words, processes are the atoms, the smallest functional units of project management. If you want to think about project management like a project management professional, think in terms of processes. Almost everything in the world of project management runs through processes.

What is a process, anyway? Step back a bit and look around. You'll see processes everywhere, not just in project management. For example, when you make coffee in the morning, you go through a process. The water, the coffee filter, and the roasted hazelnut coffee made by grinding golden beans are the inputs to that process. The coffee maker is the tool, and how you make the coffee is the technique. A cup of freshly brewed hazelnut coffee is the output of that process. So, in general, a process is a series of interrelated activities performed to obtain a specific set of products, results, or services. A project management process, as explained in the example and in Figure 1, always consists of three parts: Input, Tools and Techniques, and Output. If you like this analogy, think of a process as a chemical reaction in which tools and techniques act on the input to produce an output. The term raw data in Figure 1 means that the input is processed to produce the output.

Input	+	Tools and techniques	=	Output
Raw data or information for the process	Tools and techniques operate on input	Appropriate tools and techniques	Produces	The outcome of the operation of tools and techniques on input data or information

As illustrated in the Figure above, each process consists of three parts, described in the following list:

• **Input.** The input to a process consists of the raw data, that is, the data or information needed to start the process and to be processed into an output. For example, the project management schedule is one of several inputs to the Develop Schedule process, which is used to develop the schedule for a project.

• **Tools and Techniques.** Tools and techniques are the methods used to work with input and turn it into output. For example, the critical path method, which helps develop a schedule, is a tool used in the schedule development process.

• **Output.** The output is the output or result of a process. Every process contains at least one output element, because otherwise it would be pointless to carry out a process. For example, an output of the schedule development process is the project schedule.

Now that you know what a process is, you will probably find that you will use different processes at different stages (not phases) of a project, such as planning and execution. Actually, the entire life cycle of a project can be divided into five phases, with each phase corresponding to a group of processes.

Below are some characteristics of processes:

1. Iterations. Some processes, such as Develop Project Charter and Close Project, are executed only once or at specific times in the process, while others, such as Perform Procurement and Acquire Resources, may be executed at regular intervals, depending on the size of the project. Processes such as Define Activities may be executed even more frequently.

2. Process Interconnect. Processes relate to other processes by input or output. The output of one process becomes an input (alone or as part of another input) to another process, or it is a final output, i.e., a project or phase outcome.

3. Overlapping. Some of the elements entered may appear in more than one project. This also applies to tools or techniques. From this you can see that projects may overlap in their activities.

Now that we have a very good basic idea of projects, we can take a tour of the project life cycle.

Understanding the Project Lifecycle

As you already know, every project has a beginning and an end. The period of time from the beginning to the end of the project is called the project life cycle. If a project has multiple phases, all phases are completed during its life cycle to complete the project. Regardless of whether the project has multiple phases or only one phase, the project is started, organized and prepared, executed (the project work is performed), monitored, and closed during this life cycle. In standard terminology, a project is initiated, planned, executed, monitored and controlled, and closed.

Caution! Do not confuse the project life cycle with the product life cycle. A project is undertaken to create a product or products that will continue after the project is completed. Generally, the life cycle of a project is included in the life cycle of any product it creates. For example, a project creates a product that persists for a period of time after the project ends and is then retired. As another example, a project is undertaken to add functionality to a product that existed before the project began and continues to exist after the project is completed.

From initiation/approval to completion/completion, a project goes through a full life cycle that includes defining the project objectives, planning the work to achieve those objectives, performing the work, monitoring and controlling progress, and closing the project after receiving product acceptance.

■ *Caution! I refer to the five process groups as five phases to help you visualize a project. Technically, and in the PMBOK, they are called process groups. However, be prepared to recognize them regardless of what they are called in the audit. Do not expect that a process group or document will always be referred to by its formal technical name in the audit. This also applies to the real world out there where you will be doing projects.*

The five phases, technically called process groups, of a project life cycle are described in the following list.

Initiating a Project. In this phase, the project is defined and authorized. The project manager is named and the project is officially launched through a signed document, the project charter. This document contains elements such as the purpose of the project, a product description, project goals and requirements, and a summary of the milestone schedule. The main purpose of this phase is to align the purpose of the project with the business requirements and strategy of the company on the one hand, and the expectations of the stakeholders on the other.

It is a good strategy to involve customers and other key stakeholders in the early stages of the project. This gives them a sense of ownership that contributes significantly to the success of the project by positively influencing factors such as acceptance of the results and stakeholder satisfaction.

■ **Note** In the discipline of project management, as in many other disciplines, the term "high-level" means lacking or not referring to details. Keep this meaning in mind when reading terms in this book, such as high-level product description, high-level plan, and the like. Details are usually elaborated through a process called progressive elaboration.

■ Caution The processes in the Initiate process group, like all other process groups, can be used to initiate a phase of a project that has multiple phases.

After the project is initiated, it must be planned.

Planning the Project. In this phase, you, as the project manager, work with the project management team to develop the project scope, define and refine the project objectives, and develop activities to achieve those objectives. To this end, you develop the project management plan, a collection of various plans and other documents that provide an action plan for achieving the objectives and meeting the requirements of the project. The processes used in this phase belong to a group called the planning process group. This process group also develops some non-plan documents for the project.

The approved scope baseline, schedule baseline, and cost baseline are referred to as the Scope Baseline, Schedule Baseline, and Cost Baseline, respectively. These three baselines together are referred to as the Project Baseline or Performance Measurement Baseline (PMB). Project performance is evaluated at each point in time by comparing the results of project execution against this Performance Measurement Baseline. In other words, to see how the project is performing, compare actual project execution results to this baseline.

■ **Note** The project management plan contains plans from various project management areas called subsidiary plans, such as a project scope management plan, a schedule management plan, and a quality management plan.

You then execute the project as planned.

Executing the Project. In this phase, you, as the project manager, lead the execution of the project as envisioned in the project management plan. You will coordinate all activities that will be performed to achieve the project goals and meet the project requirements. The main output of this project is, of course, the project deliverables. Approved changes, recommendations, and bug fixes are also implemented during this phase. Stakeholders may also propose changes that must go through an approval process before implementation. Project execution is performed using processes that belong to a group called the executing process group.

Thus, the project work defined in the project management plan is executed using the processes in the executing process group. The processes in this group are used to achieve a three-stage goal:

- Coordination of resources, including budget, team members, and time used to perform project activities.

- Integrate and manage the project activities performed.

- Ensure implementation of project scope and approved changes

A large part of the project resources is consumed in the execution of the processes of the executing process group.

■ **Note** Performing processes from the executing process group may also generate change requests, which must be processed for approval in the monitor and control group.

Where do the changes and recommendations that are implemented at this stage come from? They come from the monitoring and control of the project. In general, the implementation of the project must be monitored and controlled to ensure that the project remains on the planned path.

Monitoring and Controlling the Project. They monitor and control the project throughout its life cycle, including during the execution phase. The purpose of monitoring and control is to ensure that the project stays on track, i.e., is executed as planned, and, if it goes off track, to take action to get it back on track. To accomplish this, perform the following steps on an ongoing basis:

1. Collect the actual project performance data.

2. Analyze it to compare results to project performance and measure deviation from plan.

3. Based on variances, create change requests, such as recommendations for preventive and corrective actions, and process them for approval and subsequent implementation.

Change requests can also come directly from stakeholders and should also be properly evaluated and addressed. You do all this using the processes that belong to the Monitoring and Control process group.

■ *Note Monitoring and controlling does not start only after the project begins execution. Rather, the project needs to be monitored and controlled all the way from initiation through closing.*

Whether completed or terminated, each project needs to be closed properly.

Closing the Project. In this phase, you ensure that all required project processes are completed, all project-related contracts are closed, the project deliverable is turned over to another group, such as the maintenance or operations group, and you can end the project by disbanding the project team. Completing the project also includes conducting a project report to evaluate the lessons learned. Do not forget the last - but not leastimportant - task in the closing phase: the celebration. Completed projects (i.e., projects that are terminated before completion) should also go through the closure phase. The processes that are used in the closure phase are called the closure process group. In a multi-phase project, each phase can and should be closed using the same process that is used to close the project.

■ **Caution!** What we refer to as project stages here are not the project phases. A project phase is part of the whole project in which certain milestones or project deliverables are completed. All these stages, technically called process groups, can be applied to any phase of a project that is divided into multiple phases.

■ **Note** The processes of the closing process group can be used to close a project, as well as to close a phase of a project.

Each process is a two-dimensional entity. It belongs to a certain project phase (group) and to a certain process knowledge area.

Understanding Project Management Knowledge Areas

To manage projects, you use project management knowledge, which is divided into different categories; each category is called a project management knowledge area. For example, each project has a scope that needs to be managed, and the knowledge required to manage the scope is in the Project Scope Management knowledge area. To perform the project work within the project scope, you need resources that need to be managed; the knowledge area used to manage human resources is called resource management. You get the idea. Each process belongs to one of the ten knowledge areas listed below:

Project integration management. The project is initiated, planned and executed in parts, using different areas of knowledge, and all these parts are related to each other and need to be brought together. This is where integration management comes into play. For example, efforts to develop and integrate various subordinate plans into the project management plan must be coordinated. In general, the Integration Management knowledge area provides processes for defining, identifying, coordinating, and integrating various activities and processes within each project management process group.

Project scope management. The main purpose of project scope management is to ensure that all the required work, and only the required work, is done to complete the project. Scoping a project involves drawing the lines between what belongs and what does not. During scope management, you develop the Scope Baseline, one of three very important project baselines. The other two are the Schedule Baseline and the Cost Baseline.

The work included in the project scope must be scheduled.

Project schedule management. The main purpose of project schedule management is to develop and manage the project schedule to complete the project on time as planned. It includes processes for generating the information needed to develop the schedule, a process for developing the schedule, and a process for controlling the schedule. As part of schedule management, you develop the schedule baseline, one of three very important project baselines. The other two are the scope baseline and the cost baseline.

Resources are needed to carry out the project activities in the project schedule.

Project resource management. The primary purpose of project resource management is to identify, acquire, and manage the resources needed to complete the project. The term resources refers to both human resources, e.g., the project team, and physical resources, e.g., materials, equipment, facilities, and infrastructure. It also includes the processes for procuring, developing, and managing the project team that will perform the project work.

All project resources cost money.

Project cost management. The main tasks of project cost management are to estimate and control project costs, and the main goal is to complete the project within the approved budget. During cost management, you develop the cost baseline, one of the three very important project baselines, the other two being the scope baseline and the schedule baseline.

We do all of these and other project management tasks for the project stakeholders.

Project stakeholder management. The main purpose of stakeholder management is to identify project stakeholders and to manage and monitor their engagement in the project. This includes analyzing their potential influence on the project and their expectations of the project, and developing an appropriate strategy to engage them appropriately in the project.

Not only do you need to communicate when managing project stakeholders, but also when managing all aspects of the project.

Project communication management. It is essential for the success of the project that project information be created and distributed, i.e., communicated, in a timely manner. Some would say that communication is the most important aspect of a project and the most important skill of a project manager. Without a doubt, it is an extremely important component of project management and a common thread that runs through the entire project life cycle.

This process group provides three processes: Plan communication to determine the communication approach; Manage communication to execute it; and Monitor communication to ensure it occurs. The key to a project and the mantra of effective communication is getting the right information to the right stakeholders at the right time using the right communication methods to achieve the desired impact. To achieve this, you need to be able to create, store and retrieve information. Any project is only complete to the extent that its objectives and requirements are met; this relates to project quality, which must also be managed.

Project quality management. This process group provides three processes for quality management: plan quality to determine the quality requirements and standards relevant to the project at hand; manage quality to ensure that the planned quality requirements and standards are applied; and control quality to verify that the project and its results meet the quality requirements and conform to the quality standards.

We make assumptions and estimates and face constraints. These other sources of uncertainty can lead to risks that must be managed.

There will be situations where your organization does not have the expertise to perform certain planned activities internally. For this or other reasons, you may want to purchase some items or services from an outside vendor. This type of purchase is called procurement and must also be managed.

Project procurement management. The primary purpose of procurement management is to manage the acquisition of products (i.e., products, services, or deliverables) from outside the project team to complete the project. The external provider offering the service is referred to as the vendor. Procurement management includes the processes for planning, executing, and controlling procurements.

As you have seen, managing a project essentially means performing a series of processes at various stages of the project, such as initiation and planning. Accordingly, processes are grouped according to these phases, and these groups are called process groups. Processes are also part of the knowledge required to manage projects. Each of these processes belongs to one of the ten knowledge areas listed in the PMBOK Guide, Eighth Edition. Thus, a process has a dual affiliation - first to a process group, which indicates in which phase of the project the process is performed, and second to a knowledge area, which indicates which aspect of the project is managed using the process.

■ *Note* *Not all the processes are used in all the projects. The project management team decides which processes need to be used in a given project.*

Triangular Relationship: Project, Program, and Portfolio

As a project manager, you should know the basic concepts of programs and portfolios and how they relate to each other and to projects. The actual action to achieve an organization's goals always takes place at the project level, but for good reasons a project can also be carried out as part of a program or a portfolio; the two structures are described in the following sections.

Program. A program can be defined as a series of interrelated projects all working toward the same goals. These projects are combined into a program to take advantage of coordinated management that would not be possible when managing individual projects. For example, a publisher might include several scholarly book development projects in one program and a set of web development projects related to marketing, sales, and learning in another program.

A program can also be a part of a higher-level program. Both projects and subprograms within a program are called program components. Just as a project is managed by a project manager, a program is managed by a program manager who oversees the program components and manages the project-level aspects. Program management focuses on optimally managing the interdependencies between projects in the program to align program and project goals with the organization's strategic objectives. Program managers also ensure that both program and project benefits are realized. Program manager responsibilities also include:

• Ensure that program scope is appropriately incorporated into program components and that dependencies among program components are managed to best achieve program objectives, and that budget is appropriately allocated to program components.

• Resolve resource conflicts and constraints affecting program components and manage change requests to the Shared Governance Framework.

• Resolve program-level issues between component projects and resolve constraints and conflicts affecting projects within the program.

• Management of program risks that may affect program components.

Portfolio. A portfolio is a higher-level structure that can include projects, programs, sub-portfolios, and operations, and is managed by a portfolio manager. These components are combined into a portfolio to enable effective management to implement the organization's strategic business plan.

■ *Caution!* *The portfolio components, programs, or projects may or may not be interdependent or directly related.*

Portfolio management is the centralized management of one or more portfolios, managing portfolio components at the portfolio level to achieve specific strategic business objectives. A portfolio is an interface between a company's projects and programs and its strategy. Portfolio management focuses on ensuring that programs and projects are prioritized for resources to support the company's strategy. As a result, investment decisions are typically made at the portfolio level. One role of portfolio management is to make the optimal selection of programs and projects to both meet strategic objectives and increase the likelihood of achieving the desired return on investment. It also enables the overall risk of all portfolio components to be managed centrally.

To understand the relationship of a portfolio to projects and programs, consider the following:

• Even if an organization has no programs, but only individual projects, all of these projects can be combined into one or more portfolios.

• If an organization has programs and no individual projects outside of all programs, all of those programs can be grouped into one or more portfolios.

• If an organization has some programs and some individual projects, all of these programs and projects can be grouped into one or more portfolios.

■ *Caution!* *Projects, programs, and portfolios have different lifecycles, focuses, and sets of objectives, and hence they have different sets of activities to meet those objectives and different sets of resulting benefits. However, they may share the same resources serving the same stakeholder. This underlies the importance of Intra organization coordination to avoid and resolve conflicts.*

Figure below shows the triangular relationship between portfolios, programs, and projects; in the figure, an arrow represents containment. As the figure illustrates, all portfolios consist of programs, projects, or both. A program consists only of projects and not portfolios. The figure also illustrates that both a program and a portfolio can contain projects. This means that a project can be a member of a portfolio either directly or through a program. What is not shown in this simple figure is that a program can have child programs and a portfolio can contain child portfolios and operations.

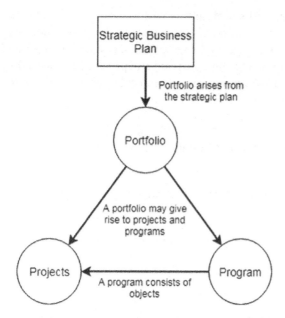

Triangular relationship between projects, programs, and portfolios.

Compared to projects and programs, a portfolio is closer to an organization's business goals, and therefore is where most investment decisions are made. If you want to learn about an organization's business intentions and direction (or strategy), you should look at its portfolio. It's also important to know that a portfolio can include operational work as part of its structure.

Characteristic	Project	Program	Portfolio
Definition	Endeavor with beginning and end to create a unique product, service, or result.	Group of related projects and subsidiary programs managed together to reap the benefits not available from managing them individually.	Collection of projects, programs, subsidiary portfolios, and other related work; managed together to meet the strategic objectives.
Management	Project manager manages the program including project team, by coordinating the to lead the project to program components' success by meeting activities to ensure the project objectives.	Program manager manages the project, delivery of planned program benefits.	Portfolio manager performs general portfolio management that may include managing or coordinating the portfolio management staff and the program and project staff with reporting responsibility to portfolio.
Scope	Project scope limited to meeting its objectives; developed throughout the project lifecycle.	A program's scope affects and encompasses the scopes of program components aimed at meeting the program benefits in the context of the strategic goals of the organization.	Portfolios have an organizational scope to produce changes in the strategic objectives of the organization.
Planning	Project manager, from high-level information, develops detailed project plans by using progressive elaboration throughout the project lifecycle.	Program has a high-level plan that includes tracking the progress and interdependencies of program components; this plan also provides guidance to plan at the component level.	Portfolio manager performs planning at the portfolio level, which includes developing and executing necessary processes, including communication in context of aggregate portfolio.
Change	Project manager expects change and perform processes to manage it.	Program manager adapts change to optimize the benefits from program components.	Portfolio manager monitors changes in the broader internal and external environments and responds to them to best serve the strategic plan of the organization
Monitoring	Project manager monitors and controls the project activities/ processes to produce the planned products, results, or services of the project.	Program manager monitors the progress of program components to make sure the overall goals and benefits will be achieved within the planned budget and schedule.	Portfolio managers monitor strategic changes, resource allocation, performance results, and risk at the portfolio level.
Success	Success measured generally by quality of project and its product, level of customer satisfaction, and whether project is completed within budget and on time.	Program success measured by delivery of planned program benefit and the efficiency and effectiveness of the delivery.	Success relates to the overall portfolio performance, which is an aggregated investment compared to the overall benefit realized.

Probability-Related Concepts

Probability theory has its roots in the early seventeenth century in the study of games of chance such as roulette and card games. Since then, a variety of mathematicians and scientists have contributed to the development of probability theory. Today, the concepts of probability appear in almost every discipline, from physics to project management. Risk (an important aspect of a project) and probability have the same origin: uncertainty. In project management, there is always an important question: what is the probability that this risk will occur? In the modern age, probability has already entered people's psyche through phrases such as "What is the probability that this will happen?"

Probability. Probability is defined as the chance that something will happen. For example, if you play the lottery and wonder what the probability is that you will win, think of probability. The simplest example of probability is the flip of a coin. If you flip a coin, what is the probability that the coin will show heads? When you flip a coin, there are only two possibilities: It will land either heads or tails. Each possibility is equally likely unless you cheat. Therefore, the probability that the coin will come up heads is 1 in 2, which is 50 percent or 0.5. In general, if there are n possible outcomes of an event and each outcome is equally likely, then the probability of a particular outcome is 1/n.

Another useful concept in probability is the combined probability of multiple events. For example, if you flip two coins, the probability that the first coin is heads and the second coin is tails is 0.5 × 0.5 = 0.25. To calculate the total probability, you generally multiply the individual probabilities. If the probability of an event X occurring is A, the probability of an event Y occurring is B, and the probability of an event Z occurring is C, then the probability of all three events (X, Y, and Z) occurring is A × B × C.

In summary, the probability that multiple independent events occur is calculated by multiplying the probabilities of occurrence of all individual events.

Random Variable. A random variable can take any value within a specified range or from a range of values. For example, you can use a random variable to represent the outcome of rolling a fair die that has six sides numbered by points from 1 to 6. The possible outcome of rolling the dice could be any number from the set of outcomes: {1, 2, 3, 4, 5, 6}.

Expected Value. This is the expected value of an outcome. Suppose you settle on a bet in which you win $10 if the coin toss comes up heads, and lose $5 if it comes up tails. Since the probability of heads or tails is 0.5 in each case, the expected value for the money you win is $10 × 0.5 = $5, and the expected value for the money you lose is $5 × 0.5 = $2.50.

Variance. The variance of a random variable is the deviation from the expected value. It is calculated as the average squared deviation of each number from its mean. For example, suppose that the values of a random variable for five measurements are 2, 4, 5, 7, and 2. The mean value for these measurements is (2 + 4 + 5 + 7 + 2) / 5 = 4

The variance of the spread of these values is V = s 2= é (2 - 4) 2+ (4 - 4) 2(7 - 4) 2(2 - 4) 2ù / 5 = 3.4

Standard Deviation. This is the square root of the variance, that is, σ. So in our example, the standard deviation is the square root of 3.4, which is 1.84.

Algebraic Equations. The Project/Program Management and some questions in the CAPM, PMP, and PgMP exams require that you can perform simple mathematical calculations. You should also have a very basic understanding of algebraic equations. You should be able to perform simple manipulations, such as the following:

CPI = EV/AC implies EV = CPI × AC

CV = EV–AC implies EV = AC + CV

Baseline

The project baseline is defined as the approved plan for certain aspects of the project, such as the cost, schedule, and scope of the project. Project performance is measured against this baseline. The project baseline is also referred to in terms of its components - cost baseline, schedule baseline, and scope baseline. How do you know how the project is performing? You compare performance to the baseline. Approved changes to cost, schedule, and scope also change the baseline.

Big Picture of Project Management

In this chapter, you learned what project management is and how project management is accomplished by applying knowledge and skills to project activities to achieve project goals. The application of knowledge boils down to the execution of processes. We also learned that projects arise out of the need to achieve the strategic goals of the organization and that they can come to you as stand-alone projects or as part of a program or portfolio.

The following figure shows the big picture of project origination and management in terms of projects, processes, the project life cycle in terms of project phases, and project aspects managed by ten different knowledge areas. There are ten important aspects of projects, and each of these ten aspects is managed by the corresponding knowledge area. For example, cost is managed by the cost management knowledge area and communication is managed by the communication management knowledge area. Thus, project management is done by applying processes from specific knowledge areas at specific stages of the project.

The three main findings from this chapter are as follows:

- A project, whether it is a stand-alone project or part of a program or portfolio, is undertaken to contribute to the achievement of an organization's strategic goals.

- The project life cycle consists of five phases, technically referred to as process groups: Initiate, Plan, Execute, Monitor and Control, and Close. Depending on the project, these phases may repeat in different sections.

- The project processes performed to manage projects make up ten project management knowledge areas: Integration Management, Scope Management, Time Management, Cost Management, Human Resource Management, Communication Management, Stakeholder Management, Quality Management, Risk Management, and Procurement Management.

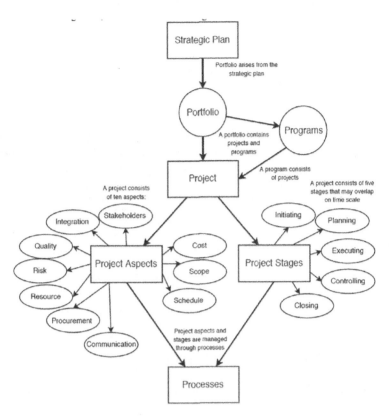

The big picture of project management: the aspects of a project that need to be managed at different stages of the project life cycle by using processes.

In short, project management and the processes carried out in project management have two dimensions: Knowledge and Process Group. This chapter has presented a big picture of project management from a more theoretical perspective.

Summary

Business activities within an organization are usually organized into groups that fall into two categories - operations and projects. Operations usually consist of ongoing routine work, while a project has the goal of producing a unique product, service, or result in a limited amount of time, i.e., it has a planned beginning and end. Companies start projects for a variety of reasons, such as to meet a business or regulatory requirement or to seize an opportunity presented by the market. However, the underlying motivation for taking advantage of these opportunities is the company's business strategy. A project, like everything else in a business, must be managed. Project management is the application of knowledge and skills to project activities to achieve project objectives. It involves a set of processes that fall into ten project management knowledge areas: Communication Management, Stakeholder Management, Cost Management, Human Resource Management, Integration Management, Procurement Management, Quality Management, Risk Management, Scope Management, and Schedule Management. Each process is two-dimensional: it is part of a knowledge area and belongs to one of five process groups: Initiate, Plan, Execute, Monitor/Control, and Close. The process groups represent different phases of a project lifecycle.

Successful project completion increases the business value of the organization, changing the state of the organization's business value to a higher level. A project can be stand-alone or belong to one of two higher-level entities: Programs and Portfolios. A program is a collection of interrelated projects and subsidiary programs and is executed to achieve benefits that would not be possible if projects were managed individually. Programs are more closely related to the company's business strategy or strategic goals than projects. A structure that is even closer to the company's strategy is the portfolio, which is generally a collection of projects, programs, subsidiary portfolios, and operations. A portfolio is a direct interface to the company's business strategy.

The Way Forward. In this chapter, we have looked at the basic framework of projects and project management. Projects are created and managed in an environment that consists of factors within the implementing organization and the outside world. We will explore this environment in the next chapter.

View from the perspective of the test

Comprehend

This is how PMI sees it: the discipline of project management is composed of ten knowledge areas: Scope Management, Cost Management, Human Resource Management, Quality Management, Risk Management, Schedule Management, Procurement Management, Communications Management, Stakeholder Management, and Integration Management.

Depending on the phase of the project life cycle in which they are executed, the processes are divided into five process groups: Initiate, Plan, Execute, Monitor and Control, and Close.

- A process belongs to exactly one knowledge area and one process group.

- The same input can occur in more than one process. This also applies to tools and techniques.

- An output from a project either becomes an input for another process or is a final output, i.e. a project or phase result.

- You do not have to perform all processes in a project, and a process can be performed more than once.

- Projects bring about change in an organization by increasing the business value of the organization, thus raising the state of business value to a higher level.

Look Out

• For a work effort to be qualified as a project, it must be temporary (that is, have a start and a finish), and the outcome must be a unique product, result, or service. Routine ongoing work is an operation, not a project.

• A project may vary in size, it may be a few days long or a few months long, and it may involve one person or quite a few individuals.

• A big project is not called a program, but a megaproject.

• A project may or may not be a part of a program or a portfolio, but a program always consists of projects or subsidiary programs, or both.

• A program may contain a subsidiary program, and a portfolio may contain a subsidiary portfolio and operation too.

Memorize

• The ten knowledge areas and five process groups listed under the "Comprehend" section of this table.

• Process groups are not project phases. A phase contains all process groups.

• Organizations start projects in response to the factors acting on them, which can be categorized into four groups: business or legal requirements; stakeholder requests or needs; business or technological strategies; and products, processes, or services.

Integration
Management

Do you see the forest or the trees when you look at a project? In other words, do you look at the broad picture, concentrating on deliverables and process, or do you concentrate on the smaller and more numerous activities that must be completed to finish the project?

The majority of project management procedures are made up of trees; nonetheless, this chapter reflects the whole forest. These seven processes concentrate on the broader, macro tasks that must be completed for the project to succeed and the company to learn from it. Whereas most of this content is arranged around the minor procedures that result in the creation of a plan or the updating of a document, the processes of integration are broader and more significant.

Integration management is the activity of ensuring that all aspects of a project are coordinated. The project is begun in integration management, the project manager creates the project plan, executes the plan, and evaluates the work outcomes, and finally the project is closed. The necessary knowledge is recorded for the organization. At the same time, the project manager must balance conflicting goals for time and resources while keeping the team focused on finishing the job.

This chapter examines seven integration management procedures and how they interact with one another.

As we begin, keep in mind that this is the one knowledge area where accountability cannot be assigned. These seven procedures are fundamental to project management, and since the project manager is ultimately accountable for the whole project, he or she is also responsible for carrying them out.

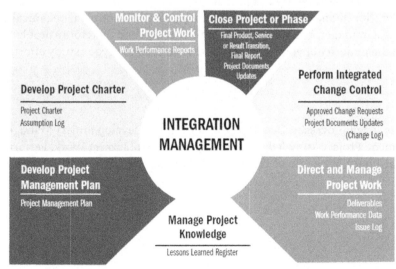

PHILOSOPHY:

From conception to completion, integration management takes a high-level perspective of the project. The term "integration" is used because any modifications made in one section of the project must be incorporated with the remainder of the project. The many systems of the human body, for example, are intimately interwoven. What you eat and drink may have an impact on how you sleep, and how much sleep you receive can have an impact on your capacity to think effectively. When assessing your physical health, consider your food, exercise, sleep, stress, and so on, since gains in one area are likely to spill over into others.

Management of integration is similar. Change does not occur in a vacuum, and although this is true for the majority of the processes discussed in this book, it is particularly true for the processes detailed in this chapter.

The philosophy behind integration management is threefold:

Decision-making throughout the project's execution procedures may be a noisy and messy occurrence, and the team should be shielded from as much of this cacophony as possible. In contrast, you want the team to be more engaged in the planning procedures. You do not want to convene a team meeting every time an issue emerges during execution. The project manager, on the other hand, should make choices and keep the team focused on completing the task packages.

The procedures that comprise project management are not distinct. That is, they do not always work from beginning to end before moving on to the next activity. It would be ideal if the scope could be specified and completed before moving on to execution without having to be reviewed; unfortunately, this is not how things usually operate. Even the most meticulously managed projects will review procedures in the planning, implementation, and control phases. This is comparable to how a symphony player may tune an instrument before the start of a concert but will most likely retune and make minor modifications numerous times during the performance. Variables and conditions vary throughout time, and when they do, a plan or method of carrying out a project must be changed.

Integration techniques must be adjusted to a project's size and complexity.

IMPORTANCE:

This part is quite important; you should anticipate numerous questions on the test that are directly related to this chapter.

PREPARATION:

This content is deemed challenging largely because there is so much information to comprehend. Earlier versions of the test did not consider integration management to be particularly tough, but much of the information from other knowledge areas has been transferred into integration management. While the material may not be as technically tough as other areas such as schedule, quality, or cost management, it may be unfamiliar to you and therefore a problem. This chapter will instruct you on where to spend the majority of your time and how to concentrate your study efforts.

INTEGRATION MANAGEMENT PROCESSES:

The integration management knowledge area has seven processes. Develop Project Charter, Develop Project Management Plan, Direct and Manage Project Work, Manage Project Knowledge, Monitor and Control Project Work, Perform Integrated Change Control, and Close Project or Phase are some of these. The following are the breakdowns that illustrate which group each process belongs to:

Process Group	Integration Management Process
Initiating	Develop Project Charter
Planning	Develop Project Management Plan
Executing	Direct and Manage Project Work, Manage Project Knowledge
Monitoring & Controlling	Monitor & Control Project Work, Perform Intergrated Change Control
Closing	Close Project or Phase

It is also essential that you know the main outputs that are produced as a result of each process. The key outputs that are created in each process are summarized in the following table.

Process	Primary Outputs
Develop Project Charter	Project Charter, Assumption Log
Develop Project Management Plan	Project Management Plan
Direct and Manage Project Work	Deliverables, Work Performance Data, Issue Log
Manage Project Knowledge	Lessons Learned Register
Monitor & Control Project Work	Work Performance Reports
Perform Integrated Change Control	Approved Change Requests, Project Documents Updates (Change Log)
Close Project or Phase	Final Product, Service or Result Transition, Final Report, Project Documents Updates

DEVELOP PROJECT CHARTER

WHAT IT IS:

Consider the project charter to be its birth certificate. It is the document that formally kicks off the project, and it is created via this procedure. Expect the charter to have a significant and conspicuous part on the test.

WHY IT IS IMPORTANT:

The charter is one of the most crucial papers on a project since it is required for the project to be created. You do not have an official project until you have a charter. As you will see later in this section, missing this step might produce issues for the project manager that may not manifest themselves for a long time.

WHEN IT IS PERFORMED:

This is one of the very first processes to be carried out. It is typical for some pre-planning to occur on a project before it becomes official, but the project will not be considered official until the charter is granted.

HOW IT WORKS / INPUTS:

Business Documents - The word "business documentation" refers to the business case and the benefits management strategy in general. Documents that define the need and how the project will meet or solve that need while benefiting the stakeholders are included in this input.

The business case describes why this project is being performed, the issue it will answer, and an estimate of the benefit-cost ratio.

The project benefits management plan is another component of these business papers. This section discusses how the project adds to the organization's strategy, as well as the predicted benefits and how to optimize those advantages. This document is often handed to the project manager at the outset of the project.

Reasons A Project May Be Undertaken

Projects may be started for a variety of reasons, which should be justified in the business case. Before proceeding with this procedure, it is necessary to discuss some of these factors as well as some of the methods for calculating benefits.

Projects are started for a purpose, and knowing that reason might help the project succeed. The following are some of the most typical motivations for starting a project:

Market Demand - A frequent situation is for a corporation to discover a market need that can be met via a project, such as an electronics company developing a new consumer gadget to suit a demand.

Organizational Need - If senior management need a new reporting tool to examine trends, this would be a solid reason to start a project to do this.

Customer Request - The most prevalent situation for new project inception is a client paying for a new project.

Technological Advance - New technical breakthroughs enable the development of new goods and services. The automobile sector is only one example of how breakthroughs in battery technology have found their way into automobiles and trucks all across the globe. Each of these undertakings began as a result of a technical advancement.

Legal Requirement - New legislation or a new interpretation of an existing law may often necessitate the need for a project to ensure compliance.

Ecological Impact - Some businesses are working on programs to lower their carbon footprint or environmental effect. This is seen as a legitimate justification for starting a project.

Social Need - Numerous groups are cropping up to promote entrepreneurship to some of the world's most destitute locations as an example of addressing social issues. Many of these objectives are also mainly met via initiatives.

Project Selection Methods

Companies choose which projects to take on in a number of ways. The most frequent approaches attempt to quantify the monetary benefits and predicted expenses of a project and compare them to other prospective initiatives in order to identify the most viable and desired ones. These are known as benefit measuring approaches.

Although the project manager may not have been officially appointed at this stage in the project, he or she may be engaged in other ways, such as creating the business case and selling the project to the selection committee or senior management.

Other approaches, such as constrained optimization, use mathematics to solve for maximizations. Constrained optimization employs a number of programming techniques. If you see the phrases linear programming or non-linear programming on the test, you will understand that they relate to a form of restricted optimization approach and that the question is about project selection strategies. For the test, you do not need to know how to compute values for restricted optimization or linear programming, but you must be aware that they are project selection approaches.

The following are additional economics, finance, management accounting, and cost accounting principles that are occasionally employed as project selection techniques. It is not required to remember these definitions word for word; nonetheless, understanding what they are and how they are used is essential.

Benefit Cost Ratio (BCR) - The BCR is the benefit-to-cost ratio. For example, if you anticipate a construction project costing $1,000,000 and selling the finished structure for $1,500,000, your BCR is $1,500,000 $1,000,000 = 1.5 to 1.

In other words, for every $1.00 spent, you get $1.50 in benefits. A benefit-to-cost ratio higher than one shows that the benefits exceed the expenses.

Economic Value Add (EVA) - When assessing the worth of a project, it is easy to lose sight of the bigger picture of generating value to shareholders. Economic Value Add (EVA) measures how much value a project has produced for its owners. It looks at more than just the net earnings. It also considers opportunity costs. EVA can effectively indicate how much wealth was gained (or lost) over time by accounting for all capital expenses. It considers the notion that every financial spend includes opportunity costs, and that if a project does not generate more money than those opportunity costs, it has not actually brought economic value to the firm.

To calculate EVA, begin with the project's after-tax earnings. Then deduct the capital invested in that project multiplied by the cost of that capital.

For example, firm XYZ spent $175,000 in a project, which generated a net profit of $10,000 in its first year of operation. Accountants would most likely rejoice at the net profit, but what does the EVA tell us about shareholder value? First, we must ascertain the true cost of that capital. In this scenario, we will estimate 6% since the organization might have invested the same $175,000 and gotten a 6% return. When calculating EVA, we use the following formula:

Profit after taxes minus (capital expenditures cost of capital), or $10,000 minus ($175,000.06) = -$500.

Even if the initiative generated an accounting net profit, XYZ would have been better off banking the funds. In other words, XYZ really lost $500 in terms of EVA since they could have gained $10,500 in interest if they had invested the money elsewhere rather than in the project.

Internal Rate of Return (IRR) - IRR, or "Internal Rate of Return," is a financial term used to quantify the returns on a project as an interest rate. In other words, what would the interest rate be if this project were a loan? Do not be concerned with the test formula; nonetheless, you should grasp that, similar to the interest rate on a savings account, larger is preferable when looking at IRR.

Net Present Value (NPV) - For an explanation of Net Present Value (NPV) and Present Value, see the section on Present Value further in this section (PV).

Opportunity Cost - Based on the idea that a dollar can only be put in one location at a time, opportunity cost asks, "What is the cost of the other possibilities we missed by spending our money and resources in this project?" The lower the opportunity cost, the better for project selection, since it is not desirable to lose up on a wonderful chance.

Payback Period - The payback period is the time required to repay an investment in a project. If you owed someone $100, you would prefer that they pay you immediately rather than $25 every month for four months. All else being equal, a shorter payback time is usually preferable to a longer one since you want to recuperate your investment as soon as possible in order to free up that money for another investment opportunity.

Present Value (PV) and Net Present Value (NPV) - PV is based on the economic principle of "time value of money," which states that a dollar now is worth more than a dollar tomorrow. If a project is predicted to generate three $100,000 yearly payments, the present value (how much those payments are worth right now) will be less than $300,000. The reason for this is that you will not get your complete $300,000 until the third year, but if you put $300,000 in the bank right now, you would have more than $300,000 in three years.

PV is a method of removing time from the equation and determining how much a project is worth right now. It is critical to remember that when it comes to PV, larger is better.

Net Present Value (NPV) is the same as Present Value, except it includes your expenses. For example, suppose you built a building with a PV of $500,000 but only spent $350,000 on it. In this situation, your net present value (NPV) would be $500,000 - $350,000 = $150,000.

Remember that a higher PV or NPV makes a project more appealing, and that NPV estimates have already taken into account the project's cost.

Return On Investment (ROI) - Return on Investment (ROI) is a percentage that reflects how much money an organization earns when it invests in something. Assume, for example, that a corporation spends $200,000 in a project. The project's advantages would save the corporation $230,000 in the first year alone. The ROI in this situation would be computed as (benefit - cost) cost, or $30,000 $200,000 = 15%.

You need not worry about remembering this equation for the test, but you should realize that greater is better when it comes to ROI.

Return on Invested Capital (ROIC) - ROIC, which is stated as a percentage, examines how a business utilizes the money spent in a project. It asks, "How much should I anticipate (or did I gain) for every dollar of cash I put in a project?" This invested money might be cash on hand or borrowed cash. The computation is quite easy for project management needs. Use the following formula:

ROIC = Net Income (after tax) from Project ÷ Total Capital Invested in the project

Fictional Enterprises, for example, spent $250,000 in a project that earned $60,000 in top-line income in its first year, with $20,000 in operating expenditures and a $8,750 tax bill. To calculate the ROIC, first deduct the expenses from the revenue to get the after-tax profits.

This is calculated as $60,000 - $20,000 - $8,750 = $31,250.

Now, use the ROIC algorithm to calculate: ROIC = $31,250 x $250,000 = 12.5%

This indicates that Fictional's project returns 12.5 percent on the money it spent to complete it.

Agreements - It is easier to consider an agreement to be a contract. Because not all projects are carried out under contract, this feedback may or may not be useful. When a project is completed under contract for another entity, the contract is usually signed before the project begins. The contract is an important contribution as we prepare to begin the project and draft the charter.

HOW IT WORKS

Project Charter - The project charter must be written whenever an organization has chosen a project or a contract to conduct a project has been signed. The following are the main points to remember regarding the project charter.

The Project Charter

Consider this the birth certificate for your project.

- It is generated as part of the Develop Project Charter process.

- It is developed in response to a need, and it should describe that need as well as how the eventual outcome will meet it.

- It is often written by the sponsor and/or customer, although in certain situations, the project manager who will be working on the project may help in drafting it.

- It is signed by the project's sponsor or another top executive in the company.

- It identifies the project manager and specifies his or her authority to allocate resources and make decisions.

- It specifies the conditions under which the project may be completed, closed, or canceled (i.e., the exit criteria).

- It should cover the project's high-level needs.

- It should offer a high-level picture of the project's milestones.

- It is a high-level document that lacks project specifics; the specifics of project activities will be established later.

- It offers a tentative project budget at the summary level.

- It includes the project's goals and performance metrics, as well as who decides if the project is successful.

- It includes a list of major stakeholders.

- It indicates who must approve the final result.

Assumption Log - The assumption log is a document that will be maintained and updated during the project. It serves as a repository for all assumptions and limitations.

Consider an assumption to be any unknown that you consider as true for the sake of planning. The assumptions may be wide and generic when the charter is created. They will be revised later in the project to be more specialized and lower level.

DEVELOP PROJECT MANAGEMENT PLAN

WHAT IT IS:

Many people wrongly associate a project plan with a Gantt chart or a timetable. The project managers who brought this misunderstanding into the exam were chewed up and vomited out by the examination! The project management plan, as you will see in this part, is a complete document that directs the project's execution and control, and it is much more than a timetable chart.

WHY IT IS IMPORTANT:

This one should be simple. The project plan directs the work of the project team. It explains who, what, when, where, and how. This paper is referenced throughout the book, so having a strong comprehension of it will be quite beneficial as you study.

WHEN IT IS PERFORMED:

Because the project management plan is not created all at once, the issue of when the process of Develop Project Management Plan is carried out is intriguing. This strategy is gradually evolved, which means it is created, polished, reviewed, and updated. Because it reflects the aggregate of the other primary planning outputs, it must be constructed after the component plans are developed.

When the project management plan is accepted, it is placed under control, which means that it is stabilized and additional modifications need a change control procedure.

HOW IT WORKS

Project Management Plan - This process's single result is the project management plan, which is one of the most essential outputs of any process.

Consider the definition of the project management plan. The project plan is defined as "a formal, authorized document outlining how the project will be managed, performed, and regulated." It may be either brief or thorough, and it can include one or more subsidiary management plans and other planning papers."

The keys to understanding this are:

- The project management strategy is formal in nature. It is critical to consider the project management plan to be a formal, written piece of communication.

- The project management plan is included in a single document. It is not 19 distinct plans. When those individual papers are authorized as the project plan, they merge into a single document.

- The project management strategy has been approved. This is the stage at which the individual plans merge to form the project plan. The persons who approve it will vary depending on the organizational structure and other considerations, but they may include:

- The project supervisor

- The project's backer

- The functional managers who are contributing project resources

- The group that will be conducting the task

- It is advisable not to consider the client or senior management as giving their approval to the project plan. The consumer will sign an agreement but will often delegate responsibility for the inner workings to the performing company (ideally, anyway). Senior management in most organizations cannot go down to the level of evaluating every component document and approving the project plan, particularly for each and every project.

- The project plan is not revised on the spur of the moment. For making modifications and updates, a change control mechanism is in place.

- The project management plan specifies how the project will be managed, carried out, and regulated. This indicates that the paper outlines how the majority of the project will be carried out.

- The project management strategy might be concise or comprehensive. Despite the fact that this term is in the definition, it is much preferable to conceive of the project management plan as always being thorough!

- The project management plan is composed of numerous components, which may be thought of as chapters in the overall plan. Longer and more formal components will be used in more formal and mission-critical projects. Not every project management plan will have all 19 components shown in the image at the conclusion of this section, but you should be acquainted with the components depicted before taking the test.

Another essential aspect of the project management plan is that the majority of its components are created in other procedures. Plan Risk Management, for example, is used to create the project risk management plan. This is the stage at which all of these plans come together.

Components of a project plan and the procedures that go with them.

Component	PROCESS
Scope Management Plan	Plan Scope Management
Requirements Management Plan	Plan Scope Management
Schedule Management Plan	Plan Schedule Management
Cost Management Plan	Plan Cost Management
Quality Management Plan	Plan Quality Management
Resource Management Plan	Plan Resource Management
Communications Management Plan	Plan Communications Management
Risk Management Plan	Plan Risk Management
Procurement Management Plan	Plan Procurement Management
Stakeholder Engagement Plan	Plan Stakeholder Engagement
Change Management Plan	Develop Project Management Plan
Configuration Management Plan	Develop Project Management Plan
Scope Baseline	Create WBS
Schedule Baseline	Develop Schedule
Cost Baseline	Determine Budget
Performance Measurement Baseline	Develop Project Management Plan
Project Life Cycle Description	Develop Project Management Plan
Development Approach	Develop Project Management Plan

MANAGE AND DIRECT PROJECT WORK

WHAT IT IS:

When studying project management methods, it is easy to get the notion that the project manager must spend the majority of his or her time planning. Fortunately, this is not the case. The Direct and Manage Project Work process consumes the majority of a project's time, money, and resources. This is the place where things get done!

The team executes work packages and creates project deliverables under Direct and Manage Project Work.

WHY IT IS IMPORTANT:

The Direct and Manage Project Work process is where roads are built, software applications are produced, buildings are erected, and items are manufactured.

WHEN IT IS PERFORMED:

This process is tough to quantify, and it is critical that you understand why. It is easy to fall into the trap of seeing project management as a linear process. That is, you plan first, then execute all of the tasks, then monitor and control, and lastly close, in that sequence. However, it is not how most projects are carried out.

On a real project, you could conduct some planning, some execution, and then some monitoring and controlling, only to go back to more planning, execution, and monitoring and controlling. In actuality, you may need to repeat this procedure many times.

As a result, while considering the process of Direct and Manage Project Work, you should not see it as a single event, but rather as something that happens whenever you implement the project management plan to achieve project deliverables.

HOW IT WORKS / INPUTS:

Project Management Plan - Remember that the project management plan directs the project's management, execution, monitoring, and control. We are focused on the implementation of the project plan in this step, therefore it should come as no surprise that it is the most important input.

HOW IT WORKS / OUTPUTS:

Deliverables - A deliverable is any product, service, or outcome that must be produced in order for the project to be finished. Some projects must also create skills in order to complete a project, and they may also be deliverables. For example, a project may need the development of a new manufacturing procedure before it can produce a product. In such situation, the competence developed by the team would be regarded a deliverable. It is also critical to comprehend what happens to the deliverables that are produced. They go through the Control Quality and Validate Scope procedures until they fulfill the standards for accuracy and completeness. The deliverables are then utilized in the Manage Project Knowledge procedure.

Work Performance Data - This is the second most essential outcome of this procedure, after the deliverables. Not only do deliverables come out of this process, but so does data regarding how those deliverables are created.

Work performance data is finally turned into work performance information when it has been examined and comprehended, as we discussed in chapter two. At this stage, the data obtained is raw and unfiltered.

Issue Log - An issue is an unsolved threat or problem on the project, or a point of contention, and the issue log is the document that records them. The issue log is vital since it not only helps to organize problems, but it also informs stakeholders and the team that they are being actively examined.

MANAGE PROJECT KNOWLEDGE

WHAT IT IS:

With this version, Manage Project Knowledge is a newly recognized procedure. This technique improves the project by using lessons acquired from past projects, as well as the performing organization by allowing it to retain the lessons learnt on this project.

WHY IT IS IMPORTANT:

Previous projects may help your project learn, and others in your company can benefit from the lessons you learn on current project. In other words, "those who do not learn from history are bound to repeat it."

WHEN IT IS PERFORMED:

Technically, this procedure may be performed whenever a project lesson is learnt; however, the most logical time is after the deliverables for each phase have been finished but before the phase or project has been concluded.

HOW IT WORKS / INPUTS:

Deliverables - This process incorporates the deliverables created in the prior phase, Direct and Manage Project Work. The reason for this is because the kind of deliverable will influence the learning that must be collected.

A new pharmaceutical product or model of car, for example, may have considerable regulatory lessons learned, but a new road may have more environmental or stakeholder-related lessons learned.

The deliverables do not dictate the lessons learnt automatically, but they will certainly flavor them.

HOW IT WORKS / TOOLS:

Knowledge Management - Knowledge management is divided into two parts: explicit knowledge and tacit knowledge.

Things that can be written down or drawn and readily saved for future lessons learnt are examples of explicit knowledge.

Beliefs, views, and talents are examples of tacit knowledge. These may be difficult to convert into an archival format.

The goal of knowledge management is to encourage individuals to engage and share their knowledge and experiences. This may involve a variety of activities such as networking, assisted seminars, and meetings, to mention a few.

Information Management - It may be perplexing to see the instrument of information management alongside the tool of knowledge management. Even if it becomes subtle, the two are distinct. If you consider knowledge to be frequently experienced, consider information to be more tangible.

Consider adopting a collaboration and document management solution like as SharePoint to think about information management. This allows you to share papers, tools, templates, and lessons learned with others in your team and across the company.

The purpose of this tool is to be deliberate in gathering this clear, defined information.

HOW IT WORKS / OUTPUTS

Lessons Learned Register - The essential idea of Manage Project Knowledge is captured in this output. The lessons learned register is a record that details what worked and what did not work. It focused on what the team would do differently if they could redo this project knowing what they know today.

It will be updated during the project and utilized as feedback for both this project and future initiatives undertaken by this organization.

The team responsible for carrying out the job should be heavily engaged in its development.

MONITOR AND CONTROL PROJECT WORK

WHAT IT IS:

The Monitor and Control Project Work method examines all of the work being done on a project to ensure that the deliverables and the manner in which they are generated are in accordance with the project plan and achieve the goals.

Monitor and Control Project Work is critical since it is another macro integration process, even if the majority of the inputs, tools, and outputs are standard. It examines how the whole project is developing and, if necessary, takes remedial action via change requests. For example, if the project is running late, you may opt to reduce the scope of the initial release or even add extra resources. If you are well ahead of schedule, you may choose to use less resources. Both of these are examples of the kind of activities associated with Monitor and Control Project Work. The project manager takes major, macro judgments regarding the project based on how things have been going and how they are expected to go in the future.

WHY IT IS IMPORTANT:

On the project, all monitoring and controlling procedures play a significant part. They compare the work outcomes to the plan and make any required revisions to ensure that the two are in sync. Any adjustments to the work or the plan that are required are recognized and requested during this procedure.

Monitoring and controlling methods like this one keep an eye on all project information to verify that risks are adequately recognized and handled, and that performance is on track.

WHEN IT IS PERFORMED:

Monitor and Control Project Work is closely related to the process Direct and Manage Project Work, and it occurs as long as there is work to be done on the project.

HOW IT WORKS / INPUTS:

Project Management Plan - The project management strategy is the most important guiding input to this procedure. It will give the framework against which the outcomes will be judged.

Assumption Log – to keep track of all the uncertainty that the team was accepting as true for planning reasons.

Basis of Estimates – Backup data demonstrating how the team arrived at estimations.

Cost Forecasts – to develop earned value calculations to indicate how the project is going versus the plan.

Issue Log - to demonstrate which problems are occurring on the project, who is in charge of them, and when a response to these concerns is anticipated.

Lessons Learned Register – to use lessons learnt from prior projects and this one.

Milestone List – to offer a simple method to monitor high-level progress versus the timetable.

Quality Reports – to illustrate actual quality against intended quality. Trends may emerge that need remedial action.

Risk Register – to demonstrate recognized hazards and risk occurrences that may need remedial action.

Risk Report – to provide information regarding high-level and specific hazards influencing the project.

Schedule Forecasts - to develop earned value calculations to indicate how the project is going versus the plan.

Work Performance Information - WPI, or work performance information, is a frequent output addressed in Chapter 2. It is highlighted as an important fact in this section because it gives real outcomes that can be compared to the project management strategy.

HOW IT WORKS / TOOLS:

Data Analysis - "Nothing speaks louder than statistics," as the adage goes. In this situation, data analysis is used to examine the data and identify patterns, as well as to find root cause, assess buffers, review variances, and verify that the project is running within performance and risk tolerances.

HOW IT WORKS / OUTPUTS:

Work Performance Reports - Take note that work performance data is fed into this procedure, and work performance reports are generated. They are used to raise awareness and aid in decision-making. Dashboards, heat reports, burn-down charts, and traffic lights are a few examples.

The most critical aspect of reports is that they should be actionable.

PERFORM INTEGRATED CHANGE CONTROL

WHAT IT IS:

For the test, certain procedures are more vital than others, and this one is one of the most crucial.

Every project change, whether requested or not, must go through Perform Integrated Change Control. This is the stage at which you evaluate each change, whether it has already happened or has been requested, to determine its influence on the project.

WHY IT IS IMPORTANT:

Perform Integrated Change Control combines all of the other monitoring and regulating processes together (i.e., integrates them). When a change happens in one area, its influence on the whole project is assessed.

Assume you arrived at work one morning and discovered that a new legal requirement required that the quality of your project's product needed to be enhanced. Would you solely consider the project's quality processes? No. Following an understanding of the quality effect of this modification, you will most likely need to examine the influence on the project scope, activity duration estimates, overall schedule, budget estimates, project risks, contract and supplier concerns, and so on. In other words, you would need to include this adjustment across the project.

Perform Integrated Change Control varies from the preceding process, Monitor and Control Project Work, in that it is largely focused on managing project change, while Monitor and Control Project Work regulates how the work is carried out.

Take, for example, a new hospital building project. If a change request was filed that added a new wing to the hospital building, it would be examined using Perform Integrated Change Control to determine its effect on the whole project. If, on the other hand, the project team members performed slower than expected, this would be accounted for in Monitor and Control Project Work, and corrective action would be sought to ensure that the plan and the execution were in sync. Despite the fact that both monitor and regulate processes, they are not the same.

WHEN IT IS PERFORMED:

The process of Perform Integrated Change Control, like the integration processes Direct and Manage Project Work and Monitor and Control Project Work, occurs as long as there is work on the project to be done.

Some organizations have a Change Control Board (CCB) that evaluates and officially accepts or rejects change proposals.

HOW IT WORKS / TOOLS:

Change Control Tools - The tools in this section are used to control information flow for the Change Control Board and the project manager. Without a system in place, the quantity of activities and accompanying workflows may become challenging to manage.

Meetings - The Change Control Board is an officially formed group that is in charge of examining modifications and change requests. A Change Control Board's degree of power varies across projects and organizations; nonetheless, it should be specified in the project management plan. The change control meetings are when these modifications are officially evaluated.

HOW IT WORKS / OUTPUTS:

Approved Change Requests - This output should be called "accepted or refused modification requests."

All modifications that have been explicitly requested must be accepted or denied. Change requests that have been granted are sent back to Direct and Manage Project Work. Change requests that are denied should be returned to the seeking party.

The change log is the primary location for tracking all modifications and change requests on a project. They are recorded as part of this product and shared with stakeholders.

Project Documents Updates- The most essential document that is updated as part of this procedure is the project's change log.

CLOSE PROJECT OR PHASE

WHAT IT IS:

One of the most important characteristics of a project is that it is transient. This implies that every project must come to an end at some point, and this is where the integration process comes into play.

Close Project or Phase is all about appropriately terminating the project (or a specific phase, which is sometimes similar to a mini-project).

This involves establishing the relevant documentation and archives, documenting and archiving the lessons learned, and upgrading all organizational process assets.

Another thing to keep in mind is that the team is discharged as part of this procedure.

The majority of the responsibilities are administrative, financial, and legal in nature. The test may refer to these operations as Administrative Closure on occasion.

WHY IT IS IMPORTANT:

Projects that miss this step are often left unfinished, dragging on for months with no formal conclusion. Taking the effort to accomplish this step correctly will guarantee that the project is concluded as cleanly and permanently as possible, and that records are made and preserved appropriately. These recordings become organizational process assets that may be used on future initiatives.

WHEN IT IS PERFORMED:

You can probably assume from the name that this procedure is completed at the conclusion of the project or at the end of each phase. Projects with six stages would most likely repeat this procedure seven times (once after each phase, and once for the project as a whole). In real life, you could complete some of the actions in this process before the project or phase is completed, but for the test, consider it the last process completed on a project or phase.

HOW IT WORKS / INPUTS:

Project Charter - The charter explained why this initiative was started in the first place and the exit criteria.

It also includes a section where someone may officially sign off on the project.

Accepted Deliverables - These are the results of the Validate Scope procedure. The deliverables will be complete, accurate, and signed off on at this stage.

Business Documents - This comprises the benefits management strategy and the business case. The business case is a great gauge for determining whether or not the project met its objectives and delivered the projected benefits. These papers were introduced into the process Develop Process Charter, and the Close Project or Phase process is the equivalent project bookend.

Agreements - When studying for the test, keep in mind that agreements are contracts. Any well-written agreement would include departure criteria, thus using them as inputs into this procedure is obvious.

HOW IT WORKS

Project Documents Updates - The major document that would be updated here is the lessons learned register. Lessons learnt are things the team would do differently if they had to redo the project.

Final Product, Service, or Result Transition - This output symbolizes the acceptance and turnover of responsibility to the receiving party, rather than the product itself (e.g., the customer, operations, support group, or another company). The transition indicates that the product has been approved and is ready for this handover.

Final Report - The final report is a project or phase recap. It will very certainly contain information regarding the scope, schedule performance, cost performance, benefit realization, and a risk summary.

Organizational Process Assets Updates - During the course of a project, lessons will be learnt, information will be gathered, tools will be acquired or constructed, expertise and experience will be gained, and documentation will be made (some of which may be reused one day). All of this should be updated as an organizational process asset and provided to the relevant group or individual(s) in charge of their upkeep. This is often the project management office.

This procedure may result in the updating of organizational process assets such as the customer's or sponsor's formal acceptance papers, project closing documents, project files, and historical information. Lessons learnt should also be documented.

THE AGILE VIEW OF INTEGRATION MANAGEMENT

Projects that use adaptive approaches such as Scrum, Lean, or others place a greater emphasis on the team than the project manager. The project manager takes crucial choices on integration activities in the prior seven processes outlined in this chapter, but on an agile project, the team is empowered to make these decisions and choose how the pieces integrate. Agile teams prefer "generalizing specialists" on the team over highly specialized personnel, so team members are typically aware of the project's demands and are tightly attached to the project, making integration challenges manageable at the team level.

Develop Project Charter

This technique lends itself well to agile. Regardless matter how you approach the task, the project charter is essential. Furthermore, much of the analysis generated throughout this approach would be useful for both predictive and agile projects. In an agile setting, the second significant output, the assumptions log, is probably somewhat less relevant.

Develop Project Management Plan

On agile projects, the significance of a project management strategy is drastically reduced. Predictive projects strive to control and manage risk by planning, therefore the project management plan is critical to them, while agile projects manage risk by being flexible and responsive. Release plans and story maps may be created by agile practitioners, but they will not resemble the project management plan employed by their predictive counterparts.

Direct and Manage Project Work

This method also adapts well to agile in general. The deliverables, work performance statistics, and problem log are the three key outputs of Direct and Manage Project Work. This approach corresponds to Agile, which generates deliverables in fewer, faster iterations. Work performance data is also gathered, consolidated, and exhibited in prominent areas so that team performance may be examined clearly.

Manage Project Knowledge

The goal of Manage Project Knowledge is to keep the lessons learned register up to date, which is especially useful for agile projects. All projects should strive to improve performance and avoid making the same errors, while also sharing best practices with other projects.

Monitor and Control Project Work

Although this approach is suitable to agile, it would appear significantly different in reality. It creates work performance reports as well as modification requests. Work performance reports transfer well to team velocity charts, and agile teams embrace continual change and adaptation as they work, searching for methods to do things better and more effectively.

Perform Integrated Change Control

Carry out Integrated Change Control is difficult to apply to agile in its current form. On the predictive side, it is used to ensure that changes, whether planned or unforeseen, go through the proper planning procedure before being integrated into the project. Because change is accepted on agile projects, the team does not do all of the necessary planning that occurs on predictive projects.

Close Project or Phase

From an agile standpoint, this is a mixed bag. All projects, agile or predictive, must come to an end. Delivering the ultimate product, service, or outcome would undoubtedly apply. If the employer requires it, a final report and project record updates would be appropriate; however, agile projects have a culture of creating "just adequate" documentation, thus this would get less priority on most agile projects.

Review Questions, Answers and Explanations (online)

Scope Management

MANAGING THE PROJECT SCOPE includes the processes required to ensure that the project includes all the work required and only the work required to successfully complete the project. Managing the project scope is primarily about determining and controlling what is and is not included in the project.

The Project Scope Management processes are:

Plan Scope Management - The process of creating a scope management plan that documents how the project and product scope will be defined, validated, and controlled.

Collect Requirements - The process of determining, documenting, and managing stakeholder needs and requirements to meet project objectives.

Define Scope - The process of developing a detailed description of the project and product.

Create WBS - The process of subdividing project deliverables and project work into smaller, more manageable components.

Validate Scope - The process of formalizing acceptance of the completed project deliverables.

Control Scope - The process of monitoring the status of the project and product scope and managing changes to the scope baseline.

Key Concepts for project scope Management

In the project context, the term "scope" can refer to:

Product scope. The features and functions that characterize a product, service, or result.

Project scope. The work performed to deliver a product, service, or result with the specified features and functions. The term "project scope" is sometimes viewed as including product scope.

Project lifecycles can move along a continuum from predictive approaches at one end to adaptive or agile approaches at the other. In a predictive lifecycle, project deliverables are defined at the beginning of the project and any changes in scope are managed incrementally. In an adaptive or agile lifecycle, deliverables are developed over multiple iterations, with a detailed scope for each iteration defined and approved at the outset.

Adaptive lifecycle projects are designed to respond to a high level of change and require continuous stakeholder engagement. The overall scope of an adaptive project is decomposed into a set of requirements and work to be performed, sometimes referred to as a product backlog. At the beginning of an iteration, the team tries to determine how many of the highest priority items on the backlog list can be delivered within the next iteration. Three processes (gather requirements, define scope, and create work breakdown structure) are repeated for each iteration. In contrast, on a forward-looking project, these processes are performed at the beginning of the project and updated as needed using the integrated change control process.

In an adaptive or agile lifecycle, the sponsor and customer representatives should be continuously involved in the project to provide feedback on the products being built and to ensure that the product backlog meets their current needs.

Two processes (Validate Scope and Control Scope) are repeated for each iteration. In contrast, in a forward-looking project, Validate Scope occurs at each review of deliverables or phases, and Control Scope is an ongoing process.

In predictive projects, the scope baseline for the project is the approved version of the project scope statement, work breakdown structure (WBS), and associated WBS dictionary. A baseline can only be changed through formal change control procedures and serves as a basis for comparison when performing the Validate Scope and Control Scope processes and other controlling processes. Adaptive lifecycle projects use backlogs (including product requirements and user stories) to reflect their current needs.

Project scope completion is measured against the project management plan, while product scope completion is measured against product requirements. The term "requirement" is defined as a condition or capability that must be present in a product, service, or deliverable to meet an agreement or other formally imposed specification.

Project scope validation is the process of formally accepting completed project deliverables. The verified deliverables from the Control Quality process are an input to the Validate Scope process. One of the outputs of Validate Scope is accepted deliverables that are formally signed off and approved by authorized stakeholders. Therefore, the stakeholder must be involved (sometimes initiate) early in the planning process and provide input on the quality of the deliverables so that Control Quality can evaluate performance and recommend necessary changes.

Trends and new practices in project scope management

Requirements have always been an issue in project management and have become increasingly important in the industry. As the global environment becomes more complex, organizations are beginning to realize how they can use business analysis to their competitive advantage by defining, managing, and controlling requirements activities. Business analysis activities can begin before a project is initiated and a project manager is appointed. The requirements management process begins with a needs analysis, which can be conducted as part of portfolio planning, program planning, or an individual project. Eliciting, documenting, and managing stakeholder requirements is done as part of the Project Scope Management processes. Trends and new practices for project scope management include collaboration with business analysis professionals:

Determine issues and identify business requirements; identify and recommend viable solutions to meet those requirements.

Capture, document, and manage stakeholder requirements to achieve business and project objectives and facilitate successful implementation of the product, service, or outcome of the program or project.

The process concludes with the completion of the requirements where the product, service, or outcome is delivered to the recipient to measure, monitor, realize, and sustain the benefits over time.

The role responsible for performing business analysis should be assigned to resources with sufficient skills and knowledge in business analysis. When assigned to a project, a business analyst is responsible for requirements-related activities. The project manager is responsible for ensuring that the requirements-related work is included in the project management plan and that the requirements-related activities are completed on time, within budget, and deliver value. The relationship between a project manager and a business analyst should be one of partnership. A project is more likely to be successful if the project manager and business analyst fully understand each other's roles and responsibilities in order to successfully achieve project objectives.

Tailoring Considerations

Because each project is unique, the project manager must customize the way Project Scope Management processes are applied. Considerations for customization include:

Knowledge and requirements management. Does the organization have formal or informal knowledge and requirements management systems? What guidelines should the project manager establish for reusing requirements in the future?

Validation and control. Does the organization have existing formal or informal validation and control-related policies, procedures, and guidelines?

Development approach. Does the organization use agile approaches in managing projects? Is the development approach iterative or incremental? Is a predictive approach used? Will a hybrid approach be productive?

Stability of requirements. Are there areas of the project with unstable requirements? Do unstable requirements necessitate the use of lean, agile, or other adaptive techniques until they are stable and well defined?

Governance. Does the organization have formal or informal audit and governance policies, procedures, and guidelines?

Considerations for agile/adaptive environments

For projects with changing requirements, high risk, or significant uncertainties, the scope is often not clear at the beginning of the project, or it evolves during the project. Agile methods intentionally spend less time defining and agreeing on scope in the early stages of the project and more time establishing the process for its ongoing discovery and adaptation. In many environments with emerging requirements, a gap often finds itself between the actual business requirements and the originally stated business requirements. Therefore, agile methods are used to purposefully create and review prototypes and release versions to refine the requirements. As a result, the scope is defined and redefined throughout the project. In agile approaches, the requirements form the backlog.

Plan Scope Management

Plan Scope Management is the process of creating a scope management plan that documents how the project and product scope will be defined, validated, and controlled. The main benefit of this process is that it provides guidance and guidelines for managing scope throughout the project. This process is performed once or at predetermined times in the project.

The scope management plan is a component of the project or program management plan that describes how scope will be defined, developed, monitored, controlled, and validated. Developing the scope management plan and detailing the project scope begins with analyzing the information contained in the project charter, the most recently approved subplans of the project management plan, the historical information contained in the organizational process assets, and any other relevant factors in the business environment.

Plan scope management: Inputs

Project charter

The project charter documents the project purpose, general project description, assumptions, constraints, and general requirements to be met by the project.

Project Management plan

Project management plan components include but are not limited to:

Quality management plan. The way the project and product scope is managed can be influenced by how the company's quality policies, methods, and standards are implemented in the project.

Project life cycle description. The project life cycle defines the series of phases that a project goes through from its beginning to its end.

Development approach. The development approach defines whether waterfall, iterative, adaptive, agile, or a hybrid development approach is used.

Enterprise environmental factors

Factors in the business environment that may affect the plan scope management process include, but are not limited to:

Organization's culture, Infrastructure, Personnel administration, and Marketplace conditions.

Organizational process assets

The organizational process assets that can influence the Plan Scope Management process include but are not limited to:

Policies and procedures, and Historical information and lessons learned repositories.

Plan Scope Management: Tools and techniques

Expert judgement

Expertise should be considered from individuals or groups with specialized knowledge or training in the following topics:

Previous similar projects, and Information in the industry, discipline, and application area.

Data Analysis

One data analysis technique that can be used for this process is alternatives analysis, but is not limited to it. Various options for gathering requirements, developing the project and product scope, building the product, validating the scope, and controlling the scope are evaluated.

Meetings

Project teams may participate in project meetings to develop the scope management plan. Participants include the project manager, project sponsor, selected project team members, selected stakeholders, anyone responsible for any of the scope management processes, and others as needed.

Plan Scope Management: Outputs

Scope Management plan

The project scope management plan is a component of the project management plan that describes how scope will be established, developed, monitored, controlled, and validated. Components of a scope management plan include:

Process for creating a project scope statement; Process for creating the work breakdown structure from the detailed project scope statement; Process for determining how the scope baseline will be approved and maintained; and Process for determining how formal acceptance of completed project deliverables will occur.

The scope management plan can be formal or informal, broad or highly detailed, depending on the needs of the project.

Requirements management plan

The requirements management plan is a component of the project management plan that describes how project and product requirements will be analyzed, documented, and managed. According to Business Analysis for Practitioners, it is also referred to as the business analysis plan in some organizations. Components of the requirements management plan may include:

How requirements activities will be planned, tracked, and reported; configuration management activities, such as: how changes will be initiated; how impacts will be analyzed; how they will be tracked, traced, and reported; and the authorization levels required to approve those changes; process of prioritizing requirements; metrics that will be used and the reasons for their use; and traceability structure that reflects the requirements attributes captured in the traceability matrix.

Collect Requirements

Collect Requirements is the process of identifying, documenting, and managing stakeholder needs and requirements to achieve goals. The main advantage of this process is that it provides the basis for defining the product and project scope. This process is performed once or at predetermined points in the project.

The PMBOK ® Guide does not specifically address product requirements as they are industry specific. Note that the Business Analysis for Practitioners book provides more detailed information on product requirements. Project success depends directly on the active participation of stakeholders in identifying and decomposing needs into project and product requirements, and on the care with which requirements for the product, service, or project deliverable are identified, documented, and managed. Requirements include conditions or capabilities that must be present in a product, service, or deliverable to meet an agreement or other formally imposed specification. Requirements include the quantified and documented needs and expectations of the client, customer, and other stakeholders. These requirements must be elicited, analyzed, and recorded in sufficient detail to be included in the scope baseline and measured once project execution begins. The requirements form the basis for the work breakdown structure. Cost, schedule, quality planning, and procurement are all based on these requirements.

COLLECT REQUIREMENTS: INPUTS

PROJECT CHARTER

The project charter documents the overarching project description and requirements that will be used to develop the detailed requirements.

PROJECT MANAGEMENT PLAN

Components of the project management plan include:

Scope management plan. The scope management plan contains information on how the project scope will be defined and developed.

Requirements management plan. The requirements management plan contains information on how project requirements are collected, analyzed, and documented.

Stakeholder engagement plan. The stakeholder engagement plan is used to understand the requirements for communicating with stakeholders and the level of stakeholder engagement in order to evaluate and adjust the level of stakeholder engagement in requirements activities.

PROJECT DOCUMENTS

Examples of project documents that can be considered as inputs for this process include but are not limited to:

Assumption Log. The assumptions protocol identifies assumptions about the product, project, environment, stakeholders, and other factors that may affect requirements.

Lessons learned register. The Lessons Learned Register is designed to provide information on effective requirements elicitation techniques, particularly for projects using an iterative or adaptive product development methodology.

Stakeholder Register. The stakeholder register is used to identify stakeholders who can provide information on requirements. It also captures the requirements and expectations that stakeholders have for the project.

BUSINESS DOCUMENTS

A business document that can influence the requirements gathering process is the business case, which can describe required, desired, and optional criteria for meeting business requirements.

AGREEMENTS

Agreements can contain project and product requirements.

ENTERPRISE ENVIRONMENTAL FACTORS

The enterprise environmental factors that can influence the Collect Requirements process include but are not limited to:

Organization's culture, Infrastructure, Personnel administration, and Marketplace conditions.

ORGANIZATIONAL PROCESS ASSETS

Organizational process assets that can influence the requirements gathering process include:

Policies and procedures, and historical and experiential information with information from previous projects.

COLLECT REQUIREMENTS: TOOLS AND TECHNIQUES

EXPERT JUDGMENT

Individuals or groups who have specialized knowledge or training on the following topics may be considered as experts:

Business analysis, requirements elicitation, requirements analysis, requirements documentation, project requirements in previous similar projects, diagramming techniques, facilitation, and conflict management.

DATA GATHERING

Data collection techniques that may be used for this process include:

- **Brainstorming.** Brainstorming is a technique used to generate and collect multiple ideas related to project and product requirements.

- **Interviews.** An interview is a formal or informal approach to obtaining information from stakeholders by talking to them directly. It usually involves asking prepared and spontaneous questions and recording the answers. Interviews are often conducted on an individual basis between one interviewer and one respondent, but may involve multiple interviewers and/or multiple respondents. Interviewing experienced project participants, sponsors, other executives, and subject matter experts can help identify and define the features and functions of the desired product deliverables. Interviews are also useful for obtaining essential information.

- **Focus groups.** Focus groups bring together prequalified stakeholders and subject matter experts to learn their expectations and attitudes about a proposed product, service, or outcome. A trained moderator leads the group through an interactive discussion that is more conversational than face-to-face.

- **Questionnaires and surveys.** Questionnaires and surveys are written questionnaires that can be used to quickly gather information from many respondents. Questionnaires and/or surveys are best suited for different audiences when quick turnaround is needed, when respondents are geographically dispersed, and when statistical analysis might be useful.

- **Benchmarking.** Benchmarking compares actual or planned products, processes, and procedures with those of comparable organizations to identify best practices, generate ideas for improvement, and provide a basis for measuring performance. The organizations being compared in benchmarking may be internal or external.

Data Analysis

Among the data analysis techniques that can be used for this process is document analysis. Document analysis consists of reviewing and evaluating all relevant documented information. In this process, document analysis is used to determine requirements by analyzing existing documentation and identifying information relevant to the requirements. There is a wide range of documents that can be analyzed to identify relevant requirements. Examples of documents that can be analyzed include:

Agreements, business plans, business process or interface documentation, business rules repositories, current process documents, marketing literature, problem/issue logs, policies and procedures, regulatory documentation such as laws, codes or regulations, etc., requests for proposals, and use cases.

- **Decision making.** Decision-making techniques that can be used in the requirements elicitation process include:

- **Voting.** Voting is a collective decision-making technique and evaluation process with multiple alternatives and an expected outcome in the form of future actions. These techniques can be used to create, rank, and prioritize product requirements. Examples of voting techniques are:

- **Unanimity.** A decision that is reached whereby everyone agrees on a single course of action.

- **Majority.** A decision made with the support of more than 50% of the members of the group. A group size with an odd number of participants can ensure that a decision is made and does not result in a draw.

- **Plurality.** A decision in which the largest bloc in a group decides, even if a majority is not reached. This method is usually used when more than two options are nominated.

- **Autocratic decision making.** In this method, one individual takes responsibility for making the decision for the group.

- **Multicriteria decision analysis.** A technique that uses a decision matrix to provide a systematic analytical approach to establishing criteria such as risk level, uncertainty, and valuation to evaluate and rank many ideas.

Data Representation

Data representation techniques that can be used for this process include:

Affinity diagrams. Affinity diagrams allow large numbers of ideas to be classified into groups for review and analysis.

Mind mapping. Mind mapping consolidates ideas created through individual brainstorming sessions into a single map to reflect commonality and differences in understanding and to generate new ideas.

Interpersonal and team skills

The interpersonal and team skills that can be used in this process include but are not limited to:

Nominal group technique. The nominal group technique extends brainstorming to include a voting process used to evaluate the most useful ideas for further brainstorming or prioritization. The nominal group technique is a structured form of brainstorming that consists of four steps:

A question or problem is posed to the group. Each person silently develops their ideas and writes them down.

The facilitator writes down the ideas on a flip chart until all ideas are recorded.

Each recorded idea is discussed until all group members have a clear understanding.

Individual participants vote privately to prioritize the ideas. A scale of 1 to 5 is usually used, with 1 being the lowest and 5 being the highest. Voting can take place in multiple rounds to reduce and focus on the number of ideas. After each round, the votes are counted and the ideas with the highest score are selected.

Observation/conversation. Observation and conversation provide a direct way to watch people in their environment and see how they do their work or tasks and carry out processes. This is especially helpful with detailed processes when the people using the product have difficulty or are reluctant to articulate their requirements. Observation is also known as "job shadowing" It is usually performed by an outside observer who watches a business expert perform a task. It can also be conducted by a "participant observer" who actually performs a process or procedure to learn how it is done in order to uncover hidden requirements.

Facilitation. Facilitation is used in focused meetings that bring together key stakeholders to define product requirements. Workshops can be used to quickly define cross-functional requirements and reconcile differences of opinion among stakeholders. Because of their interactive group nature, well-moderated sessions can build trust, foster relationships, and improve communication among participants, which can lead to greater stakeholder consensus. In addition, problems can be discovered earlier and resolved more quickly than in individual meetings.

Facilitation abilities are used in the following situations, but are not limited to them:

Collaborative application design/development (JAD). JAD Meetings are used in the software development industry. These facilitated sessions are about bringing together business professionals and the development team to gather requirements and improve the software development process.

Quality Function Delivery (QFD). In the manufacturing industry, QFD is another facilitation technique that helps determine critical features for new product development. QFD begins by gathering customer needs, also known as the voice of the customer (VOC). These needs are then objectively sorted and prioritized, and goals are set for meeting them.

User stories. User stories, short, textual descriptions of needed functionality, are often developed during a requirements workshop. User stories describe the role of the stakeholder, who will benefit from the functionality (role), what the stakeholder needs to accomplish (goal), and the benefits to the stakeholder (motivation).

Prototypes

Prototyping is a method of obtaining early feedback on requirements by providing a model of the expected product before it is built. Examples of prototypes include small-scale products, computer-generated 2D and 3D models, mock-ups, or simulations. Prototypes allow stakeholders to experiment with a model of the final product rather than being limited to discussing abstract representations of their requirements. Prototypes support the concept of incremental elaboration in iterative cycles of mock-up creation, user experimentation, feedback generation, and prototype revision. When enough feedback cycles have been performed, the requirements extracted from the prototype are sufficiently complete to move to the design or build phase

Storyboarding is a prototyping technique that shows the sequence or navigation through a series of images or illustrations. Storyboards are used on a variety of projects in a variety of industries, including film, advertising, instructional design, and agile and other software development projects. In software development, storyboards are used as models to show navigation paths through web pages, screens, or other user interfaces.

Collect requirements: Outputs

Requirement documentation

Requirements documentation describes how each requirement meets the business need for the project. Requirements can start at a high level and become increasingly detailed as more information about the requirements is known. Before serving as a foundation, requirements must be unambiguous (measurable and testable), traceable, complete, consistent, and acceptable to key stakeholders. The format of the requirements document can range from a simple document listing all requirements by stakeholder and priority to more extensive forms with an executive summary, detailed descriptions, and appendices.

Many organizations divide requirements into different types, such as business and technical solutions. The former refer to the needs of the stakeholders, the latter to how these needs are implemented. Requirements can be divided into classes so that they can be further refined and detailed as the requirements are developed. These classifications include:

Business requirements. These describe the overarching needs of the organization as a whole, such as business problems or opportunities, and the reasons why a project was undertaken.

Stakeholder requirements. These describe the needs of a stakeholder or stakeholder group.

Solution requirements. These describe features, functions, and characteristics of the product, service, or result that will meet the business and stakeholder requirements. Solution requirements are further grouped into functional and nonfunctional requirements.

Functional requirements. Functional requirements describe the behaviors of the product. Examples include actions, processes, data, and interactions that the product should execute.

Nonfunctional requirements. Nonfunctional requirements supplement functional requirements and describe the environmental conditions or qualities required for the product to be effective. Examples include: reliability, security, performance, safety, level of service, supportability, retention/purge, etc.

Transition and readiness requirements. These describe temporary capabilities, such as data conversion and training requirements, needed to transition from the current as-is state to the desired future state.

Project requirements. These describe the actions, processes, or other conditions the project needs to meet. Examples include milestone dates, contractual obligations, constraints, etc.

Quality requirements. These capture any condition or criteria needed to validate the successful completion of a project deliverable or fulfillment of other project requirements. Examples include tests, certifications, validations, etc.

Requirements traceability matrix

The requirements traceability matrix is a grid that links product requirements from their origin to the products that fulfill them. Implementing a requirements traceability matrix helps ensure that each requirement adds business value by linking it to business and project goals. It enables requirements to be tracked throughout the project lifecycle and helps ensure that the requirements approved in the requirements documentation are delivered at the end of the project. Requirements tracking includes, but is not limited to: Business needs, opportunities, goals and objectives; Project objectives; Project scope and WBS deliverables; Product design; Product development; Test strategy and test scenarios; and High-level requirements to more detailed requirements.

The attributes associated with each requirement can be recorded in the requirements traceability matrix. These attributes help define key information about the requirement. Typical attributes used in the requirements traceability matrix include: a unique identificator, a textual description of the requirement, the reason for inclusion, the owner, source, priority, version, current status (e.g., active, canceled, on hold, added, approved, assigned, completed), and status date. Additional attributes to ensure that the requirement has been met to the satisfaction of stakeholders may include stability, complexity, and acceptance criteria.

Define Scope

Define Scope is the process of developing a detailed description of the project and product. The main advantage of this process is that it describes the boundaries and acceptance criteria of the product, service or result.

Since not all requirements identified in the Gather Requirements process can be included in the project, the Define Scope process selects the final project requirements from the requirements documentation developed in the Gather Requirements process. It then creates a detailed description of the project and the product, service, or deliverable.

Creating a detailed description of the project scope builds on the key deliverables, assumptions, and constraints documented during project initiation. During project planning, the project scope is defined and described in increasing detail as more information about the project is known. Existing risks, assumptions, and constraints are analyzed for completeness and added to or updated as needed. The define scope process can be highly iterative. For projects with an iterative life cycle, an overarching vision for the overall project is developed. However, the detailed scope is determined in each iteration, and detailed planning for the next iteration occurs as work on the current project scope and deliverables progresses.

Define scope: inputs

PROJECT CHARTER

The project charter contains a detailed project description, product features and approval requirements.

PROJECT MANAGEMENT PLAN

One component of the project management plan includes the project scope management plan described in Section 5.1.3.1, which documents how the project scope will be defined, validated, and controlled.

PROJECT DOCUMENTS

Examples of project documents that may be considered as input to this process include:

- **Assumption log.** The assumptions protocol identifies assumptions and constraints related to the product, project, environment, stakeholders, and other factors that may impact the project and product scope.

- **Requirements documentation.** Documenting the requirements identifizes the requirements that are included in the scope.

- **Risk register.** The risk register contains response strategies that may impact project scope, such as reducing or modifying project and product scope to avoid or mitigate a risk.

ENTERPRISE ENVIRONMENTAL FACTORS

Factors in the corporate environment that can influence the Define Scope process include: Corporate culture, infrastructure, human resource management, and market conditions.

ORGANIZATIONAL PROCESS ASSETS

Organizational process resources that may influence the define-scope process include: Policies, procedures, and templates for defining project scope; project examples from previous projects; and lessons learned from previous phases or projects.

DEFINE SCOPE: TOOLS AND TECHNIQUES

EXPERT JUDGMENT

Individuals or groups with knowledge or experience with similar projects should be considered as experts.

DATA ANALYSIS

An example of a data analysis technique that can be used in this process is, but is not limited to, alternatives analysis. Alternatives analysis can be used to evaluate ways to meet the requirements and goals set forth in the charter.

DECISION MAKING

One decision technique that can be used in this process includes multicriteria decision analysis. Multicriteria decision analysis is a technique that uses a decision matrix to provide a systematic analytical approach to establishing criteria such as requirements, schedule, budget, and resources to refine the project and product scope for the project.

INTERPERSONAL AND TEAM SKILLS

An example of an interpersonal and team skills technique is facilitation. Facilitation is used in workshops and work sessions with key stakeholders who have different expectations or expertise. The goal is to achieve a cross-functional and shared understanding of project deliverables and project and product boundaries.

PRODUCT ANALYSIS

Product analysis can be used to define products and services. It involves asking questions about a product or service and formulating answers to describe the use, characteristics, and other relevant aspects of what is to be delivered.

In each application area, there are one or more generally accepted methods for translating high-level product or service descriptions into meaningful results. Requirements are captured at a high level and decomposed to the level of detail required to develop the final product. Examples of product analysis techniques include:

Product Breakdown, Requirements Analysis, Systems Analysis, Systems Engineering, Value Analysis, and Value Engineering.

DEFINE SCOPE: OUTPUTS

PROJECT SCOPE STATEMENT

The project scope statement is the description of the project scope, key deliverables, assumptions, and constraints. The project scope statement documents the entire scope, including the project and product scope. It describes the deliverables of the project in detail. It also provides a common understanding of the project scope among project stakeholders. It may include explicit exceptions to the project scope, which can be helpful in managing stakeholder expectations. It enables the project team to plan in more detail, serves as a guide for the project team's work during execution, and forms the basis for assessing whether requests for changes or additional work are within or outside the project boundaries. The degree and detail with which the project scope statement defines the work to be performed and the work to be excluded can contribute to how well the project management team can control the overall project scope. The detailed project scope statement, either directly or by reference to other documents, includes the following:

Product scope description. Develops step-by-step the characteristics of the product, service, or deliverable described in the project charter and requirements documentation.

Deliverables. Any distinct and verifiable product, result, or service capability that must be produced to complete a process, phase, or project. Deliverables also include ancillary deliverables such as project management reports and documentation. These deliverables can be described at a summary level or in great detail.

Acceptance criteria. A set of conditions that is required to be met before deliverables are accepted.

Project exclusions. Identifies what is excluded from the project. Explicitly stating what is not part of the project scope helps manage stakeholder expectations and prevent scope creep.

Although the project charter and the project scope statement are sometimes perceived as redundant, they differ in their level of detail. The project charter contains high-level information, while the project scope statement provides a detailed description of the scope components. These components are gradually elaborated as the project progresses.

PROJECT DOCUMENTS UPDATES

Project documents that may be updated because of carrying out this process include but are not limited to:

Assumption log. The assumption log is updated with additional assumptions or constraints that were identified during this process.

Requirements documentation. Requirements documentation may be updated with additional or changed requirements.

Requirements traceability matrix. The requirements traceability matrix may be updated to reflect updates in requirement documentation.

Stakeholder register. Where additional information on existing or new stakeholders is gathered as a result of this process, it is recorded in the stakeholder register.

CREATE WBS

Creating a work breakdown structure (WBS) is the process of dividing project deliverables and project work into smaller, more manageable components. The main advantage of this process is that it creates a framework for the deliverables. This process is performed once or at predetermined times in the project.

The work breakdown structure (WBS) is a hierarchical breakdown of the total scope of work that the project team must perform to achieve the project objectives and deliver the required results. The WBS organizes and defines the overall scope of the project and represents the work specified in the currently approved project scope statement.

The planned work is contained in the lowest level of WBS components called work packages. A work package can be used to group the activities in which work is planned and estimated, monitored, and controlled. In the context of the work breakdown structure, the term work refers to work products or deliverables that are the result of an activity, rather than the activity itself.

CREATE WBS: INPUTS

PROJECT MANAGEMENT PLAN

One component of the project management plan is the scope management plan. The scope management plan documents how the work breakdown structure is created from the project scope specification.

Projects documents

Examples of project documents that can be considered as inputs for this process include but are not limited to:

Project scope statement. The project scope statement describes the work that will be performed and the work that is excluded.

Requirements documentation. Detailed requirements describe how individual requirements meet the business need for the project.

Enterprise environmental factors

Factors in the business environment that may influence the work breakdown structure development process include industry-specific work breakdown structure standards relevant to the type of project. These industry-specific standards can serve as external reference sources for the creation of the work breakdown structure.

ORGANIZATIONAL PROCESS ASSETS

Organizational process resources that may influence the process for creating the work breakdown structure include: Work breakdown structure policies, procedures, and templates; project examples from previous projects; and lessons learned from previous projects.

CREATE WBS: TOOLS AND TECHNIQUES

EXPERT JUDGMENT

Expertise should be considered from individuals or groups with knowledge of or experience with similar projects.

DECOMPOSITION

Decomposition is a technique for dividing and subdividing the project scope and deliverables into smaller, more manageable parts. The work package is the work defined at the lowest level of the work breakdown structure for which cost and duration can be estimated and managed. The level of decomposition is often based on the level of control required to effectively manage the project. The level of detail of work packages depends on the size and complexity of the project. Decomposition of the overall project work into work packages generally includes the following activities:

Identifying and analyzing the deliverables and associated work, structuring and organizing the WBS, decomposing the upper WBS levels into lower level detail components, developing and assigning identification codes for the WBS components, and verifying that the level of decomposition of the deliverables is appropriate.

A WBS structure can be created using a variety of approaches. Common methods include the top-down approach, the use of organization-specific policies, and the use of WBS templates. A bottom-up approach can be used to group subcomponents. The WBS structure can be represented in various forms, such as: Using the phases of the project life cycle as the second level of decomposition, with the product and project deliverables inserted at the third level.

Using the main deliverables as the second level of decomposition. Inclusion of subcomponents that may be developed by organizations outside the project team, such as contract work. The vendor then develops the supporting contract WBS as part of the contracted work. Decomposing the higher-level WBS components requires subdividing the work for each of the deliverables or subcomponents into its most basic components, with the WBS components representing verifiable products, services, or outcomes. In an agile approach, the epics can be decomposed into user stories. The WBS may be structured in the form of an outline, an organization chart, or some other method that identifies a hierarchical breakdown. To verify the correctness of the decomposition, it must be determined that the lower-level WBS components are necessary and sufficient for the completion of the corresponding higher-level deliverables. Different sub deliverables may have different levels of decomposition. To arrive at a work package, the work for some deliverables only needs to be decomposed to the next level, while others require additional levels of decomposition. The more detailed the work is decomposed, the better you can plan, manage, and control the work. However, excessive decomposition can lead to unproductive management effort, inefficient use of resources, lower efficiency in performing the work, and difficulty aggregating data at different levels of the work breakdown structure.

For a deliverable or subcomponent whose completion is far in the future, decomposition may not be possible. The project management team usually waits until the deliverable or subcomponent is agreed upon so that the details of the work breakdown structure can be developed. This technique is sometimes referred to as rolling planning. The work breakdown structure represents all product and project work, including project management work. The sum of the work at the lowest levels should be carried forward to the higher levels so that nothing is left out and no additional work is done. This is sometimes referred to as the 100 percent rule.

CREATE WBS: OUTPUTS

SCOPE BASELINE

The scope baseline is the approved version of a scope statement, WBS, and associated WBS dictionary that can only be changed through formal change control procedures and serves as a basis for comparison. It is a component of the project management plan. Components of the scope baseline include:

Project Scope Statement. The project scope statement includes a description of the project scope, key deliverables, assumptions, and constraints.

WORK BREAKDOWN STRUCTURE.

The work breakdown structure is a hierarchical breakdown of the total scope of work that the project team must perform to achieve the project objectives and produce the required deliverables. Each descending level of the work breakdown structure represents an increasingly detailed description of the project work.

Work Package. The lowest level of the work breakdown structure is a work package with a unique identifier. These identifiers provide a structure for the hierarchical summation of cost, schedule, and resource information and form an account code. Each work package is part of a control account. A control account is a management checkpoint where scope, budget, and schedule are integrated and compared to the completion value for performance measurement. A control account has two or more work packages, with each work package associated with a single control account.

Planning Package. A control account may contain one or more planning packages. A planning package is a work breakdown structure component below the control account and above the work package with known work content but without detailed schedule activities.

WBS dictionary

The WBS dictionary is a document that contains detailed information about the deliverables, activities, and schedules of each component in the WBS. The WBS dictionary is a document that supports the work breakdown structure. Most of the information contained in the WBS dictionary is created by other processes and added to this document at a later time. Information in the WBS dictionary includes:

- Code of account identifier

- Description of work

- Assumptions and constraints

- Responsible organization

- Schedule milestones

- Associated schedule activities

- Resources required

- Cost estimates

- Quality requirements

- Acceptance criteria

- Technical references.

- Agreement information.

Project documents updates

Project documents that may be updated because of carrying out this process include but are not limited to:

- **Assumption log.** The assumption log is updated with additional assumptions or constraints that were identified during the Create WBS process.

- **Requirements documentation.** Requirements documentation may be updated to include approved changes resulting from the Create WBS process.

Validate scope

Project scope validation is the process of formal acceptance of completed project deliverables. The main advantage of this process is that it brings objectivity to the acceptance process and increases the likelihood of final acceptance of the product, service, or deliverable by validating each deliverable. This process is performed periodically throughout the project as needed.

The deliverables verified during the quality control process are discussed with the customer or client to ensure that they have been satisfactorily completed and formally accepted by the customer or client. In this process, the results of the planning processes in the Project Scope Management knowledge area, such as the requirements documentation or scope baseline, and the work performance data obtained from the execution processes in other knowledge areas, form the basis for performing validation and final acceptance.

The Validate Scope process differs from the Control Quality process in that the former is primarily concerned with acceptance of the deliverables, while the latter is primarily concerned with the correctness of the deliverables and the satisfaction of the quality requirements established for the deliverables. Control Quality is usually performed before Validate Scope, although the two processes can run in parallel.

VALIDATE SCOPE: INPUTS

PROJECT MANAGEMENT PLAN

Project management plan components include but are not limited to:

Scope management plan. The project management plan specifies how formal acceptance of the completed project deliverables will be obtained.

Requirements management plan. The requirements management plan describes how the project requirements are validated.

Scope baseline. The scope baseline is compared to actual results to determine if a change, corrective action, or preventive action is necessary.

PROJECT DOCUMENTS

Project documents that can be considered as inputs for this process include but are not limited to:

Lessons learned register. Lessons learned earlier in the project can be applied in later phases of the project to improve the efficiency and effectiveness of validating the results.

Quality reports. Information included in the quality report may include any quality assurance issues managed or escalated by the team, recommendations for improvement, and summary of the results of the quality control process. This information is reviewed prior to product acceptance.

Requirements documentation. Requirements are compared to actual results to determine if a change, corrective or preventive action is needed.

Requirements traceability matrix. The requirements traceability matrix contains information about requirements, including how they are validated.

VERIFIED DELIVERABLES

Verified deliverables are project deliverables that are completed and checked for correctness through the quality control process.

WORK PERFORMANCE DATA

Work performance data may include the degree of compliance, the number of nonconformities, the severity of nonconformities, or the number of validation cycles performed in a given period.

VALIDATE SCOPE: TOOLS AND TECHNIQUES

INSPECTION

Inspection includes activities such as measuring, testing, and validating to determine if work and products delivered meet requirements and product acceptance criteria. Inspections are sometimes also referred to as reviews, product testing, and walkthroughs. In some applications, these different terms have distinct and specific meanings.

DECISION MAKING

An example of decision making that can be used in this process is voting, but is not limited to it. Voting is used to reach a conclusion when validation is performed by the project team and other stakeholders.

VALIDATE SCOPE: OUTPUTS

ACCEPTED DELIVERABLES

Services that meet acceptance criteria are formally signed off and approved by the client or sponsor. Formal documentation received from the customer or sponsor confirming formal acceptance of project deliverables by stakeholders is forwarded to the Project or Phase Closeout process.

WORK PERFORMANCE INFORMATION

Work performance information includes information about project progress, e.g., which deliverables were accepted and which were not, and for what reasons they were accepted. This information is documented and shared with stakeholders as described in Section 10.3.3.1.

CHANGE REQUESTS

Completed deliverables that have not been formally accepted will be documented along with the reasons for not accepting those deliverables. These deliverables may require a change request to correct defects. Change requests are processed for review and disposition as part of the Perform Integrated Change Control process.

PROJECT DOCUMENTS UPDATES

Project documents that may be updated as a result of the implementation of this process include:

Register of lessons learned. The register of lessons learned is updated with information about challenges encountered and how they could have been avoided, as well as approaches that have been successful in validating the results.

Requirements documentation. Requirements documentation may be updated based on actual results of validation activities. It is of particular interest when the actual results are better than the requirements or when a requirement has been waived.

Requirements traceability matrix. The traceability matrix is updated with the results of the validation, including the method used and the result.

Control scope

Control Scope is the process of monitoring the status of the project and product scope and managing changes to the scope baseline. The main benefit of this process is that the scope baseline is maintained throughout the project. This process is performed throughout the project. Control Scope ensures that all requested changes and recommended corrective or preventive actions are processed through the Perform Integrated Change Control process. Control Scope is also used to manage actual changes as they occur and is integrated with the other control processes. Uncontrolled expansion of product or project scope without adjustments to time, cost, and resources is referred to as scope creep. Changes are inevitable, so some type of change control process is mandatory for every project.

CONTROL SCOPE: INPUTS

PROJECT MANAGEMENT PLAN

Project management plan components include but are not limited to:

- **Scope management plan.** The scope management plan documents how the project and product scope will be controlled.

- **Requirements management plan.** The requirements management plan describes how project requirements should be managed.

- **Change management plan.** The change management plan defines the process for managing changes in the project.

- **Configuration management plan.** The configuration management plan specifies which elements are auditable, which elements require formal change control, and how changes to those elements are controlled.

- **Scope baseline.** The baseline of the scope is compared to the actual results to determine if a change, corrective or preventive action is needed.

- **Performance measurement baseline.** Earned value analysis compares the baseline of performance measurement with actual results to determine if a change, corrective, or preventive action is needed.

PROJECT DOCUMENTS

Project documents that can be considered as inputs for this process include but are not limited to:

- **Lessons learned register.** Lessons learned earlier in the project can be applied in later phases of the project to improve control of the project scope.

- **Requirements documentation.** Requirements documentation is used to identify any deviation from the agreed scope of the project or product.

- **Requirements traceability matrix.** The requirements traceability matrix helps identify the impact of a change or deviation from the baseline scope on project objectives. It can also indicate the status of controlled requirements.

WORK PERFORMANCE DATA

Work performance data may include the number of change requests received, the number of requests accepted, and the number of deliverables verified, validated, and completed.

ORGANIZATIONAL PROCESS ASSETS

Organizational process assets that may affect the span of control process include:

existing formal and informal scopes, control-related policies, procedures, guidelines, and monitoring and reporting methods and templates to be used.

CONTROL SCOPE: TOOLS AND TECHNIQUES

DATA ANALYSIS

Data analysis techniques that can be used as part of the control scope process include:

Variance analysis. Variance analysis is used to compare the baseline to actual results and determine if the variance is within the threshold or if corrective or preventive action is needed.

Trend Analysis. Trend analysis examines project performance over time to determine if performance is improving or deteriorating. Important aspects of project scope control include determining the cause and magnitude of the deviation compared to baseline and deciding whether corrective or preventive action is required.

CONTROL SCOPE: OUTPUTS

WORK PERFORMANCE INFORMATION

Work performance information includes correlated and contextualized information on how the project and product scope compares to the baseline scope. It may include categories of changes received, scope variances identified and their causes, their impact on schedule or cost, and the forecast of future scope performance.

CHANGE REQUEST

Analysis of project performance may result in a change request to the scope and schedule or other components of the project management plan. Change requests are processed through the Perform Integrated Change Control process for review and disposition.

PROJECT MANAGEMENT PLAN UPDATES

Any change to the project management plan goes through the organization's change control process via a change request. Components that may require a change request to the project management plan include:

Scope management plan. The project scope management plan can be updated to refl ect a change in the management of the project scope.

Scope baseline. Changes to the scope baseline are made in response to approved changes to the scope, scope statement, work breakdown structure, or WBS dictionary. In some cases, scope deviations may be so severe that a revised scope baseline is required to provide a realistic basis for performance measurement.

Schedule baseline. Changes to the schedule baseline are made in response to approved changes in scope, resources, or schedule estimates. In some cases, deviations from the schedule may be so severe that a revised schedule baseline is required to provide a realistic basis for performance measurement.

Cost baseline. Changes to the cost basis are made in response to approved changes in scope, resources, or cost estimates. In some cases, cost variances may be so severe that a revised cost basis is required to provide a realistic basis for performance measurement.

Performance measurement baseline. Changes to the performance measurement baseline are made in response to approved changes in scope, schedule, or cost estimates. In some cases, performance variances may be so severe that a change request is made to revise the performance measurement baseline to provide a realistic basis for performance measurement.

PROJECT DOCUMENTS UPDATES

Project documents that may be updated as a result of the implementation of this process include:

Lessons learned register. The register of lessons learned can be updated with techniques that are efficient and effective in controlling scope, including causes of discrepancies and corrective actions chosen.

Requirements documentation. Requirements documentation may be updated with additional or modified requirements.

Requirements traceability matrix. The requirements traceability matrix can be updated to refl ect updates in the requirements documentation.

Expert Judgment

The three main findings from this chapter are as follows:

- To avoid scope creep and to ensure that scope is implemented, you must control scope. You also need to validate the scope of the project deliverable before accepting the verified product.

- The schedule must be controlled to keep the project on track, i.e., in accordance with the schedule baseline. The key outputs of the schedule control process are work performance information, schedule forecasts, and change requests that result from comparing schedule-related work performance data to the schedule baseline.

- Cost control converts cost-related work performance data into work performance information by comparing the data to the integrated baseline: Scope Baseline, Schedule Baseline, Cost Baseline.

Summary

The most important thing in doing a project is to stick to the scope and schedule, and that will cost someone. These three parameters-scope, schedule, and cost-are inextricably linked; a change in any one of them is likely to result in changes in one or both of the others. Changes in any of these parameters may result in changes in resources. Scope is controlled by the Control Scope process, and the scope of verified deliverables is validated by the Validate Scope process. You must control the schedule so that it matches the baseline schedule. This includes monitoring the status of the project progress and controlling changes to the baseline schedule. According to this triangular relationship, project cost performance is measured by comparing the results of project execution to the performance measurement baseline, which is an approved integrated plan for the scope, schedule, and cost of the project. In other words, the Performance Baseline includes the Scope Baseline, the Cost Baseline, and the Schedule Baseline. Do this with the Cost Control process. Finally, use the Resource Control process to optimize results by balancing planned, allocated, and used physical resources.

Road Ahead. For a successful controlling or process, it is critical to engage stakeholders in the project, which requires effective communication. Stakeholder engagement and communication must be monitored. The next chapter will address this issue.

View from the eye of the examiner

Comprehend

Monitoring and controlling involve monitoring and controlling project performance and managing the resulting changes.

The three project parameters-cost, schedule, and scope-form a triple constraint, meaning that if one of these three parameters changes, at least one of the other two must also change.

Performance measurement baselines and work performance data are the common input for controlling scope, schedule, and cost, and work performance information and change requests are the common output.

Project costs are measured by comparing project results from work performance data to performance measurement baselines: Scope Bases, Schedule Bases, and Cost Bases.

Look Out

All change requests generated by project scope control or any other process must go through the integrated change control process for approval, and only approved changes should be implemented using the Lead and Manage Project Work process.

The Validate Scope process is applied to project deliverables that have already been verified through the Quality Control process. The goal is to have the deliverables accepted by the appropriate party, such as a customer or sponsor.

The approved version of the project plan is called the project plan baseline, against which project progress is tracked and measured by comparing actual progress against the baseline.

Resource control is about synchronizing the planned, allocated and used physical resources with each other.

The Control Resources process refers only to physical resources.

Planned value (PV), earned value (EV), and actual cost (AC) are the three key parameters that must be closely monitored. The rest of the earned value analysis is based on these three basic parameters.

Cost variance (CV) is calculated by subtracting actual cost (AC) from earned value (EV) rather than planned value (PV).

Schedule variance (SV) and schedule performance index (SPI) are calculated with respect to cost: EV and PV.

It is possible that CV and SV run in opposite directions - for example, CV has a positive value when SV has a negative value.

The total planned value (PV) of the project is equal to the budget at completion (BAC)

Memorize

Control accounts are the points in the work breakdown structure where scope, schedule, and cost are integrated for the purpose of monitoring and controlling performance.

The Control Schedule process compares schedule-related work performance data to the schedule baseline to produce work performance information that includes the schedule variance-that is, the deviation from the schedule baseline-and schedule forecasts are based on this and past performance.

In each phase or funding period:

Cost baseline = expected expenditures + expected liabilities Funding requirements = cost baseline + management reserves

For cost trend analysis:

$EV = BAC \times (\text{Work Completed} / \text{Total Work Required})$

$CV = EV - AC$

$CPI = EV / AC$

For the analysis of the schedule performance:

$PV = BAC \times (\text{Elapsed time} / \text{Total schedule time})$

$SV = EV - PV$

$SPI = EV / PV$

EACto planned rate = AC + BAC - EV BAC - EV EACto currentCPI = AC + CPI BAC - EV EACto currentCPI and currentSPI = AC + CPI ' SPI BAC - EV TCPI = BAC - AC

Review Questions, Answers and Explanations (online)

Schedule Management

FOR MANY PEOPLE, PROJECT management is synonymous with scheduling. We know that project management is so much more than that. Nonetheless, scheduling is the foundation for many of the important functions that are part of the project management process. Without defining the scope of work and scheduling the work, we would have no basis for planning resource allocation or managing cash flow. In addition, the schedule of work and the management of the project deadline are two of the most monitored and sensitive areas of most projects. So, without falling into the misconception that schedule is everything, we must recognize that scheduling is a very important component of the project management process.

In this chapter, we discuss the importance of defining and organizing the scope of work and the importance of creating a schedule of project milestones. These are the first steps on the path to developing a detailed project schedule. It is certainly possible to develop the schedule without the use of the computer. But that would be foolish. First of all, if you did it manually, you would have to recreate the schedule every time you made a change. Of course, you could use simple bar chart software to create a manually calculated schedule. That way, you do not have to completely recreate the schedule to incorporate changes. But it would not provide the benefits of scheduling task relationships - a key component of the critical path method (CPM).

Scheduling

With the software CPM you can define the tasks, their duration and their relationships and let the program create a schedule. You can impose your will on the computer by defining restricted start dates, targeted end dates, intermediate goals, concurrent work and so on. You can test options and alternatives (what-ifs). You can use the work breakdown structure and other coding to select, sort, and summarize schedule data. I could go on and on about how useful, even necessary, critical path software is.

It's unfortunate that many people wait until there is a project crisis before they embrace CPM. Then, under the pressure of the crisis, they fail to learn the few basics necessary to use these tools effectively. Frankly, using these tools for the first time can be intimidating. The trick is to familiarize yourself with them when you are not under extreme pressure and take the time to learn some of the basics. Another good idea is to have a CPM guru on staff to guide the others. Finally, try to get into using CPM gradually, starting with a small project and the basic features and then expanding the scope and functionality.

For any science (project management is both an art and a science) there is a set of fundamentals. These include basic assumptions, algorithms, formulas, terms, and protocols. The science of critical path scheduling is not exempt. Over the past decade, a variant of critical path scheduling called critical chain project management (CCPM) has emerged as an alternative to CPM. We do not wish to take a position on this somewhat controversial topic, but instead provide a balanced, objective discussion of CCPM vs. CPM. This is a concept we can strongly support, and we outline several ways to achieve this goal.

Schedules are created by defining tasks, estimating task durations, and defining task relationships. The most difficult part is dealing with task durations. For most tasks, you can specify a range of times that can be completely different without having trouble justifying any of them. The schedule is the basis for all other aspects of the plan, including the resource allocation plan and the budget. The schedule is also the basis for measuring progress and performance. Clearly, if the schedule is poorly developed, all other aspects of the plan may not be very useful, and project control is also compromised.

Unfortunately, bad schedules are not uncommon. And the impact of bad schedules on project performance is terribly damaging. Bad schedules lead to confusion and inefficient allocation of resources. The project team becomes oriented to the schedule and discouraged when they cannot rely on this document. Finally, alternate versions of the schedule emerge from sources that are not satisfied with the official schedule, leading to even more confusion and desertion.

Developing a valid schedule is not that difficult. It just takes some knowledge of the conventions of scheduling and some patience to get it right the first time. All too often, we rush to create the first schedule and then waste even more time correcting the bad schedule later. We can not help you have patience, but we can do something for knowledge.

Now comes a boring topic: critical path scheduling! Many of you will be comfortable with this topic and can move on to more interesting topics. You can also find detailed explanations of critical path scheduling in many basic project management books, as well as in books and electronic notes that come with all project management software products. For PMP participants, we have included a brief discussion of critical path planning in this chapter.

The critical path method (CPM) is the basis for almost every project plan. Even if you do not use a computer for scheduling, you probably use CPM concepts - perhaps without even realizing it. I recommend that you get good project management software and use the critical path planning features effectively to develop and manage your project plans. Therefore, our discussion of project planning assumes that you use computers for planning and control and that you have the critical path planning features on those computers.

What is the planning of the critical path? Basically, it is the process of determining when the work can be done by identifying the priority relationships between tasks. It seems simple enough. However, many people screw up this simple process and some completely ignore the power of critical path planning, even when using critical path planning tools. What a shame!

CPM Basics

Regardless of the method you use to create a project plan, the first step is always the same. You must identify the work to be scheduled before you can determine when the work should be done. There are many ways you can create the schedule.

Review these front-end steps:

- You have identified the project goals and constraints.

- You have initiated strategic planning and conducted a stakeholder analysis.

- You have developed a set of scope of work and schedule constraints.

- You will use the work breakdown structure as a framework for identifying project tasks.

- You will use the Project Milestone Schedule as a framework for developing the detailed project plan.

The next steps include:

- Create a list of all tasks to be performed.

- Estimate the expected duration of each task.

- Determine the priority relationships between the tasks.

- Identify deadline constraints and imposed deadlines.

- Let us take a closer look at each of these points.

Defining Tasks A preferred method for creating the task list is to use a work breakdown structure based on either deliverables or phases. Where practical, I like to use a combined work breakdown structure where the first level represents the phases (or project life cycle) and the next level represents the deliverables within each phase. The WBS is then developed down to the lower levels, such as the major components, subgroups, or milestones within each deliverable, and then on down to the task groups, which I like to call work packages. A work package is a group of tasks for which a single party is usually responsible and which represent a smaller sub-performance or milestone. For each task, a single party is identified as the responsible owner. Tasks may have one or more resources assigned and may have a budget (later). Each task (like any project) has an identifiable beginning and end.

Critical Path Scheduling

Estimation of task duration;

There are several ways to assign a duration to each task. The most common is to simply determine an estimated time and set that as the task duration. Depending on the nature of the work, this duration can be expressed in days, weeks, hours, etc. In any case, we are talking about elapsed times. A task assigned a duration of 10 days is expected to take 2 weeks (assuming a calendar with 5days per week). This does not necessarily mean that the task will be worked on for the entire 10 days or that it is a 10-man-day effort. Later, when discussing schedule risk, we will introduce the concept of multiple duration estimates. But for now, let us leave that aside.

A second popular method for determining task duration is the effort-driven method. In this method, we enter the total hours to be spent by each resource working on the task and set the effort rate. For example: a wall is built by two bricklayers working full time and spending a total of 80 hours. The duration of the task is calculated as 5 days (40 elapsed hours). If there are multiple resources and effort rates, the task duration is determined by the longest assignment.

There are numerous variations and subtleties that can be introduced here, but we continue our coverage of critical path planning using these two classic methods.

Priority Relationships Between Tasks and Date Constraints Scheduling naturally involves deciding when to do the work. In a few cases, there are no constraints on this scheduling. However, this is the exception to the rule. It is more likely that the timing of the work is influenced by one or more factors. These may include:

- A contractually or otherwise established deadline.

- Dependencies on other tasks.

- Availability of required conditions (weather, space, permits, funding, etc.).

- Availability of materials.

- Availability of labor resources.

The critical path method allows all of these constraints and dependencies to be specified. The normal process requires identifying task dependencies, followed by specifying dates that force the calculated schedule to be exceeded. Let us examine these options in more detail.

Defining Dependencies - The default dependency is a Finish to Start (FS) relationship. That is, task B cannot begin until task A is finished. However, there may be conditions under which overlap is possible. For example, Task B can start 2 days after Task A starts. This is called a start-to-start relationship (SS). It is also possible that 2 tasks can start independently, but the completion of one depends on the completion of the other. In this case, you would use the Finish to Finish relationship (FF). For example, Task B may be finished 5 days after Task A is finished (FF -5). The duration of the delay (5 days in this case) is called the delay.

■ *Tip A practical way of working with critical path scheduling is to start off by defining most relationships as default FS dependencies. Then, after the project schedule has been calculated, use the ability to overlap tasks to selectively compact the project duration.*

CPM: How It Works There are several ways to impose date constraints on the schedule. To understand how this works, we need to pause for a moment and look at how critical path scheduling works.

After defining the project model for the computer (task definition, task duration, dependencies, and imposed date constraints), the computer makes a forward pass to determine the earliest start and end of all tasks. After determining the earliest date for project completion, the computer calculates the latest start and finish dates of all tasks that would support the project end date based on this end date.

The difference between the early dates and the late dates is called the total buffer or total slack. The path through the critical path network that has the least buffer or slack is called the critical path. If the user has not imposed an end date on the project, the critical path has a buffer or slack of zero. If an end date is imposed on the project that is earlier than the free calculated end date, there will be tasks that have a negative buffer. The tasks with the largest negative buffer are on the critical path. Therefore, tasks that are on the critical path cannot be moved without delaying the completion of the project.

■ *Tip* *The terms float and slack are used interchangeably. They are the same. Float had been the common usage, until Microsoft introduced their scheduling products, which substituted slack for float.*

The Forward Pass sets a pair of early deadlines for each task. These are called early start and early finish. The backward pass sets a pair of late dates. These are called Late Start and Late Finish. The difference between the early deadlines and the late deadlines is the total buffer time.

■ *Tip* *Sometimes the user does not wish to publish the late dates or the float. This is controlled in the reporting process. In such situations, it is also popular to change the name of the early dates to something like Scheduled Start and Scheduled Finish, or perhaps just Start and Finish. Just about all programs allow the user to rename the standard calculated fields.*

Also, at times, the user does not wish to calculate or publish the early dates. Instead they want to have the dates calculated and displayed as the latest dates. This would be equivalent to a just-in-time scheduling approach. Most products have an ALAP (as late as possible) calculation option that can be used to accomplish this. The default is the ASAP (as soon as possible) mode.

Date Constraints Now that we know how CPM calculates dates, we can also understand how to use imposed dates and how they affect date calculations. Of the various options for imposing dates, the most popular is the Start no earlier than (SNET) or End no later than (FNLT) option.

SNET dates are used to set a start date for a task that can be later than the earliest start determined by the computer. You can override the calculations for the forward pass. For example, the computer may determine that a trench can be excavated starting January 15 (based on the completion of identified predecessors). However, your crew may not want to start excavating until March 15 because of cold weather (in Montana). Setting a SNET date of 3/15 will override the calculated early start of 1/15. If for some reason the predecessors go beyond 3/15, the imposed date is now overridden by the naturally calculated date. For this reason, we call such an imposed date Start not earlier than and not Start on, which is an imposed date that is not overwritten by the calculations.

■ *Caution* *First-time users of project management software often tend to overuse imposed dates, especially the Start On option. In an attempt to force the schedule to predetermined dates, this improper use of the Start On option creates two problems. First, it prevents the determination of a schedule that is based on defined dependencies. Second, it makes updating the schedule much more difficult, as the user must go in and manually change all the imposed dates.*

Often, this overuse of imposed Start On dates is motivated by a desire to avoid the effort of defining all the dependencies. Ironically, the result is not only a poorly developed schedule, but also vastly increased effort to maintain it.

Furthermore, one of the great benefits of project management software comes from using these tools to help develop a supportable schedule, based on defined work, dependencies, and available resources. Ignoring all of this to create a forced schedule may be easier to do and more politically acceptable. But if it is not supported by the facts, what good is it in the long run?

The Finish No Later Than (FNLT) - works exactly the other way around than the SNET constraint. The FNLT date affects the calculation of late dates when it is imposed. This is best illustrated with an example. Let us say the calculated schedule for the construction of a house states that the roof can be completed by March 15 to meet the contractual June 30 completion date for the house. We are in Iowa and the snow is expected to increase significantly by December 1. It is decided that it is important to complete the roof by that date in order to be able to work in the house and protect the materials. By imposing an FNLT date of 12/1 on the task to complete the roof, we control all other late dates to support this imposed constraint. The FNTL date does not affect the early dates that are calculated during the forward pass.

Other Constraints Some of the constraints on planning project work may involve events and conditions that are not on the list of defined tasks. We may be waiting for the availability of the land on which we want to build the house. Or we may need the building permit. The construction of the roof truss may require the availability of a crane. Buying the building materials may depend on the availability of funds. Placement of windows may depend on completion and approval of final building plans. Availability of electricians may depend on completion of electrical work on another building.

In fact, all of these constraints should be included in the project schedule. For most in the above list, we would create a new task (which may have a duration of zero) to note the constraint. For these "dummy" tasks, we would enter a SNET date "and make them predecessors to the tasks that cannot be started until this constraint is met. For example, you can survey and lay out the site while waiting for the building permit. But the first excavation task would be constrained by a start task called Obtain Building Permit. The duration would be zero. A SNET date would be set based on the anticipated permit date. This task would be defined as the Finish to Start predecessor to the Excavation task. A task with a duration of zero is often referred to as an event because it represents a point in time.

■ *Tip* *Creating dummy tasks to meet one of the above constraints is more convenient than imposing a SNET date on the affected task. There are two reasons for this. First, by using a separate task, there is a specific, separate item where we can define the specific constraint. Second, there can be more than one such constraint for a task. We can use a separate constraint task for each one.*

Still More Constraints - Up to this point, we have calculated the schedule without considering the availability of labor resources. We have assumed that all resources needed to support the work will be available at the scheduled time. Obviously, this is not a good assumption. Ultimately, we want to create a definition of available resources and allow the program to take resource availability into account when calculating the schedule. This is called resource leveling or resource-constrained scheduling.

Once we have defined the resources needed to perform the tasks, we can have the program CPM calculate the amount of each resource needed for each date. These quantities can be the number of units of a resource (when using resource classes, such as electricians) or the number of hours per time period for named resources, such as Jack Smith, a system developer. By performing this calculation of required resource quantities, we can see and evaluate the level of resources needed to support the schedule (before adjusting resource limits). This process of calculating the resources needed against time is sometimes called resource aggregation.

If the resource compilation indicates that there is a significant period of time when resource needs will peak, you can use this as an early warning to either try to arrange additional resources or prepare for significant schedule adjustments.

Baselines -Do not expect to have an acceptable schedule after the first calculation. Even without adjusting resources, it is likely that several iterations will be required before the calculated schedule satisfies the stakeholders and the key dates in the project milestone schedule.

Once an acceptable schedule is developed, it is common to save the dates as a baseline schedule. This baseline represents a set of goals that will be used to compare progress as the work progresses. Each task is given a new pair of deadlines, usually called Baseline Start and Baseline Finish. Target Start and Target Finish are alternative headings.

■ *Tip* *It is often desirable to be able to save multiple baselines. The first is usually the initial or contract baseline. A second might be a set of negotiated revision dates. I usually reserve one baseline set for my last schedule computation. Then I can compare the next update to that baseline to analyze changes during the last period.*

This concludes our overview of critical path planning. We can go into much more detail, but that might cause even more confusion. At this point, you know enough to understand some of the issues associated with project planning.

CRITICAL PATH, CRITICAL CHAIN, AND UNCERTAINTY Exploring concepts of shared contingency

In the 45 years that formal scheduling has existed on critical paths, all current protocols have treated uncertainty in essentially similar ways. They dealt with it (if at all) on a task-by-task basis. The original PERT method had a formal mechanism for uncertainty in that it provided three task durations (optimistic, most likely, and pessimistic). Some of today's CPM programs have adopted this three duration option. In the programs that did not use three time periods, uncertainty was accounted for by adding a little extra time to each estimate of task duration.

There are several problems with this approach. In the case of the latter, arbitrary approach, there was no consistency in the treatment of unanticipatedness in the schedule and there was no documentation of what portion of the duration was actually unanticipated. In all approaches, the unpredictability (allowance for uncertainty) was allocated to each individual task, although the actual uncertainty would be better handled on a group of tasks basis.

This situation has been explored by several people, and there is growing interest in an emerging treatment of (what I call) shared contingency.

■ *Caution An unforeseen schedule is an important component of a successful project. However, these contingencies must be clearly identified and managed. Inconsistent and unstructured padding of time estimates, while a common practice, is not a good thing. There are better ways to account for the uncertainty that exists in all projects.*

Exploration of the chain theory

There is an abundance of articles, both in print and on websites, either extolling the benefits of the critical chain approach or advising restraint in its application. The discussion offered here is completely neutral and finds both praise and criticism of aspects of Critical Chain Project Management (CCPM) theory and practice as presented by Goldratt and his followers.

When I shared my thoughts with two colleagues (both of whom are involved in developing software for project management), the question came up whether there were two different camps. One said that one had to be a follower of either CCPM or traditional CPM (TCPM), but could not reconcile both philosophies. I disagree. I am not willing to give up either TCPM or adopt CCPM completely.

For example, let us consider just one of the beliefs associated with the two camps, the rules for multitasking. With TCPM, it has become common to assume that resources will move back and forth between concurrently scheduled tasks from time to time. In fact, we often find that such shifting leads to more efficient schedules and more efficient use of resources, and we have criticized software that does not support splitting resource allocation. Now Goldratt comes along and disputes that assumption. He says that multitasking is only necessary because we make the duration of tasks longer than the actual time required. He claims that multitasking is inherently inefficient. If we reduce the estimated task duration to the actual effort, Goldratt argues, we do not need to shift resources. CCPM therefore intentionally prohibits resource sharing because it is a negative attribute, not a preferred capability.

In short, Goldratt argues that project schedules are always too long because of the safety factors added to task estimates. He claims that estimates are usually based on a 90 percent confidence factor (rather than 50 percent). Also, unless the performer is confident that everything needed to complete the task is ready at the start of the task (which is usually not the case), the duration of the tasks is spiked. Also, we usually add a collection factor when a group of tasks comes together to provide some margin in case one of the tasks slips. Similarly, each level of management adds a safety margin. Finally, everyone knows that the total duration will not be accepted. They figure it will be cut by 20 percent, so they add 25 percent to the already inflated estimate.

Of course, inflated estimates are nothing new to our readers, and Goldratt's solution, which deserves our attention, is also far from original.

Another interesting approach to dealing with contingencies in schedules is presented by Bradford Eichhorn. Using the technique of considering contingencies in the schedule, Eichhorn supports my appeal to specifically identify and manage contingencies.

The Shared Contingency Idea

Basically, each of these solutions could be called a shared contingency (my term). In the Goldratt approach, it is applied in several stages. First, he determines the critical path and reduces the duration of the tasks so that they match with a probability of 50 percent instead of 90 percent. Half of the removed duration is added at the end of the path as a project buffer.

Next, feeder paths are identified and treated in a similar manner. Half of the removed duration is added as a buffer at the end of each feeder path. The overall project schedule is reduced. The focus is on monitoring the project buffer and feeder buffers (for shrinkage) rather than managing the critical path.

In general, I agree with the concept of shared contingency represented by the project buffer and feeder buffer method. But it needs to be implemented on a case-by-case basis.

On the one hand, the problem (as described by Goldratt) is that the contingency of the project schedule is usually added to the invisible task contingency, resulting in an unreasonably extended schedule and reducing the pressure to complete tasks in the shortest possible time. On the other hand, care must be taken not to be overzealous in reducing the contingency so that the project is in danger of not meeting the contracted deadlines.

The concept of taking contingency out of individual tasks and placing it in project and feeder buffers makes a lot of sense and is highly recommended. It is a simple idea that can be easily implemented. Goldratt refrains from discussing aids that help in applying his methods. We will provide such advice later in this chapter. Goldratt lists three strategies associated with the basic concept. I have some serious reservations about this.

First, he suggests using remaining duration rather than percent completion to measure task status. This makes sense, but only if you are not using earned value analysis techniques (which I almost always recommend). Remaining duration has always been a status option in most project management programs.

He also says that "we are only concerned with the critical path" But then Goldratt contradicts himself by discussing ways to use feeder buffer analysis to manage the schedule. I prefer using EVA (BCWP vs. BCWS) to analyze work production (as discussed later in this chapter and in Section 8). However, a formal application of feeder-buffer analysis can be used as an alternative method.

I strongly disagree with Goldratt's principle that we should do away with management by milestones. Milestones are good for achieving intermediate goals (they provide immediate recognition and reward). Some milestones are necessary intermediate goals. The use of selected milestones should be retained to supplement other measurements. I almost always develop a project milestone plan for initial top-down planning and to guide detailed planning.

Resource and Bottleneck Buffers

Up to this point, Goldratt is concerned with a planning model that does not take into account possible resource conflicts and limits. He now addresses the complexity of resource constraints. He introduces resource buffers and specifies that the critical path must now pass through all tasks where there is concurrent competition for scarce resources. He inserts resource buffers when the work shifts to a new resource. These resource buffers are used only in the critical chain and are placed before critical tasks to alert resources to upcoming work. Goldratt acknowledges at this point that computer support is needed for analyzing and determining resource congestion and scheduling.

As far as I can tell from his discussion of resource constraints, a method such as the well-known resource balancing technique must be used. However, the use of resource buffers in the critical chain method does not insert an actual resource contingency (no resources are allocated to the resource buffers), but only a time contingency before the planned resource consumption. This gives me cause for concern. If we acknowledge that we should assign the shortest reasonable duration to tasks and then insert a time contingency, does not the same philosophy apply to resource consumption? That is, if we are reducing task duration and the associated resource effort to trim the fat, then surely we must include some reserve for resource effort in the plan. Otherwise, we blindly go into our projects thinking we have enough resources budgeted and have no reserves to draw from when the effort (and it certainly will sometimes) exceeds the plan.

So this is a serious flaw in the critical chain theory. It takes into account the risk and unpredictability of the schedule, but ignores the risk and unpredictability of the resource effort and cost.

Software for CCPM

It is accepted that computer support is required to calculate the critical chain and manipulate the various buffers. There are options to set the parameters for the buffers and override the automatic placement or calculation. The Factor Durations option allows you to specify a multiplier for the duration. For example, you could use Factor Duration to halve the task duration, and then set the buffer options to 50 percent of the path duration. In the short test I ran, I had to reduce the durations by about half to compensate for the extra duration for all the buffers. Also, in this test, the project duration (after load balancing, but without buffers) was the same as when I called MSP's resource balancing function (which was to be expected). However, the chosen order of task execution was different.

If you do not want to use separate software for CCPM, some of the functions can be achieved by creative use of conventional CPM software that has PERT (three-time estimation). None of these products calculate and place buffers, but the PERT analysis can be used to estimate the time that should be allowed for the contingency schedule.

Planning and Tracking Issues

It should be clear by now that the road to good schedules is strewn with stones and other obstacles. Our schedules must contain a balance between reasonable task durations and reasonable contingencies. We need to squeeze the fat (or excessive unpredictability) out of estimates while still maintaining a reasonable buffer for the inevitable effects of Murphy's Law. There are several techniques to deal with these planning problems, including PERT estimates (triple time estimates) and critical chain buffers.

However, once these plans are created, we can no longer rely on just one method to track progress. Those of us who learned to work with the critical path method soon found that out. If we focused solely on maintaining margin on the critical path, eventually enough work that was not on the critical path became critical, and the ability to compensate for variances somewhere in the project disappeared. With the CCPM method, there is a similar danger when we put all our eggs in one basket by focusing only on the critical chain. I prefer to supplement the traditional critical path analysis with something I call Accomplishment Value.

Using Accomplishment Value to Supplement Float Analysis

Fulfillment value or earned value (also known as budgeted cost of work performed) refers to the measurement of fulfillment against the plan once work has begun. It is quite simple and practical to apply only a portion of the Earned Value protocol to measure work performance against the plan. To use the EV approach, you identify your tasks, assign a cost factor (or other weighting factor) to each task, and schedule all tasks (either manually or through CPM). The computer calculates the BCWS or planned output for any given time by multiplying the planned percentage of completion of each task by the value (cost) of the task. Now, when it is time to move the schedule forward, simply enter the percentage completion of the tasks that have been started. The system multiplies the percent complete by the estimated cost, which gives the completion value. This gives us a weighted measure of completion that can be compared to budgeted completion. If the completion value (BCWP) is less than the planned performance (BCWS), the work is not being completed as quickly as planned and you can say that the project is behind schedule.

Interestingly, some CCPM proponents criticize EVA 's methods on the grounds that they are not accurate because they are based on cost, not duration. This is not necessarily true.

Using Your Options

The bottom line is that you should be aware that there are several ways to plan and track project activities. There will be times when using techniques such as CCPM or PERT to plan projects will yield a better plan. Risk management and contingency planning are always warranted (not an option). Tracking options include percent complete, duration remaining, earned value, milestone tracking, critical path tracking, and buffer analysis. I could never argue that only one of these options is very important and the others should be subordinated or ignored. Each of these options has its purpose.

The concept of shared contingency is one that I can very much support, but there are many ways to do it. Critical chain theory has done a lot to bring the concept of shared contingency, leaner task duration, and risk awareness to the forefront. We can all learn from this and look for ways to address these issues.

Project success depends not so much on planning and control methods and tools, but on the behavior of managers and other employees who contribute to project performance. It is well known that traditional methods and tools tend to be intimidating to these individuals. Some claim that CCPM breaks down this barrier. I am not sure that this is true. However, I am certain that improving the way people operate in the project environment and their commitment to good planning and communication and execution according to plan are the real keys to project success.

ESTIMATING TASK DURATIONS

Think a little about the relative importance of task duration. A project schedule is the result of aggregating all task durations. If the durations are not right, then the project schedule is not right. Fidelity in estimating task durations is essential to developing a healthy project schedule. And such accuracy can only be achieved through a structured and consistent approach to task duration estimation.

How Long Does It Take to Catch a Fish?

Here's a good question. How long does it take to catch a fish? Ridiculous, you will say. You can not estimate the time it takes to catch a fish. It could be shortly after you cast your line. It could be never. Or somewhere in between. As ridiculous as that sounds, that's exactly the feeling that goes through our minds when we are asked to estimate how long a task will take. Our first thought is, how the h_ am I supposed to know? But we can not get away with that. So we set to work trying to scientifically determine the duration of the task. First, we create an estimate of the likely duration of the task. This is the time it would take us to complete the task about 50 percent of the time. But we are not comfortable with a 50 percent confidence factor. So we add a time that we think we can meet about 90 percent of the time.

ESTIMATING TASK DURATIONS

Next, we consider what we need to begin the task, including the conditions required to do so. If we are concerned that we do not have everything we need to start the task, we add a little more time to the task estimate (although these questions do not affect the actual time to complete the task itself). And then there's the gathering factor. When a group of tasks comes together, we tend to add a little more margin of safety so that one of the tasks does not get lost. Similarly, we find that we tend to lose time between tasks. I call this the 5 + 5 = 13 rule. Two tasks, each estimated to take 5 days, take 13 days in succession because we lose 3 days between the completion of the first task and the start of the second task.

So what do we do? We compensate for all these factors that are outside the immediate task by adding time to the task estimate itself. Finally, everyone knows that the total duration will not be accepted. They reckon that it will be cut by 20 percent, so they add 25 percent to the already inflated estimate.

What does the task duration really mean?

If we assign task duration as just described, do we really know how long the expected task duration is? Certainly there is a rationale for all of the above. However, most of them have nothing to do with the actual time we need to complete the task. Moreover, even the estimation of the actual task duration can take different paths. For example, there are several approaches to estimating task duration.

Elapsed Time vs. Working Time - We think it will take us 5 days to actually get the work done. But we know that we will not work on the task without interruption. So we set the task duration to 10 days to account for the time we expect.

Task Time vs. Resource Time - We estimate that the task will take 80 hours. Is that 80 hours for 2 people, which gives a time of 5 days? Or is it 80 hours for 1 person working part-time, resulting in an elapsed time of 20 days?

Interface Losses and Delays - We have noted above that we can expect some loss of time between tasks and at the convergence of multiple tasks. Should we build these expected losses into the tasks themselves or set up dummy tasks to account for these delays?

Theoretical Duration vs. Experience -Here is a situation that always frustrates me. I have a task that I have done several times. Each time I estimate how long it should take, I come up with 20 days. I just know that I can do it in 20 days. But each time I do the task, it takes about 50 percent longer than the 20 days. Each time there is a different reason for the delay. Still, on average, it takes me 30 days to complete the task. What should I do now? Do I use the estimated duration of 20 days, which I think is correct? Or do I use an estimate of 30 days - based on past experience? It is justified to use the 20-day estimate. The task should be completed in 20 days, and that is what we should use as a target. But if our experience tells us to expect 30 days, are not we deceiving the team when we say we expect the task to be completed in 20 days? And if we use the 30-day estimate, will we end up taking the 30 days because that's the time available? Is there a right answer?

■ *Caution Be careful not to misuse averaging. For example, we do not want to average performance on parallel paths. Suppose we have tasks A, B, C, and D, each of which is estimated to take 20 days. A, B, and C actually take 15 days each. Task D actually takes 35 days. The average is still 20 days, but the actual duration of the path (for the four parallel tasks) is 35 days.*

As another example, consider two serial tasks, each estimated to take 10 days. Task A is completed in 8 days. Task B takes 12 days. The chain probably took 22 days (not 20) because Task B did not start until the eleventh day. (Harvey's Law: a delay in one step is passed on to the next step. Progress made in one step is usually wasted)

Skill Levels, Learning Curves, and Priorities - How do we deal with potential performance changes? Do we add time to the estimated duration because we assume the task will require more time and effort the first time (learning curve)? Should the duration be adjusted based on the skill level of the resources expected to be used? Do we have an index of skill levels? And what if resources change? Will a higher priority task or project get done faster because of pressure and attention? These are all things that can affect how long a task takes. But rarely is there a set of guidelines to help us estimate and provide a consistent approach for the entire project and team.

PERT Method - This technique provides a quantitative method for accounting for uncertainty or risk. It requires the use of three time estimates for each task. These are called optimistic, most likely, and pessimistic. The most likely is the duration that can be expected 50 percent of the time. The optimistic value is the shortest reasonable duration that can be achieved about 10 percent of the time. The pessimistic value is the longest reasonable duration that can also be achieved about 10 percent of the time. In the PERT method, a PERT duration is calculated, usually based on the formula: $(a + 4b + c)/6$, where b is the highest probability. Using special software, it is then possible to perform a statistical analysis that provides a calculated probability of meeting any project deadline. Although it may seem that the PERT method involves a lot of extra work, the opposite is true. In reality, we tend to think about the possible range of estimates based on perceived risk and uncertainty. But having mentally derived a single duration, we fail to capture the information that went into the estimate.

Delphi Method This decision-support technique is rarely used in determining task duration, but could be used if desired. It asks each team member to submit his or her own estimate to the group. Estimates at the extremes (shortest/longest) are defended by the person who made the estimate, which often raises issues not considered by the others. Based on the new information, the team votes again (re-estimate). The process is repeated until a reasonable consensus on the task duration is reached and they are satisfied.

The Psychology of Task Durations

There is a self-fulfilling prophecy regarding the completion of tasks within the scheduled time period. A task is hardly ever completed ahead of schedule. There are several reasons for this. We can illustrate these with a task that has a 50/50 chance of being completed in 5 days, but has been scheduled for 10 days to account for uncertainties, risks, detour for emergencies, and so on.

First, there is Parkinson's Law. Work expands to fill the time available for the work. Work on the task has started on schedule and is essentially completed within the first 5 days. However, since 10 days are allotted for the task, the performer spends the next 5 days fine-tuning the result. This is a natural work ethic for most people. We achieve 98% completion of our task, and when we have more time available, we try to refine it until the deadline is reached.

The second option is procrastination. We can start the task as planned. But since we have 10 days available and we know we only need 5 days, we wait a week to start the task. Now, of course, the quota is exhausted before the task is started, and the potential for exceeding the schedule has increased. But even if there are no problems, the 5-day task has taken 10 days. Less obvious are the subtle motivators that prevent premature completion of tasks. If we estimate 10 days and complete the task in 5 days, we might be criticized for inflating the estimate, even if the extra 5 days was a legitimate allowance for uncertainty. Or we might be under increased pressure to shorten duration estimates in the future. There is rarely a reward for completing tasks early - only disadvantages for exceeding them. So where is the motivation to complete the task in 5 days?

Practical Time Estimating

Given all the possibilities for biased or spiked time estimates, how can we account for all the disruptions that may affect the schedule without obscuring the true duration of the task? Of course, if we do not account for uncertainty by planning for the unexpected, we risk being late and missing deadlines. However, if we include the contingencies in the estimates of each task, we can be almost certain that the work will be completed in the time available. This dilemma is the reason for the concepts of common contingencies. Using the various shared contingency conventions is one way to solve many of the problems raised. It is also possible to solve some of these problems using the traditional methods and tools of CPM. Here are a few examples.

- Example 1 The task is to be completed in 20 days, but based on past experience you need to allow 30 days. Enter a duration of 20 days. Create a dummy task with a duration of 10 days for contingencies.

- Example 2 Combine all contingencies for a logical group of tasks into a common contingency dummy task. Following the CCPM philosophy, add up the contingencies and halve them for the buffer task (split contingency method).

- Example 3 Use Finish-to-Start links (FS) with a delay duration to allow time for delays between tasks.

- Example 4 Freely set Finish-Not-Late (FNLT) dates to achieve earlier completions. Set the FNLT dates for tasks that you do not want to delay equal to the early completion dates.

Even more important than all of the above is the need to develop consistency in estimating task durations. There should be a general guideline for contingencies. That way, at least everyone knows on what basis the estimate is based. The project department should establish standard guidelines for estimating task duration that can be used universally.

PRACTICAL TIME ESTIMATING

When applying the guidelines, consider the key factors for project success. If getting the work done as quickly as possible is a key objective, then contingencies should be minimized and identified. If protecting the business from late penalties is a primary goal, then contingency provisions play a larger role.

Flexibility within standardized guidelines and noting and communicating the basis for estimates help reduce the potential for poor estimates and planning. But no one said it would be easy.

HOW IMPORTANT ARE SCHEDULES AND TIME COMPRESSION?

Have you ever driven along a highway where a construction project seemed to take forever? You drive for miles, past thousands of orange barrels and cones, past hundreds of barriers and signs, past dozens of expensive cranes, bulldozers, excavators and the like, and past miles of temporary concrete dividers. But there are hardly any people to be seen. Where are the workers? Why is there 10 miles of detour and only 10 yards of active work? Not only that, you drove by this site six months ago and hardly anything has changed. Aside from your immediate frustration with the traffic delays, your ever-curious mind wanders to the subject of waste. How much money is tied up in all these paraphernalia? How much money could be saved if these projects were expedited (and also reduced the inconvenience to motorists)?

Period Costs and Hammocks

A typical project consists of a combination of labor costs, material costs, and other costs such as equipment rental and consumables. Keep in mind that many of these costs are accrual-based. That is, the costs are associated with the duration of use, not the intensity or frequency of use.

If we look at highway projects, such as those mentioned above, we can list several period-related costs. These include trailers for field service, office equipment including computers and telephones, earthmoving equipment, and the like. What about all those orange barrels and cones? They must represent a reasonable capital investment. What about the foremen? The longer the job, the higher the cost.

Good scheduling software has a hammock feature. A hammock is a type of task that has no fixed duration. Instead, it automatically calculates its duration from the tasks to which it is linked (or from the group of tasks to which the hammock extends).

You can use the hammock function for any task that has resources or costs associated with time periods that are dependent on other tasks. For example, let us say we rent an excavator for $200 per day. We create a hammock task called Rent Excavator and assign it a cost of $200 per day. We note a start-to-start relationship with the first task requiring the excavator and a finish-to-target relationship with the last task requiring the excavator. That's it. If the series of tasks requiring the excavator spans 21 days, the rental cost is automatically calculated at $4,200. If the schedule is compressed to shorten that time span to 16 days, the cost of the excavator is automatically recalculated to $3,200.

When you set up these period cost tasks using hammocks, you can easily see the impact of compressing time from the schedule. Often the additional cost of overtime and/or night work can be offset by the reduction in period cost. Maybe not always, but with this method you do not have to puzzle over it. Using hammocks in this way also allows you to see the true cost of delays.

Time-to-Market

Here's another thought to ponder. We all read constantly about the importance of time to market. We hear about constant progress in shortening product development cycles. We know that there are pro-competitive incentives to shorten time-to-market. And we can assume that shortening the process might even reduce development costs.

But how much has been written so far to actually quantify the benefits of shorter development cycles? Well, we have some interesting numbers to offer on this. When a new product is developed for a new market, it's very likely that the first product to hit the market will claim at least 50 percent of the total market. The remaining 50 percent is all that is left for all the other players. No wonder the pressure on new developments is so great (and perhaps why some developers are more willing to cut corners on quality than risk delays).

Hey, there's more. If the first vendor in the market gets 50 percent of the potential revenue, while #2 grabs, say, 20 percent, that's not the likely ratio for revenue. That's because No. 1 sets the price that maximizes profit and return on investment without competition. As the other suppliers enter the fray, profit margins will fall (but only after No. 1 has made its profit). Moore assumes that No. 1 can claim at least 70 percent of the profit pie in this model.

Now I ask you - is that enough motivation to drive schedule compression and management?

Every day that can be squeezed out of the schedule improves the developer's chances of capturing the lion's share of the market. The developer of a new product must not only strive to create schedules, but must also constantly balance the schedule for opportunities to optimize (shorten) the time cycles. The reward for being first to the finish line is huge.

Schedule and Cost - Effect on Profit

Here's some more data to support our thesis about the harmful effects of schedule delays. As project managers and owners, we tend to worry equally about schedule delays and cost overruns. But according to an oft-cited study, one of the two issues is more equal than the other.

This study examines the impact of schedule delays and cost overruns on expected profit over a 5-year period. The resulting data show that cost overruns on the order of 50 percent ultimately reduce profits by about 3 to 4 percent. On the other hand, schedule delays of 6 months were found to often result in a loss of one-third of expected profit over five years.

Of course, given the general marketing models, this should not be surprising. The impact of schedule delays on cash flow and return on investment described in the following sections further supports these findings.

Effect of Project Delays on Return on Investment

I recently played with some numbers to examine the impact of extended project completion on cash flow and payback period. In doing so, I assumed that the project would be completed in two years and that I would invest $10,000 per month (at a cost of 8%). The project began on 1/1/2000 and was scheduled to be completed on 1/1/2002, at a cost of $260,000. Upon completion, the project would yield $10,000 per month and return my investment on approximately 3/1/2004, 50 months after the project began.

I then calculated the impact of a six-month delay combined with a 15 percent increase in monthly expenses. This overrun in schedule and cost is much less than the published studies suggest. When the project was completed, I had invested $381,000. At a monthly return of $10,000, starting on 7/1/2002, it will take until 9/1/2005, or 68 months, for me to recover the money.

This is just another example of the potential cost of schedule delays and cost overruns. I imagine that if I had presented such a project to the funders and offered a 68-month payback instead of a 50-month payback, I would have met with considerable resistance. After experiencing the extended payback period, how well would the project meet the criteria for project success?

Extended Cash Flow Projections

We usually use critical path planning software to plan and control a project. Usually, we define the project as everything that happens from project approval or initiation to completion of all deliverables. When we use the costing capabilities of the software, they are applied over that time period and generally include all costs incurred to complete the deliverables. But why stop here? Cash flow can be positive or negative. If the project we are managing is expected to generate positive cash flow (as with the new product developments mentioned above), then why not add pseudo-tasks that generate revenue? Now we can model different scenarios and evaluate the best actions for a project. Not only can we determine the most cost-effective plan to complete the project, but also the best plan to generate the preferred long-term cash flow.

Taking this process even further, we can evaluate a range of projects and change the mix of projects to optimize support for overall business strategies and plans. We have been hearing a lot about project portfolio management lately. A key component of this enterprise-level strategy is schedule-based cash flow analysis of multiple projects.

Risk Considerations

So far, we have been talking about schedules as if they were based on well-defined task durations. But we all know that this is an illusion. Task durations are based on estimates of time and effort. These are always based on one or more assumptions, and these assumptions are subject to interpretation. Usually, such estimates are developed with some degree of contingency. Yes, there are cases where an optimistic person makes a "best possible" estimate. But most estimates assume that there are one or more conditions that extend a task beyond its achievable duration. So to a 10-day task, 2 days are added for possible weather delays, another 2 days for resource conflicts, 1 more day for equipment problems, and maybe another 3 days just for convenience. Now that the 10-day task has grown to 18 days, we add a few days because we know the project manager will ask for a 10 percent improvement to speed up the schedule.

There are many ways to solve this dilemma, such as using multiple estimates (PERT durations) or common contingency concepts such as the Critical Chain and Project Contingency Allowance techniques. However, there is one aspect of this condition that we all need to be aware of. There is a relationship between schedule contingencies and schedule risk. Adding contingencies to the schedule is motivated by a desire to reduce the risk of failure. Although adding contingencies does not necessarily reduce risk (because we learn to use contingencies to let things slide), it provides more room for error and corrective action than a very tight schedule.

If we use contingency (which I strongly recommend), it must be controlled contingency. By that I mean a controlled contingency:

We need to know the basis for the contingency. That is, if we allow 2 days for weather and 1 day for equipment, it should be noted.

The contingency should be separated from the actual expected duration.

Pressure should be applied to achieve the most likely times.

The manager moves time from the contingency pool to the schedule and performs an analysis of schedule performance and use of contingencies.

The tighter the schedule, the less margin there is for error (less time is available for corrective action, so remediation is limited). This increases the importance of proactive risk management. Management must be fully aware of all risk areas. These risk areas must be constantly monitored. The risk-averse manager is prepared in advance to take remedial action by having alternative plans ready when needed.

PERT Analysis

As briefly mentioned in the previous section, there is a tool to help analyze schedules with varying degrees of temporal contingency. This involves the use of three time estimates for each task. This method is usually referred to as PERT analysis.

The method consists of assigning an optimistic, a most likely, and a pessimistic estimate to each task. For example, a task might have a most likely duration of 4 days and be completed in 3 days in the best case. However, there may be delays so that the pessimistic estimate is 10 days. We enter this as 3, 4, 10. The most likely estimate is weighted by 4 times the others and the sum of the estimates is divided by 6 to get a weighted estimate. Scitor's PS8 allows us to set weights other than the default values. If we want to allow for a bit more unpredictability, we can weight the pessimistic values slightly more than the optimistic ones. The calculation of the schedule based on these weighted estimates is automatic.

This method gives us at least 3 advantages. First, by setting 3 estimates, we have a better sense of the actual time estimate and the range of risks and contingencies for each task. For example, a task with an estimate of 3, 4, 10 would be more risk-prone than a task with an estimate of 5, 5, 5.

Second, we can calculate the schedule with different weights. In this way, we can determine the expected dates of completion of the project for different degrees of optimism or unpredictability. This does not change how long the project will take. But it does give us insight into the possible outcomes. Management needs this information to make intelligent decisions.

Third, using the special analysis software PERT, we can produce a statistical evaluation of the probability that each of the possible project completion dates will be met. In one of the tests I did on a model project, it turned out that the project completion date, which I assumed had a 50 percent probability (using only the most likely estimates), had only a 5 percent probability when analyzed by PERT.

The Value of Critical Path Scheduling

CPM has been around for more than 40 years, and it has been used with varying degrees of success. Although it is sometimes criticized for being too difficult to use or understand, it is almost universally used by serious project managers on serious projects. In most situations, it does the job. It is the basis for the techniques we just described: the use of hammocks, project portfolio analysis, and PERT analysis. It is also the basis for other planning techniques. When we work in a project environment where there is a strong payoff for shortening project duration, these techniques help achieve shorter times and evaluate planning options.

PRACTICAL SCHEDULING

When Will the Work Be Done?

When we talk about scheduling, we are talking about the timing of the work. We determine when the work should be done. Schedules can be determined by various factors. This can also include a combination of factors:

• **Milestone-driven** Work is scheduled to meet milestones and deadlines specified by the contract or project terms. These milestones and deadlines are usually recorded in the project milestone schedule, which serves as a guide for detailed scheduling.

• **Precedence-driven** Work is scheduled by the computer based on task durations, constraints, and defined relationships. A pure precedence schedule may not fully support the defined milestones and assumes that all resources will be available when needed. While this is not realistic, it is a good start. Even a schedule that considers the milestones and resources must also consider the priority relationships if it is to have any validity.

• **Resource-driven** The work is planned when the resources for the work are available. To do this, we must start with a preliminary (non-resource constrained) schedule, preferably one based on priority. Then we define the resources to be allocated to the work and let the computer calculate the required resource utilization. If you also define the available resources, the computer can compare the resource requirements with the resource availability. By calling the resource balancing function, the computer can then reschedule the work to stay within the defined limits.

A practical final schedule takes into account all of the above. There will be conflicts over scarce resources, conflicts with established milestones, haggling over priorities, political and territorial disputes, and consideration of risk. Task durations will be challenged, task precedence will be redefined, and even the defined scope of work may be changed. Resource availability will also be extremely dynamic, changing almost as quickly as it is defined.

It is obvious that the computer will become an indispensable tool for project planning. In this chapter, we will give you some tips on how to use these tools to take all these dynamics into account when planning and create a practical project plan.

Schedule Analysis Using Total and Free Float

The use of float for decision making dates back to the original PERT and CPM programs in the late 1950s. It is still a valuable technique when used properly and not blindly. Buffer time (also called slack in Microsoft Project) is calculated by the critical path planning function that is at the heart of virtually all project management software products. The float time is the difference between the earliest time a task can be executed and the latest time allowed. There are two types of float: total float and free float. Each type can be used differently.

The total buffer time is the amount of time a task can move without extending the end date of the project. The higher the total buffer time, the more reserve time there is in the project. We can use this information for two important purposes. First, we can determine which of the tasks are more critical. That is, which task has a smaller time margin (buffer or slack) and therefore needs to be monitored more closely. If there is a risk of missing important deadlines and milestones, we can use the total buffer time to determine which tasks need to be accelerated.

Another way to use total float is to analyze schedule risk and trends. The more tasks have low float, the higher the risk of not meeting target dates. We can compare total float values to those from the last schedule update to determine how far behind schedule a project is. Even if the most important tasks are completed on time, the reduction in margin for less important tasks could be an indication of impending problems.

It is important to remember that total buffer time should not be taken as a request to arbitrarily postpone work. It should be viewed as a reserve to be allocated as needed under management control. We must also remember that total buffer time is calculated over a chain of tasks. If someone utilizes the total buffer time for a task that is at the beginning of a chain (by letting the task slide), the total buffer time for all subsequent tasks that are in that chain will decrease.

Free float solves this chaining problem. Free float is the measure of how far back a task can slide without affecting the earliest start of another task. As an example, consider some roofing work. Laying roof shingles has two predecessors: getting shingles and laying underlayment. If the scheduled end of the underlayment is June 22 and the earliest delivery of shingles is June 8, we can say that the procurement task has 2 weeks of slack. Delaying the delivery of the shingles by up to 2 weeks will not delay any other tasks (and might even be preferable due to cost or space constraints).

Regarding these two types of buffers, we can state that the free buffer can usually be used freely by the responsible task manager, but the overall buffer should be managed at a higher level so as not to interfere with the work of others.

Working with Dependency and Due Dates

We introduced date constraints in Section 3.1. We noted that we can add date constraints to tasks and modify schedule calculations. And we discussed the most popular of these imposed date features: Start No Earlier Than (SNET) and Finish No Later Than (FNLT).

Remember to use the SNET dates to delay the start of a task beyond the earliest possible start, which is determined by the simple precedence of the task. For example: you are replacing guardrails on the expressway that carries traffic to a popular resort. Although your materials will be on site by 8/22 and other preparations can be completed by that date, you do not want to close the right lane until after Labor Day. So, set a SNET date of 9/4/01 (the day after Labor Day) for the tasks related to closing the right lane. If any of the preceding tasks go beyond the 9/4 date, the SNET date will be overridden by the precedence.

Use this SNET data as needed to express planned launch delays. However, avoid using them as an excuse to escape the need to define legitimate task precedence. Also note that the SNET constraint only affects the forward run, i.e., the calculation of early deadlines.

The Finish No Later Than (FNLT) constraint works in exactly the opposite way as the SNET constraint. The FNLT date affects the calculation of late dates when it is imposed. Let us take the same highway construction project as above and give another example. This time, work is scheduled for June, and much of the project work must continue into the summer. Again, there is pressure to minimize the impact on resort traffic, which increases around Memorial Day. So we are moving to the task that is the completion of the work that requires the lane closures and setting an FNLT date of May 24.

By imposing an FNLT date of 5/24 on these tasks, we force all other late dates to support this imposed constraint. The FNTL date has no effect on the early dates that are calculated during the forward pass. And if the defined priority is stricter than the imposed dates, the FNLT date is overridden.

Just-in-time Scheduling

The default setting for CPM is ASAP (as soon as possible). In the example above (SNET), we showed one of the ways you can override ASAP 's calculations, based on exceptions. But what if there are parts of your project that you would rather have closer to the desired time (closer to the latest dates)?

In most programs, you have the option to select ALAP (as late as possible) mode. In ALAP mode, the backward pass becomes the driver of the schedule, and the task dates are set to have no wiggle room. This can be done for the whole project or for each individual task.

But even in just-in-time (JIT) mode, I would advise against developing a schedule that reduces everything to zero buffer. We can plan for some margin or safety by using the software's delay feature or by inserting dummy tasks. For example, we have several tasks that are needed for guardrail work on our expressway project. These include things like the new guardrails, fasteners, excavators, traffic cones, and lane closure signs. We do not want to buy or accumulate these things too early, so we are listing them as ALAP tasks. But we'd like to schedule them five days before we plan to start the guardrail work. We can do this in two ways. One option is to enter a delay of 5 days (FS5) between each of these tasks and the start of the guardrail milestone. Another option is to insert a dummy task called Collect items for guardrail work and assign it a duration of five days.

Building In Schedule Contingency

Suppose you are working with the traditional tools of CPM. How can we deal with contingency? One way is to use the analysis feature PERT if it is available in the tool you are using. For a discussion of PERT, see Chapter 3.3. Briefly, if you use the three time periods of PERT mode and change the weighting in favor of the pessimistic value (as is possible with PS8 from Scitor), you can build some contingency into the schedule.

Another way to build contingencies into the schedule is to consider the situations that most often cause schedule delays. These situations include:

- Points where a large number of predecessors feed into a task. This is often where time is lost to communicate and confirm that feeder tasks are complete and the next task can begin.

- Points where the location of the next task or the parties responsible for the next task change. As with the relay race, there is often a problem with the clean handoff of the baton.

- Points where there is a known or anticipated lack of resources.

- Your project has low priority or weak sponsor support.

Key decision points. These may include design reviews, funding reviews, permit reviews, or anything that may temporarily stall the project while you wait for approval to proceed.

Experience has shown that there is a high potential for delays in these situations. Nevertheless, we do not want to factor in such delays by extending the duration of the associated tasks. We can not see why the task duration was increased and by how much. Instead, it looks like we are using the extra time to complete the task. And (due to Parkinson's Law) we take the allotted time instead of using it for the purpose for which we had scheduled the extra time.

The better idea is to add a dummy task at each of these potential delay points. The task should describe the purpose of the delay and be set to a duration that accommodates the potential situation without unduly delaying the schedule. Another method is to add a delay between the start and end.

And then there is the issue of shared contingency buffers. I really like the idea of shared contingencies, whether you use CCPM or traditional tools. There is nothing wrong with taking a set of tasks, pulling the contingency out of the individual task estimates, and creating a dummy task at the end of the set that contains the sum of the contingency. Using Goldratt's approach, I would reduce the sum of the individual contingencies by 50 percent.

For example, in our highway project, there are the following tasks associated with guardrail construction: staking and marking the site, digging the holes for the support posts, erecting the posts, installing and securing the guardrails, painting, completing the landscaping. Each of these tasks has a probable duration of 4 days, but the schedule identifies them as 6-day tasks (with 50% contingency for each task). As an option, you can reduce the duration of each task to 4 days and insert a dummy task at the end with a duration of 6 days. The total duration of the task series is reduced from 36 days to 30 days (24 days for the 6 tasks plus 6 days for the contingency task). Psychologically, we needed the 2-day adder to feel comfortable with each task, but the 6 days for the task series is within a reasonable range.

Since the duration of the tasks is fixed at 4 days, we maintain the pressure to fulfill the most probable duration. The buffer task (contingency) ensures that the task is scheduled early enough to allow for reasonable slippage (even if you use the ALAP mode). If one of the tasks slips, the amount of slippage is removed from the buffer. In this way, the entire chain schedule is preserved (until all contingencies are exhausted). By reviewing and managing the buffers, we can keep track of the contingency situation. Granted, these concepts of buffer management come from Goldratt's dissertations on critical chains. However, practical application of some of these concepts is possible with traditional tools from CPM.

In terms of schedule contingency, there are three things you can be sure of.

1-If there is no schedule contingency, the end date of the project will not be met.

2-If there is no schedule contingency, the schedule will falter and the project will be completed even later than if there was no schedule.

3-Murphy is working on your project.

The Magic of Hammocks

We have already introduced the hammock function. This feature, which by the way is not found in many packages from CPM, has several practical uses. A hammock is a type of task that has no fixed duration. Instead, it automatically calculates its duration from the tasks it is associated with (or from the group of tasks that the hammock spans). Let us go back to the highway project for an illustration. There are a number of tasks associated with putting up the new guardrails. We determine the location and mark it. We drill holes for the support posts. We place the posts. We install the guardrails and fix them. We paint them. Finally, we finish the landscaping. During all this time, we have to close the right lane and put up a flashing sign warning of the closure.

How long do we need the sign and traffic cones? This is a specification we need to make when we add these activities. The answer is: the duration is the time it takes to complete the tasks described above. With hammocks, we do not need to calculate this duration. We create a task Put up traffic diversion signs and traffic cones. We create a start-to-start relationship with the first guardrail task and a finish-to-finish relationship with the last guardrail task. The computer sets the task duration equal to the duration of the series of tasks it spans.

If the work is to begin on 6/1 and continue until 6/22, the duration of the hammock task is set at three weeks. If the duration of any of the tasks within the chain changes, either during planning or execution, the Hammock task will automatically take these changes into account.

If there are daily costs associated with the hammock task, these will also be calculated automatically. So if the signs and cones are calculated at $2,000 per week, the budget will be set at $6,000. If the task chain is extended to four weeks, the budget changes to $8,000. The same approach applies to the resources allocated to the hammocks.

Hammocks can be stretched between any two points in the project network. They do not have to be a connected set of tasks or fall under the jurisdiction of a single responsible party. Hammocks can also be used as auxiliary collection tasks to show the time span between the two anchor points.

Practical Uses of the Baseline

Most products from CPM have a Set Baseline feature. A baseline is a snapshot of the project schedule at a particular point in time. The early and late dates are saved as baseline or target dates for later comparison with the current dates after the schedule has been updated. There should always be an original baseline. This is a set of project target dates at the time the official project schedule is adopted. When the schedule is updated, a variance report can be generated to show the changes from the original schedule. The report can be set up to select only the deviations that exceed a certain threshold, and the tasks can be sorted by the amount of the deviation (largest first).

If your product supports multiple baselines, consider these additional baseline options. Create a new baseline (keeping the original one) each time a major change to the plan is approved. I also like to create a rolling baseline. This is a snapshot of each update as it is completed. The next time I update the schedule, I compare the new dates and float to the last set (the rolling baseline) to note any variances during this last update. Once the update is complete and verified, I replace the previous rolling baseline with a snapshot of the current update to use for the next round.

Practical Options to Shorten Schedules

So they have done all the things that we have suggested here. They have made a list of all the tasks. You have estimated the duration of the tasks, defined the relationships between the tasks, set deadline constraints where necessary, and considered contingencies. You have a reasonable schedule. Except for one small problem. The resulting end date of the project is unacceptable.

Is there anything you can do to shorten the schedule? Our goal is to maintain a reasonable schedule. It should still represent something that can reasonably be achieved, not something we wish would happen. It does not take long for the team to see through a storefront schedule. Here are a few options you can consider.

Shorter deadlines Are task estimates really based on the most likely deadlines, or are they provided with some margin? Some contingency is important, but check to make sure it has not been overdone. Do you want 90 percent certainty? 80 percent? 50 percent? Keep it reasonable and consistent. Check the critical path first, i.e., the task chains with the least margin. It does you no good to reduce times on the non-critical paths.

Overlaps Again, check the critical paths first to see if some of the series tasks can overlap. Does task B really have to wait until task A is completed? Or can it start when task A is about 50 percent complete? Selectively overlapping critical tasks is a great way to shorten the schedule. But remember that these overlaps need to match actual circumstances and should not be forced just to make the schedule fit.

Reduce scope Is the schedule too long (or over budget)? Perhaps one option is to reduce the scope. This is done all the time, but usually only after some of the work has already been promised and executed. Why not address this issue early on? If the total scope of work does not fit into the time available, negotiate to reduce some of the scope or defer it to a later phase.

Change the strategies The schedule is based on the work identified and the strategies selected to complete that work. If the schedule is not acceptable, it may be useful to review the strategic alternatives. There may be other ways to accomplish the goal that result in a shorter schedule. For example, reusing older code rather than starting from scratch. Or buying an off-the-shelf component instead of making a custom one. The original strategies may have been chosen without considering the impact on schedule. Now that the problem is known, reevaluate your choices. Again, focus on the critical paths first.

Ranting and raving Well, that will not help the schedule. But sometimes you just need to blow off some steam.

The Useful Schedule

In my travels, I have seen more bad schedules than I care to admit. I have seen schedules created by computers that bore no resemblance to reality. Sometimes this was because the developers of the schedules did not understand what the computer was doing with the information they provided. In other cases, the schedule was so heavily manipulated that it was impossible to support and difficult to update. In either case, the result of the scheduling work is completely unusable, forcing staff to resort to alternative means and documents to work with a more usable schedule. In the first case, training helps (see Chapters 1.4 and 13.1). In the second case, the planner must resist the temptation to take shortcuts by forcing deadlines rather than defining realistic task durations and priorities. Only then can override features such as date constraints, ALAP modes, and dummy tasks be used to modify and improve the schedule. A schedule developed in this way is the only one that can contribute to project success.

Summary

Developing a project schedule is a journey that begins with decomposing the work packages in the work breakdown structure into project activities and ends with an approved schedule for performing those activities, called the schedule baseline. Once the schedule is developed, it must be controlled to ensure that actual project execution is consistent with this baseline. Of course, all processes related to the schedule are performed according to the schedule management plan developed prior to the application of these processes.

The Define Activities process is used to break down the work packages in the work breakdown structure into activities that must be scheduled later. The resulting activity list is used by the activity sequencing process to create network diagrams showing the dependencies between activities. The network diagrams are created using the Priority Diagram Method (PDM) and other techniques. The activity list and attributes are also used to determine the resource requirements for the project. Based on the available resources, you can estimate the duration of the activity, i.e. the time needed to complete the activity.

All the pieces developed in these processes are brought together to create the project schedule using the Develop Schedule process and a variety of techniques. For example, you can start with the critical path method to develop the project schedule from a network schedule. After you create this schedule, you can use schedule compression methods, such as fast tracking and crashing, to ensure deadlines are met. Schedule development is an iterative process that may continue throughout project execution, for example, due to approved changes and the emergence of risks.However, the approved planned project schedule is used as the basis for tracking project progress. You need to control the schedule so that it matches the schedule baseline, which we will discuss in detail later in this book.

Road Ahead. Duration is an important attribute of an activity because the schedule depends directly on it. The duration is estimated for the given resources available for the activity. In the next chapter, we will discuss the procedure for estimating activity resources along with other procedures for scheduling the resources needed for the project.

Exam's Eye View

Comprehend

The schedule management plan is developed from the project charter, scope management plan, and product development approach and serves as the foundation for all other schedule management processes.

The main task of the Define Activities process is to create the activity list by breaking down the work packages from the work breakdown structure into activities.

The main task of the Activity Sequence process is to determine the dependencies between the activities in the activity list, put them in an appropriate order, and display this order in the network diagrams.

Network diagrams with the activity durations assigned to each activity can be used to develop the schedule.

To estimate the duration of an activity, we need to know the resource requirements of the activity.

Look Out

Because deliverables are divided into work packages and activities that are developed incrementally, there may be change requests that require updating the scope and cost basis.

A key benefit of sequencing activities is that it provides a way to deal with project constraints in the most efficient manner.

The activity duration is estimated for a specific resource assigned to the activity. If you change the quantity or capability of the resource, the estimated duration also changes.

Any operation on a critical path has a float time of zero and therefore represents a schedule risk.

Therefore, you must monitor the activities on all critical paths very closely during the execution of the project.

The approved version of the project plan is called the project plan baseline, which is used to track and measure project progress by comparing actual progress against the baseline.

Memorize

The project milestone schedule, an output of Define Activities, is from the WBS dictionary, a component of Scope Baseline.

Dependencies have four attributes: internal mandatory dependencies, external mandatory dependencies, internal discretionary dependencies, and external discretionary dependencies.

In PDM, end-to-beginning is the most commonly used dependency relationship, while beginning-to-end is the least commonly used.

Activity duration measured in work periods does not include holidays, while duration measured in calendar units does. For example, the activity duration from Friday to the following Tuesday is three days when measured in work units and five days when measured in calendar units, since there is no work on Saturday and Sunday.

The approved project schedule, called the Schedule Baseline, becomes part of the Project Management Plan.

Fast tracking compresses the schedule by performing activities simultaneously that would otherwise be performed sequentially, while crashing compresses the schedule by allocating more resources.

Review Questions, Answers and Explanations (online)

Cost Management

MONEY. CASH. GREENBACKS. DEAD presidents. It's all the same thing when you get right down to it: Projects need finances to get from start to finish, and it's often the project manager's job to estimate, control, and account for the finances needed for a project. Projects consume project budget during execution when all the project management plans we discussed are put into action, and the project budget is monitored and controlled during the monitoring and control processes.

What are you saying? You have no control over the money your project requires? Management gives you a set budget and it's up to you to make it happen? Yes! This book may be about your Project Management Professional (PMP) exams, but that's always one of the scariest things I hear. Or is it? If management's decision is based on previous projects, business analyst research, or expert cost estimates, then it's not so scary. I can tell you this much: a pre-determined project budget is always a constraint and rarely a pleasure for the project manager. And what about those projects that do not have money set aside for project work? You know... the projects where the project scope is only covered by the project team's time and there are no materials or items to purchase. That's fine - there are still costs associated with the project because someone, somewhere, is paying for the project team's time. Salaries can also be considered a project cost. After all, time is money.

Finally, and this is the kicker, it does not matter where your project funds come from, whether you actually control them, or what procedures your organization uses to spend them. With the Project Management Institute (PMI) exam, you need to understand all the appropriate processes and procedures for how projects are estimated, budgeted, and then financially controlled. And that's what we'll discuss in this chapter.

Determining the Project Costs

I assume that by now you know that there are various project management processes. Guess how many of them revolve around cost? Three: cost estimating, cost budgeting, and cost control. Is not that reassuring? Your PMI exam will undoubtedly include questions about cost, but much of the content in this chapter relates to your organization's environmental factors. Your cost management plan defines and outlines your organization's and project's procedures for managing and controlling costs. I am not going to pass the buck anymore.

One of the first questions a project manager is likely to be asked when starting a project is, "How much to completion?" This question can only be answered by working it out step by step. To answer this question, the project manager or project estimator must first examine the cost of the resources needed for each of the project's activities. Resources are people, of course, but also things: equipment, materials, training, and even pizza if the project requires it.

In addition to the cost of resources, there are all the variances that must be accounted for: Project risks, variations in material costs, the appropriate human resources for each activity, and special factors such as shipping, insurance, inflation, and monies for testing and evaluation.

Cost estimates are usually prepared through a series of refinements in one of three ways. As more details become known during the project, the estimates are refined. Industry guidelines and company policies may dictate how estimates are refined.

- **Rough order of magnitude** This estimate is "rough" and is used during initiation processes and top-down estimates. The variation of the estimate can range from -25% to +75%.

• **Budget estimate** This estimate is also somewhat broad and is used at the beginning of planning processes and for top-down estimates. The variation of the estimate can range from -10% to +25%.

• **Definitive estimate** This type of estimate is one of the most accurate. It is used late in the planning process and is associated with bottom-up estimating. You need the work breakdown structure (WBS) to produce the final estimate. The variance of the estimate can range from -5 percent to +10 percent.

While project managers typically think of project estimates in terms of a unit of measurement such as dollars, euros, yen, or others, it is possible and often feasible to estimate project costs based on labor hours. Think of the number of hours the project team will have to work on developing a new piece of software. You can also estimate costs based on the number of full-time employees assigned to the project for a given duration.

Estimating the Project Costs

Assuming that the project manager and the project team work together to produce the cost estimates, there are many inputs to the cost estimating process. For your PMI exam, you should be familiar with these inputs as they are often the supporting details for the cost estimate produced by the project management team. Let us take a look at them, shall we?

Relying on Enterprise Environmental Factors

Every time I have to say or write "corporate environmental factors," I cringe. That's just a highfalutin euphemism for how your company runs the show. In every business, there are "factors" that affect the costing process. Surprise, surprise. There are two for your audit:

• **Marketplace conditions** When you need to buy materials and other resources, the market determines the price, what is available and from whom you will buy. There are three conditions that can affect the price of anything your project needs to buy:

Sole Vendor There is only one vendor that can supply what you need to buy for your project. Examples include a specific consultant, a specific service, or a specific type of material.

Sole Source There are many vendors who can supply what you need for your project, but you prefer to work with one particular vendor. He is your favorite.

Oligopoly This is a market situation where the market is so tight that the actions of one vendor influence the actions of all the others. Can you think of any? How about the airline industry, the oil industry, or even training centers and consultants?

Commercial databases One of my first consulting jobs was for a large commercial printing company. We used a database based on the type of material the job was to be printed on, the number of inks and coatings to be used, and the press to determine the cost of the job. This is a commercial database. Another accessible example is any price list that your suppliers provide you with so that you can make an accurate estimate.

Using Organizational Process Assets

Here's another term that makes my teeth hurt. Organizational process assets are simply things your organization has learned, created, or purchased that can help the project management team better manage a project. When it comes to costing, there are many resources that an organization can leverage:

• **Cost Estimating Guidelines** An organization can and often will create a guideline for how the project manager or cost estimator should prepare the project cost estimate. This is just a rule. Do you have something like this in your organization?

- **Cost Estimating Templates** In case you have not noticed, PMI and the Project Management Body of Knowledge (PMBOK) love templates. Templates in project management are not usually about a shell, the way Microsoft Word thinks of templates. It's about using previous similar projects as a template for the current project.

- **Historical Information** Aside from the specific costs of previous projects, historical information is pretty much anything that happened prior to this project that can help the project manager and project team create an accurate cost estimate.

- **Project Files** Project archives and files from previous projects can be helpful in estimating costs. Specifically, the project manager looks for the performance of previous similar projects in the areas of cost control, risk costs, and quality issues that could affect costs.

- **Project team knowledge** Your project team is usually made up of the experts closest to the project work and can provide valuable input into the project cost estimation process. Be warned - in the real world and in your PMI review, project team recollections, while great, are not the most reliable input. In other words, Marty's war stories about the project XYZ being $14 billion over budget do not compare to historical information that says the project XYZ was $14 over budget.

Lessons learned It is always good to draw on lessons learned when planning. After all, it is better to learn from the mistakes of others.

■ *Tip Sometimes an organization has two projects or opportunities, and it can only choose one of the projects to complete. Example: project A is worth $75,000 and project B is worth $250,000. The organization will likely choose Project B because it is worth more and drop Project A because it is worth significantly less. Opportunity cost is a term used to describe the total amount of the project that was abandoned instead of the selected project. In this case, the opportunity cost is $75,000, the value of Project A.*

Relying on the Project Scope Statement

Specifying the scope of the project is also an input to the cost estimate. What a surprise! The project scope statement is needed because it defines the business case for the project, the project justifications, and the project requirements - all things that cost money to accomplish. The project scope statement can help the project manager and stakeholders negotiate funding for the project based on what has already been agreed upon. In other words, the size of the budget must be in proportion to the requirements of the project scope.

While the project scope defines the constraints, it also defines the assumptions. If the assumptions in the project description turn out to be wrong, the project manager must estimate the financial impact.

Include all elements in the project scope statement that may contribute to the project cost estimate:

- Contractual agreements

- Insurance

- Health and safety issues

- Expenditure for the environment

- Safety concerns

- Intellectual rights costs

- Licenses and permits

Finally, and perhaps one of the most important elements in the project scope statement, is the requirement for acceptance. The estimate must reflect the monies needed to meet the project client's expectations. If there are insufficient funds to accomplish all elements of the project scope, the project scope must be adjusted to reflect the available funds, or more money must be put into the project.

Examining Other Cost Estimating Inputs

I have covered the major inputs to cost estimating, but there are still some minor, common sense inputs that the project manager or cost estimator must rely on to complete the cost estimating process. Do not worry - it's nothing you have not seen before, and it's all pretty straightforward:

• **Work breakdown structure** The work breakdown structure is needed to prepare a cost estimate, especially for the final estimate, as it clearly defines all the deliverables that the project will provide. Each of the work packages in the work breakdown structure incurs costs in the form of materials, time, or often both. You will find the work breakdown structure a common thread throughout this chapter, because the money you spend on a project is for the things you promised in the work breakdown structure.

• **WBS dictionary** The work breakdown structure's buddy, the work breakdown structure dictionary, is needed because it contains all the details and related work for each deliverable in the work breakdown structure. As a rule, the work breakdown structure dictionary is always with you when you use the work breakdown structure.

• **Project management plan** The project management plan defines how the project will be carried out and at the same time monitored and controlled. Recall that the project management plan includes all the subordinate plans for the project, i.e., at least one for each project management knowledge area and a quality process improvement plan. Since project management is inherently integrative, the outputs from each knowledge area are considered as inputs to the cost estimate. Specific project management plan content you should consider for the PMI exam includes the following:

• **Schedule management plan** The availability of resources, the time when resources are to do the work, the time when investments are to be made, and so on. The schedule may also take into account contracts with collective bargaining agreements (unions) and their deadlines, seasonal labor and material costs, and other timing that may affect the total cost estimate.

• **Staffing management plan** We have already established that time is money because the project pays for the labor to create the items promised in the project description. The staffing plan determines when project resources, specifically people, will be needed on the project team and the cost of engaging those people. Chapter 9 discusses the staffing plan in more detail.

• **Risk register** A risk is an uncertain event that can cost the project time, money, or both. The risk register is a central repository for the project's risks and the associated status of each risk event. For some risks, the project team can buy its way out, while other risks will cost the project when they occur. The risk register is needed because the cost of the risk helps the project management team create an accurate cost estimate.

■ **Tip** Risks may not always cost monies directly but could affect the project schedule. Keep in mind, however, that this could, in turn, cause a rise in project costs because of vendor commitment, penalties for lateness, and added expenses with additional labor.

Estimating the Project Costs

All cost information is needed so that the project cost estimator, probably the project management team, can produce a reliable cost estimate. The cost estimates you should know for the CAPM and PMP exams and for your career reflect the accuracy of the information on which the estimate is based. The more accurate the information, the better the cost estimate will be. Basically, all estimates are developed as you go along: The more details available, the more accurate the estimate is likely to be. Let us look at the most common methods for determining how much a project is likely to cost.

Using Analogous Estimating

The analogous estimate relies on historical information to predict the cost of the current project. It is also known as top-down estimating and is the least reliable of all cost estimating methods. The cost of the historical project is applied to the cost of the current project, taking into account the scope and size of the current project and other known variables.

Analog estimating is considered a form of expert judgment. This estimation approach takes less time than other estimation models, but is also less accurate. This top-down approach works well for quick estimates to get a general idea of what the project might cost. However, the problem or risk with using an analog estimate is that the historical information on which the estimate is based must be accurate. For example, if I were to prepare an estimate for the NBG project based on a similar project Nancy did two years ago, I would assume that Nancy kept accurate records and that her historical information was correct. If that is not the case, then my project cost will not be accurate and I will be very angry with Nancy.

Determining the Cost of Resources

One of the project management plans needed for cost estimating is the personnel management plan, which identifies all the characteristics of the project staff, including staffing rates. Using this plan and determining what resources are needed to complete the project, the project manager can project what the cost of the staffing element of the project is likely to be.

Resources include more than just the people who will perform the project work. The cost estimate must also account for all equipment and materials needed to complete the work. In addition, the project manager must identify the amount of resources needed and when the resources will be needed for the project. The identification of resources, the quantity needed, and the timing of resources are directly related to the expected cost of the project work.

There are four variations of project costs that you should consider:

Direct costs These costs are directly attributable to the project work and cannot be shared between projects (airfare, hotel costs, long distance phone charges, etc.).

Indirect costs These costs are representative of more than one project (utilities for the implementing organization, access to a training room, project management software license, etc.).

Variable costs These costs vary depending on the conditions that apply to the project (number of meeting participants, supply and demand of materials, etc.).

Fixed costs These costs remain constant throughout the lifecycle of the project (cost of equipment rented for the project, cost of a consultant hired for the project, etc.).

And yes, you can mix and match these terms. For example, you can have variable costs based on shipping costs that are also direct costs for your project. Do not worry too much about these types of costs, but familiarize yourself with these terms for your PMI exam.

Using Bottom-Up Estimating

Bottom-up estimation starts from zero, considers each component of the work breakdown structure, and arrives at a total for the project. It is performed with the project team and can be one of the most time-consuming methods for predicting project costs. While this method is more expensive due to the time required to prepare the estimate, it is also one of the most accurate. An added benefit of a bottom-up estimate is that it allows the project team to be engaged in the project work, seeing the cost and value of each cost within the project.

Using Parametric Estimating

That would be $465 per ton.

You can buy our software for $765 per license.

How about $125 per network drop?

These are all examples of parameters that can be incorporated into a parametric estimate. Parametric estimating uses a mathematical model based on known parameters to predict the cost of a project. The parameters in the model can vary based on the type of work to be performed and can be measured by cost per cubic yard, cost per unit, etc. A complex parameter can be unit cost, with adjustment factors based on the conditions of the project. Adjustment factors may have several modifying factors depending on additional conditions.

There are two types of parametric estimating:

• **Regression analysis**This is a statistical approach that makes predictions about the future based on historical values. Regression analysis makes quantitative predictions based on variables within one value to predict variables in another value. This form of estimation relies solely on pure statistical mathematics to uncover relationships between variables and predict future values.

• **Learning curve** This approach is simple: unit costs decrease the more units workers do, because workers learn as they do the required work. The more a person does an activity, the easier it is to do. The estimate is considered parametric because the formula is based on repetitive activities, such as wiring telephone jacks, painting hotel rooms, or other activities that are performed repeatedly within a project.

■ *Tip Don't worry too much about regression analysis for the exam. Learning curve is the topic you're more likely to have questions on.*

Using Good Old Project Management Software

Who creates estimates with their abacus? Most organizations rely on software to help the project management team produce an accurate cost estimate. Although the CAPM and PMP exams are vendor-neutral, a general knowledge of how computer software can assist the project manager is required. There are several computer programs that can be used to streamline the estimating of project work and increase its accuracy. These tools include project management software, spreadsheet programs, and simulations.

Examining the Vendor Bids

Sometimes it is simply more cost-effective (and easier) to hire someone else to do the work. In other cases, the project manager has no choice because the skills needed are not available within the organization. In either case, vendor proposals must be analyzed to determine which vendor should be selected based on its ability to meet the project scope, expected quality, and cost for its services.

Creating a Reserve Analysis

Do you think it will snow in Michigan next December? I do believe it will. But do we know on what date exactly? That's a quick and easy example of a "known unknown" You know something is likely to occur, but you do not know when or to what extent. Projects are full of known unknowns, and the most common one involves cost. Based on experience, the nature of the work, or fears, you suspect that some activities in your project will cost more than expected - that's a known unknown.

Instead of addressing known unknowns by supplementing costs with additional money, the PMBOK suggests that we establish "contingency reserves" to account for these cost overruns. Contingency reserves are used at the discretion of the project manager to offset cost overruns in schedule activities.

This is a related concept when it comes to project cost reserves. This reserve is sometimes referred to as a contingency reserve and is traditionally set aside for cost overruns due to risks that have impacted the project's cost base. Contingency reserves can be managed in a number of ways. The most common method is to set aside a contingency for identified risks within the project. Another approach is to set aside a fund for the entire project for identified risks and known unknowns. The final approach is to allocate funds to categories of components based on the work breakdown structure and project schedule.

Considering the Cost of Quality

Quality cost is a term that defines the money that the project must spend to achieve the expected level of quality in a project. For example, if your project is using a new material that no one on the project team has ever worked with, the project team will likely need to be trained to use the material during project implementation. Training, as you can imagine, costs something. This is an example of the cost of quality.

On the other side of the coin (the cost pun is intentional, thank you) is the cost of poor quality, sometimes referred to as the cost of not meeting quality. This is the cost your project incurs when you do not meet quality on the first try. In our example with the project team and the new materials, failure to train the team on the new materials means that the team will likely not install the materials properly, will take longer to use the materials, and may even waste materials. All of these negative conditions cost the project time, money, team frustration, and even lost revenue.

Examining the Cost Estimate

Of course, once all the inputs have been evaluated and the process of preparing the estimate is complete, you will receive the estimate. The estimate represents the anticipated cost of the project - it is not a guarantee, so there is usually a modifier, sometimes called an acceptable variance. This is the plus/minus on the estimate, e.g., $450,000 +$25,000 to -$13,000, depending on the conditions attached to the estimate. At a minimum, the estimate should include the estimated cost for all of the following:

- Labor

- Materials

- Equipment

- Services

- Facilities

- Information Technology

Special categories, such as inflation and contingency reserve.

It is possible that a project may have other cost categories, such as consultants, outsourced solutions, and others, but the above list is the most common. Consider this list when studying for your exam. Along with the estimate, the project management team includes the basics of the estimate. These are all the supporting details about how the estimate was arrived at and why the confidence in the estimate is as high as it is. Supporting details typically include all of the following:

- A description of the work to be performed in consideration of the estimate.

- Explanation of how the estimate was prepared.

- What assumptions were used in preparing the estimate?

- The constraints that the project management team had to take into account when preparing the cost estimate.

A project's cost estimate can lead to unpleasant news in the form of change requests. I say "unpleasant" because changes are rarely pleasant. Changes can impact scope in two ways when it comes to cost:

We do not have enough funds to meet the cost estimate, so we have to cut the scope.

We have more than enough funds to meet the estimate, so we add to the scope.

All change requests must be documented and routed through the integrated change control system. What the project manager should guard against is goldplating. Goldplating means that the project manager, project sponsor, or even a stakeholder adds extras to the project that eat up the entire project budget. This is essentially adding unneeded features to the product in order to use up all the funds allocated for the project. While this often happens in the final stages of a project, it can also start when the project is being costed. Gold plating delivers more than is needed and can create new risks, work, and contribute to a decline in team morale.

When changes are approved, integrated change control is enacted and the project scope and work breakdown structure and work breakdown structure dictionary are updated, and so on, as needed through all project management plans. The cost management plan must also be updated to reflect the cost of the changes and their impact on project costing.

Budgeting the Project

Now that the project estimate has been prepared, it is time to prepare the official cost budget. Cost budgeting is actually cost aggregation, meaning that the project manager assigns specific dollar amounts to each of the planned activities or, more likely, to each of the work packages in the work breakdown structure. The aggregation of costs for the work packages equals the total budget for the entire project. Through this process, the cost basis is established.

Cost budgeting and cost estimating can go hand in hand, but estimating is completed before a budget is created - or assigned. In cost budgeting, cost estimates are applied over time. The result is a time-phased cost estimate that allows a company to predict cash flow, a project's return on investment, and forecasts. The difference between cost estimates and cost budgeting is that cost estimates break down costs by category, while a cost budget presents costs over time.

Creating the Project Budget

Good news Many of the tools and techniques used to create project cost estimates are also used to create the project budget. Below is a brief listing of the tools you can expect to use in the CAPM and PMP exams:

Cost Aggregation Costs are calculated in parallel with each WBS work package. The cost of each work package is aggregated to the appropriate control accounts. Each control account is then aggregated to the total project cost.

Reserve Analysis Cost reserves are for unknown unknowns within a project.

The contingency reserve is not part of the project's cost basis, but is included as part of the project budget.

Parametric Estimating This approach uses a parametric model to extrapolate costs for a project (e.g., cost per hour and cost per unit). It may include variables and points based on conditions.

Funding limit reconciliation Organizations only have a certain amount of cash they can commit to projects - and no, you can not have all the money immediately. Funding limit reconciliation is an organization's approach to managing cash flow against project deliverables based on a schedule, milestone achievement, or data constraints. This helps an organization plan when to use funds for a project rather than using all available funds at the beginning of a project. In other words, funds for a project budget become available based on dates and/or deliverables. If the project does not meet the specified dates and products that have been established as milestones, the additional funding becomes questionable.

Examining the Project Budget

As in most parts of the PMBOK, when you complete a process, you get not just one result, but several. Project budget preparation is no different, as there are four outputs you need to know for the PMI audit. The following sections look at these in detail.

Working with the Cost Baseline

The cost baseline is actually a time lapse showing when project funds are to be spent relative to the cumulative values of the work completed in the project. Most baselines are presented in the form of an S-curve, where the project starts on the left and works its way to the upper right corner. When the project starts, it is not worth much and usually not much has been spent. As the project nears completion, the money for labor, materials, and other resources is consumed in proportion to the work. In other words, the money spent on the project over time equals the work that is completed with the project.

On some projects, especially high priority or large projects, there may be multiple cost baselines to track labor costs, material costs, and even internal resource costs versus external resources. This is all well and good as long as the values in each baseline are maintained and consistent. It would not do a project manager much good if the cost baseline for materials was regularly updated and the cost baseline for labor was politely ignored.

■ *Tip Funds that have already been spent on a project are considered sunk into the project. These funds are called sunk costs - they are gone.*

Determining the Project Funding Requirements

Projects require a budget, but when the funds are made available in the project depends on the organization, the size of the project, and simply common sense. For example, if you were building a skyscraper that cost $850 million, you would not need all the funds on the first day of the project, but you would predict when those funds would be needed. That's the cash flow forecast. The project can be funded incrementally based on the cost basis and the expected project schedule, or based on the conditions within the project. Typically, funding requirements have already been included in the cost basis. The release of funds is treated like a step function, which it is. Each step of project funding allows the project to move to the next milestone, deliverable, or other "step" of the project agreed upon by the project manager and stakeholders.

Project funding requirements also take into account contingency reserve amounts. This is a pool of funds for cost overruns. Typically, the contingency reserve is allocated to the project at each step. However, some organizations choose to spend contingency funds only as needed - it's simply part of the organizational process. To be clear, the cost base is what the project should cost in an ideal, perfect world. The contingency reserve is the "gap filler" between the base cost and the maximum funding. In most cases, the contingency reserve bridges the gap between the project's cost base and the maximum funding to complete the project.

The Usual Suspects

There are two other outcomes of the cost budgeting process. Guess which two? Here are the common expenses:

• **Change requests** Did you guess that? Just about any activity in a project can generate a change request, and cost planning is no different. Of course, the change request must be documented and go through the integrated change control system. There are no free rides, especially in cost management.

• **Cost management plan updates** If a change request is approved, you probably need to update the cost management plan. Fascinating.

Controlling the Project Costs

Once a project is funded, the project manager and project team must work effectively and efficiently to control costs. This means getting the job done right the first time... It also means, and this is not easy, avoiding expanding the scope of the project and undocumented changes, as well as eliminating any activities that do not add value. When the project team adds components or features that are not required for the project, they waste time and money.

Cost control focuses on controlling the possibility of cost changes and how the project management team can allow or prevent cost changes. If a change does occur, the project manager must document the change and the reason for it and, if necessary, prepare a variance report. Cost control is about understanding why the cost variances, both good and bad, occurred. The "why" behind the variances allows the project manager to make appropriate decisions about future project actions.

Ignoring cost variances in the project can cause the project to suffer from budget shortfalls, additional risks, or schedule problems. When cost variances occur, they need to be investigated, recorded, and studied. Cost control allows the project manager to address the problem, find a solution, and then act accordingly. Specifically, cost control focuses on:

- Controlling the root causes of changes to ensure that the changes are actually necessary

- Controlling and documenting changes to the cost base as they occur

- Control of changes in the project and their impact on costs

- Perform cost monitoring to identify and understand cost variances

- Record appropriate cost changes in the cost baseline

- Preventing unauthorized changes to the cost baseline

- Communicating cost changes to the right stakeholders

- Work to keep costs within an acceptable range

Controlling project costs is more than a philosophy - the project manager works with the project team, stakeholders, and often management to ensure that costs do not creep into the project and to manage cost increases as they occur. To implement cost control, the project manager must rely on several documents and processes:

• **Cost baseline** You already know that. The cost basis is the expected costs that will be incurred for the project and when those expenses will be incurred. This phased budget reflects the amount that will be spent over the course of the project. Remember that the cost baseline is a tool that can be used to measure project performance.

• **Project funding requirements** Funds for a project are not allocated all at once, but in stages depending on the project's results. Thus, the closer the project gets to completion, the more funds are allocated. This allows for cash flow forecasting. In other words, an organization does not have to have the entire project budget at the beginning of the project, but can predict that the budget will be available incrementally based on expected revenues.

• **Performance reports** These reports focus on project cost trends, project scope, and planned performance versus actual performance. Reports may vary depending on stakeholder needs. We will discuss performance reporting in detail in Chapter 10, and we will get to everyone's favorite, earned value management, in a moment.

• **Change requests** When changes to the project scope are requested, an analysis of the associated costs to implement the proposed change is required. In some cases, such as when a portion of the project deliverable is eliminated, a change request may reduce the project cost. (I know this is wishful thinking, but in the world of PMI it is possible)

• **Cost management plan** The cost management plan specifies how cost variances are to be handled. A variance is a difference between what was expected and what occurred. In some cases, the contingency reserve may "cover" the cost overruns. In other cases, depending on the reason for the overrun, funding must be provided by the project client. Take a customer who wanted the walls painted green and changed their mind after the work was completed and wanted the walls orange. This cost overrun is only due to a change request and not a defect.

Creating a Cost Change Control System

Whenever some joker wants to add something to the project scope or even take something out of our project scope, the scope change control system is turned on. Similarly, the cost change control system checks all changes associated with changes in project scope, material costs, and costs for any other resources you can think of.

When a cost change is entered into the system, there is appropriate documentation, a tracking system, and procedures that the project manager must follow to get approval for the proposed change. When a change is approved, the cost basis is updated to reflect the approved changes. If a request is denied, the denial must be documented so you can refer back to it later. You do not want a stakeholder at the end of the project wondering why their change was not included in the project scope without documentation of why.

Using Earned Value Management

When I teach a PMP Trunk Camp, attendees perk up when it comes to Earned Value Management and their exam. This topic is foreign to many people and they understandably want a detailed explanation of this arcane collection of formulas. Perhaps you find yourself in the same situation. Here's the good news: it's not so bad. Relax - you can memorize these formulas, answer the exam questions correctly, and take care of the more difficult exam topics. I'll show you how.

First of all, Earned Value Management (EVM) is a process of measuring the performance of project work against plan to identify variances and opportunities to improve the project, or simply to review the state of the project. EVM can help predict future variances and final cost at completion. It is a system of mathematical formulas that compares work performed to that planned and measures the actual cost of the work performed by your project. EVM is an important part of cost control because it allows the project manager to predict future variances from past expenditures on the project.

Learning the Fundamentals

EVM, in terms of cost management, addresses the relationships between three formulas that reflect project performance. The relationship between the following EVM values:

- **Planned value (PV)** The planned value is the work planned and the budget approved to carry out that work. For example, if a project has a budget of $500,000 and the sixth month is 50 percent of the project work, the PV for that month is $250,000.

- **Earned value (EV)** Earned Value is the physical work completed to date and the approved budget for that work. For example, if your project has a budget of $500,000 and the work completed to date is 45 percent of the total project work, the earned value is $225,000. You can determine EV by multiplying the percentage of work completed by the project's budget at completion (BAC).

- **Actual cost (AC)** Actual cost is the actual amount of money the project has required to date. For example, in your project, your BAC is $500,000 and your earned value is $225,000. As it turns out, your project team wasted something, and you actually spent $232,000 in actual funds to reach the 25 percent completion milestone. Your actual cost is $232,000.

These are the basics of earned value management. All of our other formulas are based on these simple formulas. Just remember that earned value is always the percentage of work completed times the specified budget at completion. In your PMI audit, you will always be presented with the actual cost, the money that has already been spent on the project. To determine the budgeted value, you will need to do a little math. This is the value your project should be at at a certain point in time. The formula for planned value is the percentage of project completion based on where the project should be at a certain point in time. For example, let us say you are scheduled to be 80 percent complete by December 15. If your budget is $100,000, your projected value in this case is $80,000.

Finding the Project Variances

I am sure that in the real world, your projects will never be late and never go over budget... For your audit, you need to be able to determine the cost and schedule variances for your project. I'll stick with the same $500,000 budget I worked with in the previous examples. Identifying variances helps the project manager and management determine the condition of a project, set goals for project improvement, and compare projects based on the variances identified.

Finding the Cost Variance

Let us say your project has a $500,000 BAC and you are 40 percent complete. However, you have spent $234,000 in real funds. To determine the cost variance, we determine the earned value, which is 40 percent of the $500,000 budget. As Figure 7-7 shows, this is $200,000. In this example, you spent $234,000 in actual costs. The formula for determining the cost variance is earned value minus actual cost. In this case, the cost variance is negative $34,000.

This means that you spent $34,000 more than the work you performed was worth. Of course, the $34,000 is relative to the scope of the project. On this project, that's a significant error, but on a billion-dollar project, $34,000 may not mean that much. On both projects, a $34,000 cost variance would likely result in a cost variance report (sometimes called an exception report).

Finding the Schedule Variance

Can you guess how plan deviation works? It is basically the same as cost variance, only this time it is about the planned value rather than the actual cost. Let us say your $500,000 budgeted project is supposed to be 45 percent complete by today, but we know you are only 40 percent done. We have already determined the earned value as $200,000 for the budgeted value.

Remember that the planned value, the value you are supposed to achieve, is equal to the planned completion times BAC. In this example, it is 45 percent of the $500,000 BAC, or $225,000. Uh-oh! You are behind schedule. The formula for schedule variance, as Figure 7-8 shows, is the earned value minus the planned value. In this example, the schedule variance is $25,000.

Finding the Indexes

Mathematically, an index is an expression that indicates a ratio - and that's what we do with these indices. Basically, in earned value management, an index shows the state of the project's time and cost. The index or ratio is measured at a value of one: The closer the index is to one, the better off the project is. As a rule, you definitely do not want to be below one, because that means the project is doing poorly. And, believe it or not, you do not want to be too far above one, because that shows that the estimates were inflated or way too pessimistic. Really.

Finding the Cost Performance Index

The cost performance index (CPI) measures the project by its financial performance. The formula is simple: earned value divided by actual cost, as Figure 7-9 shows. In this example, your project has a budget of $500,000 and you are 40 percent done with the project work. That's an earned value of how much? Right. It's 40 percent of the $500,000, so it's an earned value of $200,000.

Your actual cost to date on this project (the cumulative cost) is $234,000. Your PMI exam will always tell you your actual cost for each exam question. Let us finish the formula. To find the CPI, we divide the earned value by the actual cost, or $200,000 divided by $234,000. The CPI for this project is 0.85, which means we are 85 percent on track financially, which is not healthy for any project, regardless of its budget.

You can also look at the value of 0.85 as losing 15 cents of every dollar you spend on the project. Yikes! That means that for every dollar you spend on work, you actually only get 85 cents. Not a good deal for the project manager. As you can guess, the closer to one the project is, the better.

Find the Schedule Performance Index

The SPI (Schedule Performance Index) measures the overall health of the project schedule. The formula, as Figure 7-10 shows, is earned value divided by scheduled value. In other words, you are trying to determine how accurately your project work is being completed relative to the project schedule you created. Let us give this formula a try.

Your project with a budget of $500,000 is 40 percent complete, which equates to an earned value of $200,000. However, you are scheduled to complete 45 percent by today. That's a projected earned value of $225,000. The SPI for this project at this time is determined by dividing the completion value of $200,000 by the planned value of $225,000, which yields an SPI of 0.88. This means that the project is 88 percent on schedule, or if you are a pessimist, that the project is 12 percent off schedule.

Predicting the Project's Future

Note that I said "at this time" in the previous paragraph This is because the project will hopefully continue to progress and the numbers for projected value and earned value will change. As the project nears completion, the amounts for earned value will naturally increase and so will the figures for planned value. Typically, these indices, for both schedule and cost, are measured against milestones and allow the project management team to forecast where the project is likely to end up when it is completed. That's right - we can make a forecast.

Finding the Estimate to Complete

So your project is in trouble and management wants to know how much more this project is going to cost. They depend on the cost estimate equation (ETC). There are three variations of this formula depending on the conditions of your project.

ETC based on a new estimate Sometimes you simply have to accept the fact that all previous estimates are flawed and you need a new estimate. Imagine a project where the project manager and project team assume the work will cost $150,000. However, once they start the project, they find that it will actually cost $275,000 because the work is much more difficult than they expected. That's one reason ETC for a new estimate.

ETC Based on Atypical Variations This formula, shown in Figure 7-11, is used when the project has experienced some crazy cost fluctuations and the project manager does not believe the anomalies will continue throughout the project. For example, lumber was estimated to cost $18 per board. However, due to a hurricane in another part of the country, the lumber cost has increased to $25 per board. This variation in material cost has changed, but the project manager does not believe the cost change will affect the cost of delivering the other work packages in the WBS. Here is the formula for atypical variances: ETC =BAC-EV.

Let us say this project has a $500,000 BAC and is 40 percent complete. The earned value is $200,000, so our ETC formula would be ETC = $500,000-$200,000, or ETC of $300,000. Of course, this formula is very superficial and will not be the best forecasting formula for every scenario. If material costs have changed dramatically, a completely new estimate would be more appropriate.

ETC based on typical variances Sometimes a variance will surface in a project and the project management team will determine that it will continue as the project progresses. Figure 7-12 illustrates the formula: ETC = (BAC-EV)/ CPI. For example, consider a project to install 10,000 light fixtures across a college campus. You and the project team have estimated that 12,000 labor hours will be required to install all the lights, and your cost estimate is $54 per hour, which equates to $648,000 for the entire installation. However, as the project team begins the installation, you find that it takes a little longer than you expected to install the light fixtures. You realize that your estimate of how long it will take is incorrect and that the project team will probably need 16,000 man-hours to install all the light fixtures.

The ETC in this formula assumes that the project manager knows the Earned Value and Cost Performance Index. Let us assume that this project is 20 percent complete, so the EV is $129,600. Since the work takes longer, the actual cost until the 20 percent mark is reached is $172,000. The CPI is determined by dividing the earned value, $129,600, by the actual cost of $172,000. The CPI for this project is 0.75.

Now let us try the formula ETC: (BAC-EV)/ CPI, or ($648,000-$129,600)/.75, which equals $691,200. That's $691,200 more than is budgeted for this project to complete the rest of the project work. Yikes

Finding the Estimate at Completion

One of the most basic predictive formulas is the estimate at completion (EAC). This formula takes into account all the pennies you lose on every dollar if your CPI is less than one. It's an opportunity for the project manager to say, "Hey! Based on the current state of our project, this is probably how we'll do at the end of the project. I'd better work on my resume." Let us take a look at these formulas.

EAC with a new estimate Just like with the estimate to completion formulas, sometimes it's best to just create a whole new estimate. This approach with EAC is pretty simple - it's the actual cost plus the estimate for completion. Let us say your project has a budget of $500,000 and you have already spent $187,000 of that. For whatever reason, you have determined that your estimate is no longer valid and your ETC for the project will actually be $420,000 - that's how much you'll need to complete the project. The EAC in this case is the actual cost of $187,000 plus your ETC of $420,000, or $607,000.

EAC with Atypical Variances Sometimes there are anomalies within a project that can distort the estimate of the project at completion. The formula for this scenario is actual cost plus budget at completion minus completed value. Let us try this out. Your project has a $500,000 budget at BAC and the completion value is $100,000. However, you have spent $127,000 in actual costs. The EAC would be $127,000+$500,000-$100,000, or $527,000. This is your new estimate at completion for this project.

EAC using the CPI If a project has a CPI of 0.97, you could say that the project loses three pennies per dollar. These three pennies will add up over time. This approach is most often used when the project manager recognizes that cost variances are likely to continue throughout the life of the project. This formula is EAC = AC +(BAC-EV)/ CPI. Do not you just love nested formulas? Let us give this formula a try.

Your project has a BAC of $500,000 and your earned value is $150,000. Your actual cost for this project is $162,000. Your CPI is calculated as .93. The EAC would be $162,000+(($500,000-$150,000)/.93), or $538,344. Was not that fun?

■ *Tip* *There will not be as many questions about these EVM formulas as you might hope, but knowing them can help clarify the few questions you are likely to have.*

Finding Big Variances

Two deviations apply to the entire project, and both are easy to learn. The first variance you will not learn until the project is 100 percent complete. This is the project variance, and it is simply BAC-AC. If your project had a budget of $500,000 and you spent $734,000 to complete it, then the project variance is $500,000-$734,000, which of course equals -$234,000.

The second variance is part of our forecasting model that predicts what the project variance is likely to be. It is called the variance at completion (VAC) and the formula is VAC =BAC-EAC. Let us say your project has a BAC of $500,000 and your EAC is predicted to be $538,344. The VAC is $500,000-$538,344, which is a predicted variance of $38,344. Of course, this formula assumes that the rest of the project goes smoothly. In the reality that you and I hang out in, the VAC can swing one way or the other depending on the overall performance of the project.

Using Earned Value Management Variations

As with most things in project management, there is usually more than one way to do the same job. I am happy to report that Earned Value Management works the same way. The formulas I gave earlier are accurate, reasonably reliable, and come directly from the PMBOK. However, there are some alternative formulas you can use to save yourself memorizing these complex formulas, especially for the ETC and EAC formulas.

Summary

Projects require resources and time, both of which cost money. Projects are estimated or predicted how much the project work is expected to cost. There are several types and approaches to project estimating. Project managers can use analog estimating, parametric estimating, or the most reliable method, bottom-up estimating. Regardless of which approach the project manager chooses, the basis of the estimate should be documented in case the estimate is ever questioned.

When preparing the project estimate, the project manager should also include a reserve for project risks and cost overruns. Depending on a company's environmental factors and often project priority, the process for creating and maintaining the contingency reserve can fluctuate. The contingency reserve is not a carte blanche to spend at the discretion of the project manager, but rather a safety net in case the project goes awry. Variances covered by the contingency reserve cannot be swept under the rug, but must be accounted for and hopefully learned from. Cost budgeting is the summary of costs to create work packages in the work breakdown structure. Sometimes cost budgeting is also referred to as "rolling up" the costs associated with each work package. Cost budgeting is the process of applying cost estimates over time. Most project managers do not receive total project funding in one fell swoop, but in increments over the life of the project.

Once the project moves from planning to execution, it also moves to monitoring and control. The project manager and the project team work together to control project costs and monitor the performance of the project work. The most accessible method for monitoring project costs is earned value management. Earned value management shows the performance of the project and allows the project manager to predict where the project is likely to end up financially.

Key Terms

Actual cost (AC) The actual amount of money the project has spent to date. Analogous Estimating An approach that relies on historical information to predict the cost of the current project. It is also referred to as top-down estimating and is the most unreliable of all approaches to cost estimating.

Bottom-up estimating An estimation approach that starts from zero, considers each component of the work breakdown structure, and arrives at a total for the project. It is performed with the project team and can be one of the most time-consuming and reliable methods for predicting project costs.

Budget estimate This estimate is also somewhat broad and is used at the beginning of planning processes and also in top-down estimates. The range of variation of the estimate can be between -10% and +25%.

Commercial database An approach to cost estimating in which a database, usually software-driven, is used to generate the cost estimate for a project.

Contingency reserve This is an allowance for contingencies to account for cost overruns. Contingency reserves are used at the discretion of the project manager and with management approval to offset cost overruns on schedule activities.

Cost aggregation The costs are parallel to each WBS work package. The cost of each work package is aggregated to the appropriate control accounts. Each control account is then aggregated to the total project cost.

Cost baseline A temporal representation of when the project's funds are to be spent in relation to the cumulative values of the work performed under the project.

Cost budgeting Cost aggregation is accomplished by allocating specific dollar amounts to each of the planned activities or, more likely, to each of the work packages in the work breakdown structure. Cost budgeting applies cost estimates over time.

Cost change control system A system that reviews all changes related to changes in project scope, material costs, and costs for other resources, and the associated impact on the overall cost of the project.

Cost management plan The cost management plan determines how cost variances are to be handled.

Cost of poor quality The money spent to recover from failure to meet the expected level of quality. Examples include rework, troubleshooting, loss of life and limb because safety precautions were not taken, loss of revenue, and loss of customers.

Cost of quality The money spent to ensure the expected level of quality within a project. Examples include training, testing, and safety precautions.

Cost performance index (CPI) Evaluate the project based on its financial performance. The formula is $CPI = EV/AC$.

Cost variance (CV) The difference between the earned value amount and the cumulative actual cost of the project. The formula is $CV = EV-AC$.

Final estimate This type of estimate is one of the most accurate. It is used late in the planning process and is associated with bottom-up estimating. You need the work breakdown structure to create the final estimate. The variance of the estimate can range from -5 percent to +10 percent.

Direct Costs Costs that are directly attributable to project work and cannot be allocated between projects (e.g., airfare, hotel costs, long distance charges, etc.). Earned Value (EV) Earned Value is the physical work completed to date and the approved budget for that work. It is the percentage of BAC that represents the actual work completed on the project.

Estimate at completion (EAC) These forecast formulas predict the probable cost to complete the project based on the current scenarios within the project.

Estimate to complete (ETC) An earned value management formula that predicts how much funding the project will take to complete. There are three variations of this formula based on the conditions under which the project is running.

Fixed costs Costs that remain constant throughout the life of the project (the cost of rented equipment for the project, the cost of a consultant brought in for the project, etc.).

Funding limit reconciliation An organization's approach to managing cash flow for project deliverables based on a schedule, milestone achievement, or data constraints.

Indirect costs These are costs that are representative of more than one project (e.g., utilities for the implementing organization, access to a training room, project management software license, etc.).

Known unknown An event that is likely to occur in the project but is not known when or to what extent it will occur. These events, such as delays, are usually risky.

Learning curve An approach in which unit costs are assumed to decrease as workers complete more units because workers learn while doing the required work. Oligopoly A market condition in which the market is so tight that the actions of one supplier affect the actions of all others.

Opportunity cost The total cost of the opportunity rejected to realize an opponent's opportunity.

Parametric estimating An approach that uses a parametric model to extrapolate costs for a project (e.g., cost per hour and cost per unit). It may include variables and points based on conditions.

Parametric estimating Uses a mathematical model based on known parameters to predict the cost of a project.

Planned value (PV) The planned value is the planned work and the approved budget to perform that work. It is the percentage of BAC that reflects the status of the project at that time.

Project variance The final deviation discovered only when the project is completed. The formula is VAR = BAC-AC.

Regression analysis This is a statistical approach to predicting future values based on historical values. Regression analysis makes quantitative predictions based on variables within one value to predict variables in another value. This form of estimation relies solely on pure statistical mathematics to uncover relationships between variables and predict future values.

Reserve analysis Cost reserves are for unknown contingencies within a project. The contingency reserve is not part of the project cost basis, but is included as part of the project budget.

Rough order of magnitude This rough estimate is used during initiation processes and top-down estimates. The range of variation in the estimate can be from -25 percent to +75 percent.

Schedule performance index (SPI) Evaluates the project based on its schedule performance. The formula is SPI = EV/PV.

Schedule variance (SV) The difference between the earned value and the projected value. The formulas are SV = EV-PV.

Single source Many vendors can provide what you need for your project, but you would prefer to work with a specific vendor.

Sole source Only one vendor can deliver what you need for your project. Examples include a specific consultant, a specific service, or a specific type of material. Sunk costs Money that has already been invested in a project.

Variable costs Cost that varies according to the conditions of the project (number of meeting participants, supply and demand of materials, etc.). Variance A variance is the difference between what was expected and what occurred.

Variance at completion (VAC) A predictive formula that predicts what the project's variance will be based on current conditions within the project. The formula is VAC = BAC-EAC.

Review Questions, Answers and Explanations (online)

Quality Management

THE PROJECT QUALITY MANAGEMENT knowledge area consists of three processes, as shown in the Table below.

Process Name	Project Management Process Group
Plan Quality	Planning
Perform Quality Assurance Perform Quality Control	Executing
	Monitoring and Controlling

■ *Tip The cost of quality can be affected by project decisions. Let us say you are producing a new product. Unfortunately, the product scope or project scope description was inadequate to describe the functionality of the product. And the project team produced the product exactly as stated in the project scope statement, work breakdown structure, and other planning documents. Once the product hit the shelves, the company was bombarded with returns and warranty claims due to poor quality. So their project decisions impacted the cost of quality. Product recalls can also impact the cost of quality.*

1.

Control Charts

Control charts help you determine whether a process is stable and whether process deviations are under control or out of control.

Benchmarking

Benchmarking is a process of comparing past similar activities to current project activities to provide a standard against which performance can be measured. This comparison also helps you derive ideas for quality improvements in the current project. For example, if your current printer can print 8 pages per minute and you are considering a new printer that prints 14 pages per minute, the benchmark is 8 pages per minute.

Design of Experiments

Design of experiments (DOE) is a statistical technique used to identify the elements - or variables - that will have the greatest impact on the overall outcome of the project. It is most commonly used in relation to the project's product, but can also be applied to project management processes to examine tradeoffs. DOE designs and creates experiments to identify the ideal solution to a problem based on a limited number of example cases. Multiple variables are analyzed simultaneously, allowing you to change all (or some) variables at once and determine which combination provides the best result at a reasonable cost.

■ *Tip For the exam, remember that the key to DOE is that it equips you with a statistical framework that allows you to change the variables that have the greatest effect on overall project outcomes at once instead of changing one variable at a time.*

Statistical Sampling

Statistical sampling involves taking a certain number of parts of the total population and examining them to see if they are within an acceptable variance.

Flowcharting

A flowchart graphically represents the relationships between and among steps. They usually show activities, decision points, and the flow or sequence of steps in a process.

Proprietary Quality Management Methodologies

We have already covered most of these methods in our discussion of the cost of quality. Proprietary quality management methods include Six Sigma, Lean Six Sigma, Total Quality Management, Quality Function Deployment, and others.

Additional Quality Planning Tools

The final tool and technique of the quality planning process are additional quality planning tools. The PMBOK ® Guide lists these additional tools as follows:

- Brainstorming

- Affinity diagrams

- Force Field Analysis

- Nominal group technique

- Matrix diagrams

- Priority matrices

We have already looked at brainstorming and the nominal group technique. Now let us take a quick look at the remaining tools.

Planning Project Resources

Affinity diagrams are used to group and organize thoughts and facts and can be used in conjunction with brainstorming. After brainstorming all possible ideas, summarize similar ideas in an affinity diagram.

Force field analysis is a way to examine the drivers and resistors of a decision. You could use the old T-square approach and list all the drivers in the left column and all the resistors in the right column. Determine which of these elements in the list are obstacles and which are enablers for the project. Assign a priority or rank to each element and develop strategies to leverage the strengths of the high-priority enablers while minimizing the high-priority obstacles.

Matrix diagrams are also used as decision aids, especially when multiple options or alternatives are available. In a spreadsheet format, list the common elements in the first column of the row and then list each alternative in its own column to the right. You then place each alternative in the appropriate cell where the common element and the alternative overlap.

Prioritization matrices are useful when you need to prioritize complex issues for which there are numerous decision criteria. They are best used in situations where you can use data or inputs to evaluate the criteria. They work much like a weighted scoring model, where the most important criterion has the greatest weight.

You should memorize the names of these additional plan quality tools for review, but more importantly, you should understand both the names and the concepts of the other tools and techniques I talked about earlier in this chapter.

Plan Quality Outputs

As you have seen, Plan Quality uses many techniques to identify areas of quality improvement that can be implemented, controlled, and measured as the project progresses. These are recorded in the primary deliverable of this process, which is called the Quality Management Plan. The following list contains all of the deliverables of this process:

- Quality Management Plan

- Quality Metrics

- Quality checklists

- Process improvement plan

- Project document updates

Project document updates include updates to the Stakeholder Register and RAM and may also include updates to the Quality Management Plan and Process Improvement Plan as a result of changes or corrections resulting from the quality assurance process.

Quality Management Plan

The quality management plan describes how the project management team will implement the quality policy. It should document the resources needed to carry out the quality plan, the responsibilities of the project team in implementing quality, and all the processes and procedures that the project team and the organization should use to meet the quality requirements, including quality control, quality assurance methods, and continuous improvement processes.

The project manager, in collaboration with the project team members, writes the quality management plan. Based on the requirements of the quality plan, you can assign quality measures to the activities listed on the WBS. Is not this work breakdown structure practical? As the Perform Quality Control process continues, measurements are taken to determine whether the quality to date is consistent with the quality standards defined in the quality management plan.

■ *Tip The knowledge area of project quality management, which includes the processes of planning quality, performing quality assurance, and performing quality control, includes both the quality management of the project and the quality aspects of the product or service to be created as part of the project.*

Quality Metrics

A quality metric, also called an operational definition, describes what is measured and how it is measured as part of the Perform Quality Control process. For example, let us say you are managing the opening of a new restaurant next July. One of the deliverables might be the procurement of flatware for 500 place settings. The operational definition in this case might include the date the flatware must be delivered and a count or inventory process to ensure you have received the number of place settings ordered. The measurements of this variable consist of actual values, not "yes" or "no" results. In our example, the receipt of the flatware is a "Yes" or "No" attribute result (you have it or you do not), but the date of delivery and the number of pieces delivered are actual values. Defect rates are another type of quality metric that is measurable, as are reliability, availability, test coverage, and defect density measurements.

Quality Checklists

If you are like me, you start your day at the office with a long to-do list that has so many items on it that you are unable to complete them all. Yet, you conscientiously write down the list each day and check off the items that you have completed during the day. Checklists are similar in that they provide a way to determine if the required steps in a process have been followed. As each step is completed, it is checked off the list. Checklists can be activity-specific or industry-specific and can be very complex or simple to follow. Sometimes organizations have standard checklists that they use for projects. You may also be able to obtain checklists from professional organizations.

Real World Scenario Fiona Walters is a contract project manager at Candy Works. She is leading a project to introduce a new line of candies in a variety of exotic flavors: Café Latte, Hot Buttered Popcorn and Jalapeño Spice, to name a few.

Fiona is writing the quality management plan for this project. After interviewing stakeholders and key team members, she has found several quality factors that are important to the business. Quality is measured by the following criteria:

Candy size Each piece should measure 3 mm.

Appearance No visible cracks or breaks should appear in the candy. Flavor Flavor must be distinguishable when taste tested.

Number produced The production target is 9,000 pieces per week. The current machine has been benchmarked at 9,200 candies per week.

Intensity of color There should be no opaqueness in the darker colors.

Wrappers The candies are wrapped in snug-fitting packages that are folded over twice in the back and twisted on each side. There is a different wrapper for each flavor, and they must match exactly.

The candies are cooked and then pulled into a long cylindrical mold that is about 6 feet long and 2 feet in diameter. This cylinder is inserted into the machine that shapes and cuts the candies into drops. The cylinders vary a little in size because they are stretched by hand by experienced candy makers before they are inserted into the machine to make the candies. As a result, the end of one batch - the Café Latte flavor - and the beginning of the next batch - the Hot Buttered Popcorn flavor - blend together. This means that the drops that fall into the collection containers are mixed during the last run of the first flavor. In other words: In the last container of the run for the Café Latte flavor, a few drops are mixed with hot butter and popcorn. And there is no way to separate the drops once they enter the container. From here, the candies enter the packaging machine, where the colorful packages are adjusted to each flavor. According to the quality plan, the hot butter popcorn candies cannot be packaged as café latte candies. Juliette thinks about what to do. As she tosses and turns in the night thinking about the problem, it occurs to her to present this problem to the company as an opportunity. To keep production at 9,000 candies a week, the machines can not be stopped every time a new batch is introduced. So Fiona comes up with the idea of putting packaging that says "Mystery Flavor" on the candies from the mixed bins This way, production can keep up with the schedule and the problem with the quality of the packaging and the flavors is alleviated.

■ *Tip Be aware that a checklist occurs as an input, as an output, and as a tool and technique. Quality checklists are an output of the process Plan Quality and an input to the process Perform Quality Control, and checklist analysis is a tool and technique of the process Identify Risk.*

Process Improvement Plan

The process improvement plan focuses on finding inefficiencies in a process or activity and eliminating them. The idea is that if you are doing activities or processes that do not add value, you should either stop doing them or change the process to add value. Note that the process improvement plan is a secondary plan to the project management plan. Some of the elements you should consider when thinking about process improvement are the process boundaries, which describe the purpose of the process and the expected start and end dates; the process configuration, so you know which processes will be performed when and how they interact; the process metrics; and any specific elements you want to improve.

Quality Baseline

The quality baseline is not a listed result of this process. But almost everything you did during the Plan Quality process culminates in the Quality Baseline. The quality baseline is the quality goal of the project. You will measure and report on quality against it when you perform the other quality processes. For review purposes, you should understand the definition of the quality baseline.

■ *Tip One of the outcomes of the quality planning process is that your product or process may need to be adjusted to meet quality policy and standards. These changes may result in cost and schedule delays. You may also find that you need to apply risk analysis techniques to problems you uncover or adjustments that result from this process.*

Bringing It All Together

Believe it or not, you have officially completed the group planning process. Along the way, I mentioned that you need to get approvals for parts of the project plan such as the schedule and budget.

The Project Plan is the approved, formal, documented plan that guides you through the Project Execution process group. The plan consists of all the deliverables from the Planning process groups, including the Project Management Plan. It is the map that tells you where to go and how to perform the activities of the Project Plan during the Project Plan Execution process. It serves several purposes, the most important of which is tracking and measuring project performance through the Execute and Monitor and Control processes and making future project decisions. The project plan is critical to all communication you will have with stakeholders, management, and customers from now on. The project plan also documents all project planning assumptions, all project planning decisions, and important necessary management reviews.

The project plan includes everything I have talked about so far and is presented in a formal document or collection of documents. This document includes the statement of the project scope, deliverables, assumptions, risks, work breakdown structure, milestones, project schedule, resources, and more. It provides the basis against which you can measure and track progress. It also helps you control the components that deviate from the original plan so you can bring them back into alignment.

The project plan serves as a communication and information tool for stakeholders, team members, and the management team. They will also use the project plan to review and evaluate progress.

Remember, releasing the project plan is important to the success of the project. Your final step in the planning process group is to have the stakeholders, sponsor, and management team sign off on the project plan. If these people have been involved in the planning process from the beginning (and I know you know how important that is), approving the project plan should be a mere formality.

Note that you will use all of the management plans I discussed during the planning processes - the project management plan and its sub-plans, including the scope management plan, schedule management plan, etc., as well as the cost budgeting baseline, schedule baseline, and quality baseline - throughout the Execute process group to manage the project and align the project's performance with the project objectives. If you do not have a project plan, you have no way to manage the process. You will find that even with a project plan, the project scope is always changing. Stakeholders and others tend to sneak in a few "Oh, I did not understand that before" statements and hope they pass you by. With the signed and approved project plan on file, you can gently remind them that they have read and agreed to the project plan and that you will stick to it.

Real World Scenario Project Case Study: New Kitchen Heaven Retail Store

You are finishing a phone call with Jill and see Dirk walking toward your office.

Dirk walks in, crosses his arms in front of his chest, and stands next to your desk with a "I am here to get answers" look.

"I thought I'd stop by to see if you have signed a lease yet and Jake has started the build-out," Dirk says.

"I just got off the phone with Jill," you reply. "The realtor found a great location and we have scheduled a showing for tomorrow."

"What took you so long?" Dirk asks. "I thought we could start the build-out now."

"I have been working on the project plans."

"Project plans," interrupts Dirk. "We already have a plan. The timeline, risk, and budget thing you have been doing for the last couple of weeks has made things pretty clear."

"I am almost done with the project plans. I want you to take a look at the staffing plan after I go over with you what we have done so far."

"I do not understand why you are wasting so much time on planning. We all know what the goals are, do not we?"

"Dirk," you reply, "if we put the right amount of time and effort into planning, the actual work of the project should go pretty smoothly. Planning is probably one of the most important things we can do on this project. If we do not plan properly, we could miss something very important that could delay the opening of the store. The date is set, I thought."

"Yes, the date is fixed. But I do not see how we could miss anything. You and I have met several times, and I know you have met with Jill and Jake as well. They are the other key players in this."

"Let me finish," you reply. "I have met with all the key stakeholders and after you review these last documents I have for you, we are done with the planning phase of this project. Ricardo has created a work plan for procurement. He needs to hire some outside staff - by the way, I have noted that in the staff management plan - to run Ethernet cable, procure T1 line, and purchase some routers and switches. The purchase of the routers and switches will be done through a fixed price contract and the staff needed will be procured through a time and materials contract. Jill also prepared a statement of work for the purchase of the gourmet and cookware lines. I documented much of the staffing plan when we did the activity and duration estimating exercise and put the finishing touches on it yesterday. It includes a RACI chart for all major project deliverables." You take a quick breath, not wanting Dirk to interrupt. "And the quality management plan is ready. After you review it, I'll distribute it to key stakeholders. The quality management plan describes how we will implement our quality policy. You know the old saying, 'Do it right the first time' I have taken the time to write down the specific quality criteria we are looking for, including the date for signing the lease (it has to start and end on time) and the specifications for the IT equipment, and Jill has documented the specifications for the gourmet products and the cookware line."

Dirk looks impressed, but it's hard to say for sure.

"Once I look at the last of these planning documents, can we start work?" "Yes, as soon as the lease is signed. I expect that to happen by the end of this week. Tomorrow's tour is the fifth site Jill will be looking at. She's very pleased with the third property she saw, but wants to look at this last one before making her final decision." "Great. Let us look at the human plan or whatever it is"

After reviewing the final planning documents, Dirk signs off on the project plan.

Understanding How This Applies to Your Next Project

In my organization, the process of plan procurement comes right after defining the scope of the project, because procuring goods and services is very time-consuming and labor-intensive. This means that we need to start procuring resources as early as possible in the project to meet project deadlines.

In all the organizations I have worked in, someone has always been responsible for procurement - whether it was a single person or an entire department. Usually, the procurement department determines many elements of the procurement management plan. Sure, the project team determines how many vendors need to be involved and how they will be managed along with the deadlines, but many other elements are predetermined, such as the type of contract to be used, the project team's authority over the contract, how multiple vendors will be managed, and the identification of prequalified vendors.

The procurement department will also determine what type of procurement document you should use, depending on what type of resources you want to acquire and how much money you want to spend. They will usually provide you with a template with all the legal sections already filled out. You then work on the sections that describe the work or resources you need for the project, milestones or dates, and evaluation criteria.

Do not make the mistake of thinking that your procurement department will do all the paperwork for you. At the very least, you will likely be responsible for writing the statement of work, the RFP, the contract requirements (related to the project work), the vendor selection criteria, and setting the dates for the contract work.

Developing the staffing plan is a process that you may not need to complete depending on the size and complexity of the project. I typically work with the same team members over and over again, so I know their skills, abilities, and availability. However, if you are hiring contract resources for the project or typically work with new team members on each project, I recommend you complete a staffing plan.

The quality management plan is another important element of your project plan. You should consider the end result or product of the project and the complexity of the project to decide if you need a multi-page document with detailed specifications or if the plan can be more informal and general. Depending on the complexity of the project, the measurements or criteria you use to determine the quality objective may be a few simple sentences or bullet points or a more formal, detailed document. The quality baseline should also be documented during this process.

Summary

The focus of this chapter has been on project resource planning. This planning involves several aspects, including the procurement of goods and services, the planning of human resources, and the determination of the activities in which human resources will be involved.

This chapter began with the Plan Procurements process. This process identifies the goods or services you will purchase from outside the organization and determines what requirements the project team can meet. This includes tools and techniques such as make-or-buy decisions, expert judgment, and contract types. The procurement management plan is one of the outputs of this process and describes how procurement services will be managed throughout the project. The procurement SOW (another output of this process) describes the work to be contracted.

In discussing contract types, we covered fixed-price, cost-plus, and time-and-materials contracts and the benefits and risks of using them.

As part of the Develop Human Resource Plan process, roles and responsibilities and reporting relationships are identified and assigned. In many cases, the roles and responsibilities are mapped in a Responsibility Assignment Matrix (RAM) or RACI chart. The staffing plan describes how and when project team members will be recruited and is part of the output of the staffing plan of this process.

The quality plan defines the quality standards that are relevant to your project. The quality management plan defines how the project team will implement the quality policy.

You must consider the cost of quality when considering stakeholder needs. Four men originated the theories of the cost of quality. Crosby is known for his zero defect theory, Juran for the serviceability theory, Deming for attributing 85 percent of quality costs to the management team, and Shewhart for the plan-do-check-act cycle. The kaizen approach states that the project team should constantly look for ways to improve the process and that people should be improved first, followed by product or service quality. TQM and Six Sigma are examples of continuous improvement techniques.

Cost-benefit analysis considers tradeoffs in the plan quality process. Benchmarking compares past similar activities with current project activities to provide a standard against which performance can be measured. Design of experiments is an analytical technique used to determine which variables have the greatest impact on project outcomes. This technique gives you a statistical framework that allows you to change all the important variables at once, rather than changing one variable at a time.

Quality costs include three types of costs: prevention costs, assessment costs, and failure costs; the latter are also referred to as poor quality costs. Error costs include the costs of internal and external errors.

The process improvement plan is a subsidiary plan of the project management plan and targets inefficiencies in a process or activity. The quality baseline is used to document the project's quality objectives and is used as the basis for future quality processes.

Exam Essentials

You can state the purpose of the plan procurement process. The purpose of the plan procurement process is to determine what project needs should be procured from outside the organization. Make-or-buy analysis is used as a tool and technique to determine this.

You can identify contract types and how they are used. Contract types are a tool and technique of the plan procurement process and include fixed-price contracts and cost-based contracts. Use fixed-price contracts for well-defined projects with high value to the business, and use cost-based contracts for projects with uncertainty and large investments early in the project life. The three types of fixed-price contracts are FFP, FPIF, and FP-EPA. The four types of cost-reimbursable contracts are CPFF, CPIF, CPF (or CPPC), and CPAF. Time and materials contracts are a hybrid of fixed-price and cost-reimbursable contracts.

You can state the results of the plan procurement process. The outputs of plan procurement are the procurement management plan, work instructions, make-or-buy decisions, procurement documents, source selection criteria, and change requests.

You can name the purpose of the Develop Human Resource Plan process. Develop Human Resource Plan involves defining roles and responsibilities, reporting relationships for the project, and creating the Human Resource Management Plan, which describes how team members will be recruited and the criteria for their dismissal.

You can cite the benefits of meeting quality requirements. The benefits of meeting quality requirements include increased stakeholder satisfaction, lower costs, increased productivity, and reduced rework. These benefits are identified as part of the quality planning process.

Be able to define the cost of quality. COQ is the total cost of producing the project's product or service to quality standards. This cost includes all work required to meet the quality requirements for the product. The three costs associated with quality costs are prevention, evaluation, and defect costs (also known as poor quality costs).

Can you name four people associated with COQ and some of the techniques they introduced. They are Crosby, Juran, Deming, and Shewhart. Some of the techniques they helped establish are TQM, Six Sigma, cost of quality, and continuous improvement. The Kaizen approach deals with continuous improvement and states that people should be improved first.

You can name the tools and techniques of the plan quality process. The plan quality process consists of cost-benefit analysis, cost of quality, control charts, benchmarking, design of experiments, statistical sampling, flow charts, proprietary quality management methods, and additional quality planning tools.

Key Terms

In this chapter you have seen how important communication is to any successful project. You have learned how to plan, what work needs to be done, how to communicate during the project, and how to evaluate whether the project is successful. The following processes will enable you to accomplish these parts of project planning. Understand them well and know each process by the name used in the PMBOK ® Guide:

Plan Quality

Develop staffing plan

Plan procurements

Before taking the exam, you should also be familiar with the following terms:

assessment costs benchmarking checklists continuous improvement cost of quality (COQ) cost plus fee (CPF) cost plus fixed fee (CPFF) cost plus incentive fee (CPIF) cost plus percentage of cost (CPCC) cost reimbursable contract trial design (DOE) failure cost fixed fixed price contract (FFP) fitness for purpose fixed price plus incentive contract (FPIF) fixed price with economic price adjustment (FP-EPA) kaizen approach lump sum contract make-or-buy analysis

operational definition organizational structure (OBS) prevention process improvement plan procurement documents procurement management plan procurement work instruction (SOW) quality fundamentals quality management plan quality metrics RACI chart regulation resource structure plan (RBS) responsibility assignment matrix (RAM) Six Sigma standard time and material contract (T&M) total quality management (TQM) zero defects.

Study Hints

The project quality management questions on the PMP® certification exam are easy to answer - especially if you know the definitions of terms and understand statistical process control. You do not have to solve quantitative problems, but there are questions on statistical methods of quality measurement and control.

The exam will likely have a strong emphasis on customer satisfaction and continuous improvement through the use of quality tools such as Pareto analysis and cause-and-effect diagrams. You will also need to know the differences between planning quality management, performing quality assurance, and performing quality control.

Key quality planning documents

Quality Management Plan

Quality Metrics

Quality checklists

Process improvement plan

Quality management and control tools

Affinity diagrams

Process Decision Program Diagrams

Relationship diagrams

Tree diagrams

Prioritization matrices

Activity network diagrams

Matrix diagrams

Quality audits

Process analysis

Variable sampling

Attribute sampling

Tolerances and control limits

Prevention

Probability

Standard deviation

Validated changes

Verified results

Approved change requests Review Impact of motivation on quality Prioritize quality over cost and schedule Design and quality.

Review Questions, Answers and Explanations (online)

Resource Management

RESOURCE PLANNING IS A strange fish. We all know that efficient staffing and resource planning is critical to project success. Millions of dollars are spent on tools to support this function, and countless hours are spent developing pragmatic resource plans.

The embarrassing truth is that much of this effort is in vain. First, when I ask project managers about their use of resource planning systems, I get almost no responses. That is, hardly anyone uses these features, even when they are available. When I ask why, one response is that it's too much trouble to learn the system and describe the allocation details to the computer. But an even more common complaint is that these systems do not provide a usable solution. Personally, I have conducted numerous tests of resource scheduling systems over the past 40 years, and my results agree with those of the testers. However, I believe that the use of resource planning systems is quite reasonable, even if they are not perfect.

In what follows, we describe the basic elements of such resource planning systems and discuss the issues involved in using them, as well as the various components of a resource planning system and how they work. We cover both traditional and some experimental approaches and comment on their effectiveness.

Resource management (RM) means different things to different people in an organization. In this chapter, we take a role-based look at managing resources in a project-oriented organization. We look at resource management from the perspective of managers, participants, and other stakeholders.

During the first four decades of modern project management, the traditional view of resource management was that of schedule-driven management. That is, we first defined the work, then we planned the work, and then we adjusted the schedule to account for resource constraints. This was fine for typical project-oriented conditions where resources were primarily available to complete projects. More recently, a new model has emerged in which greater emphasis is placed on managing resources (rather than managing project schedules). This is not to say that the latter gets short shrift. Rather, the focus is on managing the workforce.

There is a subtle but very significant difference between managing project resources and managing manpower. This difference stems from the nature of the organization at issue and its primary focus. When we talk about project resource management, we are typically talking about an organization whose business strategy is based on delivering projects. If it is a for-profit organization, the focus is on successfully completing projects on time and on budget so that the projected profit margin is maintained. When we talk about workforce management, we are usually talking about a service company. The company is made up of skilled workers who are employed at billing rates that provide for a margin above their actual costs. These service companies focus on maximizing the time these skilled workers are deployed and finding the most productive opportunities for each person - the ones that bring in the maximum margin.

In each case, we are dealing with the allocation of resources to work. However, in the first case, managing project resources, we tend to focus on work and meeting project goals. In the other case, managing labor, we focus more on resources and improving productivity. Nevertheless, the approach we take to planning and monitoring resources for tasks is not that different, and we can address the practices and issues in a common section of this book.

As mentioned earlier, the algorithms built into most traditional CPM programs generally do not provide the optimal solution for resource utilization. Recently, however, this has improved somewhat. In the section Resource Leveling and Gaming, we present the results of some tests conducted a few years ago and comment on these results. In this chapter, we find fault with how many of these products handle resource scheduling. But we also give tips on how you can make sense of the processes.

As we are always keen to provide guidance on the practical application of project management, we offer advice on resource planning and management in the final chapter of this section. We recognize that traditional resource planning has limited value, but nevertheless believe that it is a worthwhile and important part of project planning and management. In this chapter, we summarize all the useful aspects of these tools to provide you with guidance on practical resource planning.

AN OVERVIEW OF THE DIFFERENT ELEMENTS OF RESOURCE MANAGEMENT

Resource Analysis

Part of this topic has already been covered. It is about being able to query the various resource data to analyze resource utilization and demand, resource performance, and so on. The data must be accessed from different (even remote) locations, and there must be control over who accesses the data and what data is retrieved. It requires that big data be sliced and diced, suggesting that some kind of online analytical processing (OLAP) would be useful. Resources and capabilities are required to provide a hierarchical roll-up and drill-down capability.

The Requestor/Allocator Approach

Occasionally, a vendor takes a different approach to allocating resources to work. Resource View, for example, developed by Artemis as part of the Artemis Views suite, has two components. In the request module, anyone can identify work to be done (projects or individual tasks) and add them to a list that goes to the resource owners. In the assignment module, resource managers assign resources to tasks. Resources can also be requested by adding a project from Project View or Microsoft Project. Microsoft took a similar approach with Team Manager. ABT developed a similar resource manager component. Although the concept seems sound, on the surface something is not working. Both the Artemis and Microsoft tools failed to catch on, and ABT was acquired by Niku, presumably primarily to add a scheduling engine to the Niku PSA (professional services automation) package. The Artemis product was pulled from the market. And the Microsoft and ABT capabilities are not advertised.

I suspect that the lack of centralized control is one reason for this failure. Managing resources requires some structuring, supervision, direction and coordination, like we get from a central project office. These requester/allocator concepts suggest that the system can operate successfully outside of a CPO. This failure also indicates that marketing research can sometimes produce the wrong results.

ROLE-BASED NEEDS FOR MANAGING RESOURCES IN A PROJECT-DRIVEN ORGANIZATION

Let us shift down a gear. In the previous chapter, we looked at the mechanisms of a resource planning system. This was intentionally a narrow view. Our main focus was on linking resource allocations to defined tasks and creating resource-loaded schedules. But the topic of resource management in projects encompasses so much more. So we need to look at the topic through the eyes of the various resource groups and examine their needs.

In this section, we review the goals and needs of the various disciplines in the organization associated with managing project portfolios and the resources used to support them. We then discuss the problems and solutions associated with these needs.

Each discussion addresses a specific segment of the business, such as Operations, Strategic Planning, Projects, and Functional Management. We cover a wide range of stakeholders, both at different management levels and with different contributions, as well as external and internal stakeholders.

A common denominator is the urgent need for fresh, high-quality information, accessible to a large community, in forms that support free and clear communication and promote good decision-making and choice of alternatives.

Introduction

Today's typical organization is much more complex than it was in the 1960s (when organizational structure and boundaries were relatively well-defined) or in the 1980s (when matrix concepts allowed for greater flexibility in the use of human resources within the organization while maintaining defined lines of communication and responsibility). Today, we contribute to this complexity by deploying employees in different team configurations, for temporary assignments, and for different periods of time. We also try to use employees more effectively by recognizing multiple skill sets and assigning those employees to work based on their skills rather than departmental structure. When we then bring in outside staff, we create an environment where loss of control is all too common and communication is a screaming, jumbled mess.

Add to that poorly defined goals at both the mission and project levels, as well as weak definition of the customer or client and what they want, and chaos is inevitable. Oh, and one more very important thing. In most organizations today, selecting and executing projects is not just about completing them on time and on budget so they are profitable. Rather, the success of the projects is critical to the survival of the company and/or positioning the company for the next big technological and business breakthrough.

And so it happens that the management of such companies involves an extensive universe of people who contribute to, benefit from, or are otherwise affected and impacted by the company's project-oriented activities. These personnel span a wide range of positions within the company and may well be external to the company. They will involve multiple disciplines, each with a different set of needs and goals and a different definition of project success. The group will likely cross numerous traditional boundaries: physical, such as location; cultural, such as language; economic, such as cost or profit motive; and technical, such as methods and hardware.

Each member of this vast, involved information universe has a specific, distinct role in supporting the system, as well as a different, specific set of needs for the system. Only by clearly identifying these roles and needs can we expect to be able to implement a set of practices with supporting tools to further the organization's goals in this regard.

These practices and tools must facilitate the production of needed information of high quality and timeliness, and make it readily available to all stakeholders on a need-to-know basis. They must enable open communication based on current, shared knowledge that allows stakeholders to respond to changing situations and allows management at different levels and across disciplines to make effective decisions while considering the impact on all stakeholders and objectives. That's a tall order. But the technology is available to meet this need, and if you fail to implement such practices and tools, the chaos and lack of communication will have an unfavorable impact on the future of the organization. Let us now examine the goals and needs of the various disciplines in the organization, addressing the issues related to managing project portfolios and the resources used to support them.

Stakeholders

When we talk about roles, we also need to talk about stakeholders. First of all, why are stakeholders so important? Because the community that cares about your project, that contributes to your project, or that can determine the success or failure of your project is larger than you think. Who are these stakeholders? They are people who will have an impact on the success of the project. They are the project managers, sponsors and owners. They are the various senior managers whose valuation (and stock bonuses) depend on project success. They are the project participants, including suppliers and customers. They are ancillary groups such as end users, regulators, and the public. And, of course, they include everyone directly involved in defining, planning, and executing the project.

If we look at the traditional view of project success, we might say that it consists of achieving all schedule, budget, and technical objectives as planned. However, an alternative view of project success is to achieve the goals of all those involved in the project.

From a strategic perspective, we need to consider who they are, what they want, how they can influence success, and how they can be satisfied. After all, whether your project was successful depends at least in part on how those involved perceive what was actually achieved.

Each stakeholder has a specific role in one or more aspects of the business. These may include: the individual project, the project portfolio, the human resources supporting the projects, the capital investments in the portfolio, the technical deliverables, the long-term growth or survival of the business, to name a few examples. Because these roles (as well as the definition of success) differ, the way these stakeholders interact with the project management system also varies. What stakeholders bring to the system and what they need and expect from the system depends on their particular role. For the project management system to work, each role must be addressed and supported.

Classifications of Role-based Groups

For the purposes of this chapter on role-based needs for managing resources in a project-oriented organization, we will create a group of role sets based on the general nature of needs and participation in the project management system. There is no standard classification, so we will set up some.

The Management Groups Within the general classification of management, we have several subgroups. We have general management, including all the senior executives who are charged with the overall execution of the business. Within that group, I would include the executives who are responsible for strategic planning, the senior VPs of the major divisions, and other operationally oriented functions. There are the managers of the operational functions. There are the managers of the project function and the project managers. Finally, there are the managers of the staff functions.

The Participant Groups Another classification consists of the groups that are directly involved in the projects. These are the people who are likely to spend time on the projects (when time tracking is in effect). These are people who are directly involved in planning the work and providing the status.

Other Stakeholders As mentioned earlier, the universe of people who care about or influence projects is quite large. Often their role in the success is as important as that of the people mentioned above. One such group is the owner of the project. This may be an external customer or an internal sponsor. It is the person who represents the organization, who pays directly or indirectly for the work, and who (most likely) has the greatest interest in successful completion. Other internal departments that may have more than a passing interest in ongoing projects include human resources, accounting, and information systems. And many organizations depend on external functions as well.

The Roles

If we look at all of the possible classifications above, it becomes clear that each group has a very different need for and relationship to the project information system. We now proceed to examine each of these roles and discuss the needs, problems, and proposed solutions related to the use and support of the project process.

Processes, Not Job Titles, Define Roles

In their 1993 book Reengineering the Corporation (HarperBusiness), Hammer and Champy offer the revolutionary concept of treating the corporation as a process rather than a function. They identify segmentation as a major barrier to change and innovation.

What do these well-documented observations of how the way we run businesses is changing mean for the way we manage projects? First, we learn from this that it is not necessarily the position or job title that determines a person's role in projects. It is the role in the process that is critical. Second, projects are more than an independent function. Their impact extends across all segments of the organization and affects a variety of so-called functions and roles. And as traditional segmentation is pushed aside, improved communication between segments is essential.

All of this points to the need to identify all the roles associated with the project environment and define how those roles impact the design and use of project processes and the information system.

The Management Groups

First, within the general classification of management, we have perhaps four definable subgroups. We have the general senior management. This includes the CEO and COO, the chairman or the president, and all other executives who are charged with the overall execution of the company. I would include in this group the executives responsible for strategic planning, the senior VPs of the major divisions, and other operationally oriented functions. Then there is direct functional management. This includes the managers of the operational functions, such as engineering, marketing, production, software development, and information technology.

The third management category would be project management. In a formal project environment, this would be the Chief Project Officer or the head of the central project office. It also includes all managers of individual projects. The last group is the managers of staff functions, such as the Chief Financial Officer, the Chief Information Officer, and the Chief Risk Officer.

Remember, we are not so much interested in identifying job titles as we are in identifying the roles that are involved in managing the business. We have established these groups for the sole purpose of providing a basis for discussing the needs of individuals at the management level with regard to the project and resource management process.

Common Needs

What do these groups have in common? First of all, they are primarily interested in a big picture. Although each group must have a different perspective on the project portfolio, these views would include a high-level overview of data, generally across programs, projects, functions, cost accounts, locations, etc. Another common condition is that these groups are largely viewers of the information, not suppliers of data.

There is no need for these individuals to interface directly with the planning and scheduling tool. If the only way to access the information is to work directly with the critical path planning software, they are likely to be discouraged from such activity. The reason is that the complexity of these formats tends to intimidate the casual user. Rather, what these users need is access to project information in formats that are not intimidating and do not require learning new computer protocols.

Given today's technology, the natural solution is to build the management layer subsystem around a web page format. When properly designed, these formats have the opposite effect - they draw managers to the information instead of scaring them away. However, the solution is more complicated than just outputting data in a web page format. It requires the publisher to specify for each user exactly what they want to see. This does not meet the needs of these users. Their needs are dynamic, and access to information must support those needs. The web browser must be a gateway to the vast system of project data, not just a snapshot. While each user should have access tailored to their specific perspective, once they pass through, they should be able to choose between different information spaces and drill down, filter, and rearrange the data according to their specific knowledge needs.

Specific Needs

The formats described above provide a simple but effective way to access essential project portfolio data. However, they do not guarantee that the desired information will be available, and available in a way that provides the information needed for the day-to-day decisions of these executives. There is a big difference between data and information. If the data cannot be prepared in a way that provides insight into the state of the projects, it is essentially useless. For example, the CFO needs to see the data organized by different budget categories and cost accounts. The person responsible for strategic planning needs the data broken down by program initiatives. This cross-section would also be of interest to several other senior managers.

The functional managers are most interested in seeing the data by skill and resource classification. We could go on and on describing how the data could be broken down to meet the needs of different managers. The list is limited only by one's imagination. The key to supporting all of these possibilities is whether the project database is designed to input all of the required data classifications and whether the web-based output systems are designed to take full advantage of such data coding.

The following is a partial list of the types of information that management level personnel might expect from a project management information system.

General Senior Management CEO, COO, Chairman, President, Strategic Planning executive, Senior VPs of key business units, other operations-oriented functions.

- Project information, organized by program initiatives.

- Project information organized by organization, location, sponsor, customer.

- Analysis of project performance, based on deviation from time and cost targets.

- Summary, action and alert reports.

- Analysis of overall performance against key business objectives.

Direct function management Manager of operational functions such as engineering, marketing, manufacturing, software development, and information technology.

- Deployment of resources by skill, department, trade, location.

- Analysis of overloads and underutilizations.

- Analysis of outsourced resources.

- Analysis of performance according to different resource classifications.

- Commitment of resources, by project and program.

- Overview of billed time versus plan/budget/commitment.

Project Management Chief Project Officer, Project Manager.

- Analysis of project performance against variance of time and cost targets.

- Analysis of performance against targets.

- Use of resources for project planning and control.

- Analysis of overloads and underutilizations.

- Audit of project management implementation (actual vs. target).

ROLE-BASED NEEDS FOR RESOURCES

Officer for personnel functions.

Chief financial officer, chief information officer, chief risk officer

- Analysis of costs versus budgets, organized by all budget/cost account designations of the organization.

- Advance notice of upcoming major cost commitments and decision points to proceed/stop.

- Advance notice of decision points related to risk mitigation plans.

- A repository for or link to project risk planning and mitigation documentation.

- Analysis of key impacts to IT /IS resources and technology.

Implications for Tool Selection

There is no reason why all of the above needs cannot be met by a single, highly usable software system. There is also no reason why such a system cannot be used in a way that provides individualized, non-intimidating access to this data.

However, an important consideration is that the project information system cannot be an isolated desktop solution. In addition, you cannot expect people in the above roles to work directly with traditional critical path planning formats. Rather, a less obscure model, such as the Web page metaphors so popular today, would support both the format and access requirements of these groups.There is no reason why all the above needs cannot be satisfied by a single, highly usable software system. There is also no reason why such a system cannot be applied in such a way as to provide customized, non intimidating access to these data.

However, an important aspect is that the project information system cannot be an isolated desktop solution. In addition, you cannot expect those in the above roles to work directly with traditional critical path planning formats. Rather, a less arcane model, such as the web page metaphors so popular today, would support both the format and access requirements of these groups.

Making It Work

Finding appropriate software products that support these defined management roles is not difficult, nor is it the only key to success. While it is important to select tools that support the defined requirements, it is equally important to use these tools to bridge the gap between the various management groups (many of whom are defending their territory rather than seeking the synergy of shared management). Because of differing needs, goals, and metrics, operations management, financial management, functional management, and project management often work at cross purposes, each supported by a separate information system, none of which communicates with the other.

By considering the roles of each group and designing/selecting a project information system that respects and supports those roles, we can bridge this harmful divide. Such a solution facilitates comprehensive and effective communication using up-to-date data that is consistent across groups and trusted and shared by all.

The Changing Environment

The world of project management has changed. While this is no surprise, the pace of change and the dramatic impact it is having on all aspects of this particular discipline is quite astounding. It impacts how we organize for projects and how we communicate project information. It is especially impacting the roles that people play in projects. Because of these changes and the latest developments in computer technology, change is also affecting the development and use of the tools that support project and people management.

If we trace the stream of names given to these project management tools, we can get an idea of the ever-changing model of the project management world. For the longest time, we simply called all tools project management software. Whether they were developed for mainframes, minicomputers, or personal computers, they focused on the project as the center of the universe and treated each project individually. Resources were either dedicated to the project or lent to the project.

Over the past decade, this model has changed several times as the relative importance of projects to a typical company's bottom line and future has been recognized. The first sign of growth was the ability to handle multiple projects (although one of the most popular PM tools remains remarkably weak in this area). Next, we began to move beyond the project-centric view and embrace enterprise project management. A few years ago, the scope expanded to include elements of accounting and human resources when we integrated project management capabilities into enterprise resource planning (ERP).

With the realization that projects were becoming an essential element of business success, we recognized the need to bridge the traditional gap between the project side and the operational side of the business. Soon, project portfolio management became the buzzword of the year.

In recent years, another model has been born: professional services automation (PSA). What makes this new trend special is that it focuses on human resources. In all previous forms of project management, more and more attention was paid to the resource side of projects. However, with PSA and its counterpart, workforce management, we are focusing more on what is called human capital. In many ways, the PM/PSA solution meets the needs of service-oriented industries, just as PM/ERP solutions did for the product-oriented sector.

While all this was happening, the workforce environment itself was also changing. One very important element of change was the increasing shortage of labor. Another was the increasing specialization of workers. Both often meant that a company had to look outside itself to find workers with the right skills for a particular job. In addition, these temporary workers and many of the regular employees may have been located outside the company, or at least far from their supervisors. Communication, always a critical factor in project success, became more difficult.

Impact of the Changing Environment

Now let us look at what might be a typical scenario for today's participants in projects. They are temporarily assigned to one or more projects. They may not work directly for the implementing organization. They are removed from management and receive their direction from a team leader. They are independent and know that their skills are in demand and that they have a choice of where to work.

Even in a more structured environment, there was resistance to supporting traditional project control activities, such as status and time reports. So in this more informal environment, how do we get today's individuals to support traditional project and resource management activities? As we pay more attention to the human resources involved in projects, we need to recognize that there are many different roles and that our tools need to address the needs of each individual. We also need to make the process as simple and as less cumbersome as possible. And one more thing: It has been my experience that people are much more willing to provide information to a system if that system can also provide them with information that allows them to make an informed contribution.

The Participant Groups

In our introduction, we have chosen to define three classifications of roles related to project management. These are: the management groups, the participant groups, and the other stakeholders. We have looked at the roles of the management groups. Now we'll look at the next classification: the participant groups.

This is about the people who are directly involved in the projects. These are the people who are likely to spend time on the projects (when time tracking is in effect). These are people who are directly involved in planning the work and providing the status. Depending on the level of involvement in the project information system, we can divide these people into subgroups. Key members of the project team or leaders of the primary supporting functions need broader access to the system than those who primarily provide status and time effort data.

■ *Tool Tip PlanView Inc. is a project management tool that intentionally uses a role-based design when using the system. In its default roles, PlanView recognizes these two levels of contributors and calls them Deluxe Contributor and Contributor. A basic Contributor would be expected to feed regular time and cost data into the system, and possibly work status data as well. A Deluxe Contributor or Team Leader would also need to be able to add or change work items.*

Both levels of contributors need easy access to data through a process we call reports. Of course, the concept of reports has changed considerably since the early days of 11" × 14" green-bar computer sheets. Today, reports are likely to be screen views that give the user almost instant access to all the data. However, the big advantage of today's reporting technology is not speed, but customization. Back when we printed large reports, we tended to create a one-size-fits-all output. Everyone, regardless of their role or need, received the same package of reports. So they received much more than they could use, usually in a format where they had to search through the reports to get the information that was useful to them.

This is self-defeating. Today, there is no reason to create reports for general use that contain too much data. Reports can and should be created for each individual user. To do this, we would first identify the roles that should receive the data and create a set of sample reports for each defined role. Then we can move on. Each individual can have their own set of reports using a personal selection criterion.

■ *Tool Tip* *The capability, in PlanView, of having a HomeView for each individual epitomizes this concept. This not only provides access to the specific information needed by each contributor, but also limits access to the data that the individual needs.*

Access should not be overly restrictive. The information available to contributors should be rich enough to inform them about both the big picture and their specifics. They should also include alerts about current and upcoming critical articles, missing articles, and news of general interest. Again, we would expect Deluxe Contributors to have a broader range of interest and responsibility than Basic Contributors. Access and scope of information may vary for internal employees, external employees, contractors, and customers.

Remember, the well-informed Contributor is likely to feel more a part of the organization and therefore participate with more enthusiasm. On the other hand, we should avoid information overload so we do not confuse and discourage employees. We need to strive for a reasonable balance.

Of course, getting data out of the system assumes that data has been entered into the system. Therefore, it is critical that we encourage the input of good and timely data. Again, this is a result of designing appropriate and personalized data entry screens. The same principle applies here as with reports. We develop models for each role and for each type of data required. Then we further individualize them by customizing them for each employee. This usually means we use selection criteria that create a timesheet (or an expense sheet or a status update sheet) that already lists the items the employee should report on. There is no reason to require employees to enter descriptions of work tasks or task codes. The predefined list should include non-project tasks.

Team leaders need more than just input screens. Depending on the scope of their role, they may need access to work planning and resource allocation screens to add or change this data. They should have the ability to analyze performance, review alternatives, and communicate progress, problems, and issues.

Summary Comments—Participant Groups

A key to employee engagement (and project success) is a project management information system that enables frequent and accurate data entry and provides customized information to participants. Such a system is role-based, personal, and easy to use. It is accessible from off-site locations, but secure from accidental entry and unauthorized viewing. It supports the needs and participation of all interested parties while providing tailored access for the many different roles.

Other Roles

We have looked at the increasing role of project participants in the twenty-first century. We have noted the shift from a project-oriented to a resource-oriented view and the emergence of modern workforce management. We have noted a revolution in the concepts and technologies of communications, particularly as they relate to project and workforce management. And we have taken note of the expansion of the concept of stakeholders, recognizing that the success of your project depends, at least in part, on how stakeholders perceive what has actually been accomplished.

So far, we have discussed the role-based needs of two segments of the stakeholder community: the management groups and the participant groups. We conclude this chapter with the needs of the remaining stakeholders.

Other Stakeholders

As mentioned earlier, the universe of people who care about or influence projects is quite large. This goes far beyond the management groups involved and the participants directly involved. More importantly, these other stakeholders can be just as important to success as the management and participant groups. One of these groups is the owner of the project. This may be an external customer or an internal sponsor. This is the person who represents the organization, pays directly or indirectly for the work, and (most likely) has the greatest interest in successful completion. Other internal departments that may have more than a passing interest in ongoing projects include human resources, accounting, and information systems. And many organizations also depend on external functions, such as professional services organizations, outsourcing groups, and business-to-business alliances.

Communicating with Stakeholders

One of the main causes of project failure, especially information technology projects, is the lack of continuous participation and communication on the part of this rather remote segment of the project community. In fact, it seems ridiculous to call the owner or sponsor remote. However, in practice, these individuals are often out of the loop. We accept the project and then limit communication to short, disjointed, periodic reports.

One thing managers and clients abhor is surprises. But we tend to blithely go on and report that everything is fine until we can no longer hide the delays, overruns and technical problems. Then, suddenly, we announce that the customer is not getting what he expected. Such problems are to be expected on most projects. If communication and disclosure are regular, these problems become part of a natural, collaborative resolution process. But the sudden shift from a state of "no worries" to one where "all hell breaks loose" leads to a breakdown in trust.

This state of regret can be avoided. A key to this is communication. This communication should be frequent, concise, and consistent. It should allow for discussion and two-way exchange of information.

In the past, our culture seemed to support concealment. We often believed that we should tell people as little as possible. But this protectionist attitude often backfired. Today, we tend to be more open and share information with others. This has led to better participation and more trust. Let us take a closer look at this new communications environment by looking at the role-based needs of customers, sponsors and peripheral stakeholders.

Fidelity in Communications

Looking back over the four decades I have been involved in managing projects, I recall far too many instances where communication and trust broke down. The first (communication breakdowns) leads to the second (loss of trust). We all know the story of the project that quickly reaches 90 percent and then stays there forever. Obviously, the earlier 90 percent figure was more wishful thinking than fact. In another common scenario, the sponsor inquires (regularly) about the project status and is told that things are going well. Then, when the fantasy can no longer be sustained, the project suddenly jumps to negative variances that obviously did not just happen. It's just as bad when multiple data sets simply do not match. The information is unreliable and trust is completely lost.

The Need to Communicate

Regular and trustworthy communication with all stakeholders is of great benefit to project success. That is what the stakeholders need. And that's what we can give them with the help of today's improved communications technology. I know I am repeating myself here, but for such communication to work, it needs to be regular and consistent (to maintain credibility). It must also be consistent with all other data about the project. The data itself should be supported by narrative discussions about the impact of the data. These discussions should alert recipients to things that require their action or response and provide early warning of potential actions. Remember, a primary goal is to avoid surprises. (Another goal is to allow broad participation in problem solving)

Maybe data is not the right word. I remember a cartoon I saw many years ago that showed a man up to his ears in computer-generated characters exclaiming, "We are drowning in data and starving for information!" This is a great message. The data we provide must have meaning. It must have a connection to the recipient's areas of interest. For the owner, this means linking the data to their goals. The customer or sponsor wants to know how we are achieving those goals. It's not enough to say The project will be completed on 9/1/21 or We spent $120,000. Is that good or bad? If the latter, will action be taken to change the situation? Does the owner have to do something?

Similarly, reporting that a technical target is at risk is not complete communication. Again, the owner should be informed of the prognosis and possible remedial actions, as well as the diagnosis. And again, the owner should be invited to participate in the solution. This philosophy has at least two advantages. First, the customer/sponsor may actually be able to contribute to the remedy. Second, the customer/sponsor is less likely to take all the blame for the failures if he/she is invited to participate (and if mutual trust is maintained).

All too often, the project team wrestles with a problem, such as trying to achieve a desired technical goal. After investing a lot of effort and money, the team communicates the problem to the sponsor, who responds, "This goal was not that important" Imagine what could have been saved if the sponsor had known about the situation earlier.

Other Internal Operations

Most projects require the assistance of multiple internal support functions. This may be human resources or training, finance, information systems, graphics and printing, or one of the traditional internal support groups. Again, the tendency is to keep these groups in the dark until we need their services. Then we ambush them with a request for immediate support and complain that they will not respond to us unless they drop everything for your project. Lack of upfront communication on your part should not be a reason to call in the in-house graphics group on a weekend to meet your needs.

If you maintain a project plan, there is no reason not to include these internal support groups in the distribution of selected information. The goal is to identify the parts of the project that will impact these groups and provide regular updates on the status of these items.

Other External Operations

In some companies, some support functions may be external or outsourced. This should not make much difference. Similar communication is appropriate. A supplier may require that you be notified two weeks in advance of the start of a contracted service. Why not provide an estimate early and update it regularly? The contractor will appreciate this and provide better service. Again, the key is to create a customized view of the appropriate data for each stakeholder.

Software Systems Considerations

A key factor in designing the system for this other stakeholder group is whether the communication is unidirectional or bidirectional. For the subscriber groups, we obviously need bidirectional. For other stakeholder groups, this may not be necessary. If this is the case, an effective method of communication is to publish on the Internet. This would allow recipients of the information to access the data through a web browser. Web pages are developed specifically for each destination, and there are no security issues. If reverse communication is required, the web pages can contain email links to the people most likely to be contacted.

One disadvantage of web publishing is that the publisher determines what the viewer sees and when it is updated. However, this can also be seen as an advantage, as the publisher has the opportunity to review and validate the data before broadcasting it. Another advantage of web publishing is that the format is preset and the reader only needs to know how to access the web pages.

Of course, all parties can be included in the complete, bidirectional system. Security can be set so that queries are allowed, but data entry is not. This provides full (or limited) access to the data as needed without exposing the database to unauthorized input. For the most extensive access from remote locations, a web-based system is generally better suited for these users than a client/server system. With the former system, users do not need PM system software on their computers.

Role-based Needs

This concludes our section on role-based needs for managing resources in a project-driven organization. We have attempted to show that there is a large community of stakeholders supporting or influencing projects-each with an information need and many with information contributions. An effective system designer will consider and meet the specific needs of each stakeholder. The design will consider both the type of information needed and the best format to facilitate the delivery and receipt of that information.

RESOURCE LEVELING AND GAMES OF CHANCE

Potential shortcomings in conventional resource planning software are usually referred to as resource leveling. In this section, we address this issue in more detail by disclosing the results of tests of various products and looking for remedies for such shortcomings. The tests were conducted several years ago, so we will not mention the actual products (those versions are no longer available). However, the test results serve to illustrate the problem and provide a basis for discussion of techniques that work. You will benefit from this discussion by learning more about what resource balancing is all about, becoming aware of critical issues in software selection and deployment, and finding practical approaches to achieving reasonable schedules with high resource loads.

Is It Blackjack?

We begin this section with a trick question. Suppose you play a game 30 times. Thirteen times you get 17. Nine times you get 16. Six times you get 18. Once you get 20 and once you get 15. Which game are you playing? Sounds a bit like blackjack, does not it? But it's not! How about roulette? Wrong again! I know - it's the game of balancing resources. Exactly right! These are the actual results I got from a resource balancing test. In life, they say two things are certain: Death and taxes. In computerized resource leveling, there are also a few things you can bet on. First, do not expect to get an optimal solution. Second, you will rarely get the same solution, even within the same program. And we'd like to add that there's no guarantee that the more expensive or feature-rich products will deliver shorter or more consistent results. This is not to say that the software developers are sloppy or inept when it comes to the resource balancing feature. On the contrary, a lot of effort has gone into most of these products to support effective resource planning, and excellent resource balancing features have been available for more than 20 years. The problem is primarily a matter of tradeoffs and real-world realities. It may very well be possible to create an optimized solution. However, you may not want to pay the price of running such routines. First, it would usually require extensive computer resources. Second, it would require so many iterations that it would slow the process to an unacceptable level. More importantly, it would require the user to make critical and unnecessary decisions long before they are required, and then relinquish control of this complex process to the computer. And as conditions change during the planning and execution of the project, the decisions made at the beginning may not be appropriate after the fact. The user may have to intervene to create the right resource plan. The problem with this is that there are usually sensitive criteria that must be considered when deciding which task should receive the limited resources. First of all, it would be tedious to define all of these decision factors for the computer (after all, we already protest the amount of detail that must be entered to create a reasonable project model). But it would be even more difficult and unrealistic to make these decisions far in advance, before the work is done. Using computerized routines for resource reconciliation is undoubtedly beneficial, especially when it comes to getting the big picture. However, if we are to be realistic about detailed resource planning, we must take a short-term perspective and interact fully with the computer.

Wheel of Misfortune: The Resource Leveling Process

I have been researching this topic for some time, and the more I look into it, the more I find it Byzantine and fascinating. It's a pretty complex subject. There is probably more information here than you need to know. We'll start by looking at some of the issues and problems associated with leveling resources. Then we look at the resource leveling process itself and examine the results of 13 products in some test projects. Next, we look at the attributes and calculations of these products for resource planning. We also look at some alternative software for resource management. Finally, in the next section, we address the practical uses of resource scheduling.

Resource balancing is certainly not new, nor is the question of the best and most practical methods to use. I was recently leafing through an old manual that ran on IBM mainframes and the DEC VAX at the time that offered powerful resource scheduling options. The user had a choice of four leveling methods, two parallel and two serial modes. The parallel mode, which is rarely used today, usually (but not always) results in a schedule with shorter duration and limited resources. In the parallel method, the project is considered by time periods. For each time period, all tasks that are scheduled to be worked on are considered and resources are allocated according to the user's preferred ranking criteria. Activities that cannot be scheduled in this time period because resources are insufficient are postponed to a later time period. Then the system moves to the next time period and considers the next group of tasks that can be processed. Serial mode considers the project for each activity and generally takes less time to process. For a given time period, it begins as described above. However, if an activity cannot be scheduled for the earliest start period, it looks for the first available period (availability of resources) and immediately schedules that activity for that future time. Therefore, it is possible that when the system arrives at a later time period, one or more tasks are already scheduled before it looks for the best choice or the closest support for the ranking criteria. We will note that the serial method of resource leveling is almost universally used in today's popular products. Both methods often allow the user to specify a set of ranking factors (sometimes referred to as ordering, prioritization, or heuristics). These are conditions that affect task selection when some tasks must be deferred. Common factors include date values (ES, EF, LS, LF), buffer values, task durations, assigned priorities, task IDs, and user sort orders. During resource matching, the system first looks at the results for the priority and imposed date (the CPM schedule) and then at the ranking factors. There is no sure way to tell (in advance) which ranking criteria will yield the shorter or smoother schedule. (The seemingly random 30 numbers mentioned earlier are from running the same test project with 13 programs. The programs that allowed the setting of preferred ranking criteria gave different answers depending on the setting.) Experiments with different ranking factors are needed to approximate the best solution. Furthermore, in the serial method, the ranking criteria are only used when a task is first considered for resource scheduling. Tasks are not re-ranked during the process. Even with the numerous options for advanced resource matching, the system is not designed to produce optimal results. In addition to the computer resource requirements, they suggested that the process must be timely and dynamic. Today, a decade later, this reasoning is still valid, and optimization is not expected with the general use of the serial method.

We cannot hope in this book to resolve all issues of efficient and effective resource balancing. However, we will strive to help you understand the realities of resource balancing and the capabilities and limitations of current project management software products with respect to resource balancing. Perhaps as a by-product, we will keep the pressure on ourselves and the software developers to make resource balancing a more useful feature than it is today.

Place Your Bets: A Review of Resource Leveling Results

When you look at the results of resource balancing tests conducted on 13 project management software products, you are amazed at the range of responses and the impact on project duration and resource utilization. Here's an overview.

Test Model A (which yields the results mentioned earlier) consists of 14 resource-intensive tasks requiring either 1 or 2 units of a single resource. The total effort is 30 MDs. The unleveled CPM is 11 days. Leveling with 2 units of available resource should be able to result in a 15-day schedule. However, in 30 trials (excluding the splitting options where available), only 1 iteration was able to achieve the 15-day result. The others ranged from 16 to 20 days. (The splitting options available in 6 of the programs resulted in schedules of 15 and 16 days. However, activity splitting was not required to achieve a result of 15 days with manual reconciliation) Suppose you are the project or resource manager for this job. Would you be willing to pay for 40 days of effort (20 days for 2 people) when you could complete the job with 30 days of effort?

Test Model B consists of 7 tasks and 2 resources. Unsmoothed, the CPM duration is 4 weeks, but there is a resource overload in week 1. After leveling the resources, the result should still be 4 weeks because 1 task can still be moved within the available margin. However, for several products, more than 1 task was postponed, resulting in underutilization of available resources in week 1 and extending the project duration by 1 week.

In both test cases, it was possible to obtain the optimal solution manually by following a set of predefined ordering rules. However, the process of serial matching (routines to immediately place tasks ready for processing) often resulted in times when resources were underutilized, which was unnecessary.

Test model C is the most informative. It consists of only 3 tasks and 1 resource. Only 2 of the tasks require the resource. Depending on the ranking factors used, resource matching can extend the schedule by either 1 day or 5 months. For the programs that offer a choice of ranking factors, the user has to decide for himself which method of prioritization gives the better result.

And do not look to user manuals and other documentation for help in determining ranking factors for resource allocation. I read in one manual that Late Start (LS) usually yields the shortest resource-constrained schedule. Another source suggested that the lowest Total Float (TF) should be your first attempt. However, in my experiments, the best results were obtained in Test Model A with Early Start (ES) and Test Model C worked best with Late Finish (LF) or the least (shortest) duration.

Better Odds at Blackjack?

In my research and testing, I have found that the odds of getting 21 are far greater than the odds of getting an optimal, balanced schedule from project management software. Oh! If only we could use elastic resources, I thought wistfully. But resource pools that grow as needed are even rarer than successfully cloning project managers. No, the only immediate, practical solution (other than software improvements) is to recognize the limitations of today's project planning systems and work within those limitations. This requires interaction between the person managing the resources and the project management software system.

■ *Tool Tip Good news Although the serial leveling algorithm still dominates the traditional tools from CPM, the results from the latest versions are more likely to provide a better solution than the products I reviewed for my testing. The calculated results of these latest versions, while still benefiting from user interaction, are much more reliable than they were a few years ago*

Options That Affect Resource Leveling

Before we get into practical techniques for resource management, let us look at the various differences in the resource planning and leveling capabilities of project management software products. In addition to the basic leveling methods we have already discussed, we can identify several dozen design attributes that can affect the ability to define a project's resource parameters and influence the outcome of resource leveling. The variations are extensive.

Practical Uses of Resource Scheduling

In the previous section, we looked at the practical uses of resource planning. Here is a preview of some things you should find interesting.

Long-term/short-term Practical resource planning is best achieved by balancing long-term resource aggregation (analysis of projected resource utilization) with short-term resource balancing (possibly with user intervention). We outline a recommendation that should be suitable for most applications.

Using Total and Free Float Were you taught that we use CPM scheduling to get a measure of float? And that we use these float values to make decisions about priorities and to analyze the risk of the project plan? Be prepared to learn it all over again. If we use resource balancing, we can forget about using the resulting float values as a time management tool. I'll explain why in the next section.

Using Fulfillment Value Instead of Float There are other techniques to analyze project progress. Fulfillment value (based on common earned value protocols) can be used, even without the cost management features of your project management software.

A blueprint for streamlined resource planning Is there a better way to do resource planning with project management software? We present some ideas on this topic.

Options That Affect Resource Leveling

Here is a list of attributes for resource planning that you can find in the traditional products of CPM. The range of attributes is quite wide. Some of them are included in only one product. Most of the items on the list are present in many products, but in less than half of them. So when choosing project management software, you cannot assume that even the most popular and rudimentary features are supported by every product. By the way, the price is not directly related to the number of supported resource planning functions.

- User choices for ranking.

- Multiple iterations or ranking calculations.

- Effect of imposed dates (Note: Some products use fixed dates that interfere with resource leveling).

- Trial and Error—Perform what-if, but do not replace until accepted by user (or perform undo).

- Manual (interactive) adjustment (most Windows products).

• Activity splitting entire project only (this is useless - must be able to select by task). By task with definable conditions. Automatic contouring (system varies loading by time period to adjust for resource availability). Discrete loading via spreadsheet.

• Overtime.

• Activity Stretching (called Stretching or Re-profiling in some products or Flex in another). Reduces loading per time period and increases time periods (I wonder if we want to let the computer make this decision without human interaction).

• Min-Max or Threshold Options. Defines preferred limits and maximum.

• Limit for resource.

• Resource substitution (rare).

• Leveling audit or results report.

• Depletable resources.

• Producer resources (unique to SuperProject).

• Span dates for resource leveling (if we can choose to limit our resource leveling to a reasonably short time frame, then we can afford to implement more exacting leveling algorithms).

• Minimum crew size (available in a few packages).

Trends in Resource Management

Resource management is perhaps the truly oldest profession. Certainly it is not a new function. I'll bet that even when the pyramids were built, there were fairly well-structured procedures for managing projects and resources. Frederick Taylor published new concepts for more efficient use of resources in the early twentieth century. When the first systems of CPM appeared in the late 1980s, it did not take long for tool developers to add resource planning features. Currently, a most interesting trend can be observed. It concerns the new practitioners of project management and the new users of project management software. Companies are finding that their work revolves around projects. For those of us who have been on the project management scene for a while, this is no great revelation. But what is happening is that project orientation is now a normal modus operandi rather than a special situation. As a result, there has been a growing interest in project management and in computerized systems that help plan and schedule this work. The fact that they are turning to project management software for this purpose is basically a good thing! But wait! There's more (why keep it simple?). These companies have also realized that the allocation and use of resources for these projects is an important item to plan and manage. Again, companies are turning to project management software, and that's a good thing. There is no doubt that traditional project management software packages can be excellent tools to support this important function. In our model project environment, we need to do critical path planning and align schedules with limited resources. We need software that allows us to do the following:

  • Identify the scope of work for the project.

  • Organize the identified work (outlines and work breakdown structures).

  • Plan the work.

  • Identify the resources available.

  • Allocate resources to the work.

  • Evaluate and adjust schedule and resource allocations.

  • Analyze and report schedule and resource information oriented to the project and resource structures.

These are all features that are fully supported by project management software, and I would recommend using such software for most applications. However, traditional project management software is not necessarily the ideal solution for every application. There are certain advantages and disadvantages that need to be considered, especially when alternative software solutions are available. The strength of project management software is its ability to perform critical path planning. These tools are optimized for creating and displaying work plans based on defined task durations, dependencies and date constraints (and optionally resource constraints). They are designed to analyze and display resource schedules and workloads (as well as costs). They appear to be complete systems for planning and control. The problem is that these project management software systems are rarely linked to the company's accounting systems. Yet the latter are usually the only complete and reliable repositories for resource accounting (timesheets) and cost data.In addition, many of these project management software systems are optimized to present a project-centric view of the work, often leaving functional and resource managers with less information and control than is desirable. So our discussion of computer support for resource management functions would not be complete without mentioning some of the tools that are available for this purpose (CPM). Here are some options for software that can be used in place of or complement our traditional project management software products.

Summary

Companies today recognize the importance of project management and hiring a Project Management Professional to do a human resource management presentation. A PMP human resource management presentation gives companies confidence that the person managing the company's projects has the necessary skills and knowledge to implement the principles of project management in the organization.

A PMP people management presentation adds value to the company's initiative to improve people management by helping companies get started with project management in their organization.

It is often said that planning, research, communication, and review are essential elements of project management, and yet these very elements are usually set aside in a hurried or time-limited project. However, with a PMP people management presentation, this mentality of delivering projects in a way that is not cost effective is replaced with successful delivery of projects that are on time, on budget, and within the standards of all stakeholders.

A PMP Human Resources Management presentation uses a tool or method that applies the best practices, procedures, and rules that every successful company uses. The PMP Human Resources Management Presentation adds value to human resources management by carefully examining the feasibility of a project and then performing a cost-benefit analysis before setting expectations for the desired outcome. In this way, the objectives of the project are defined and, finally, the steps required to achieve the set goals are determined.

After the initial planning, a PMP human resource management presentation also applies tracking and follow-through to each project to ensure it meets the organization's standards.

Exam Essentials

Unlike other areas of this book where commonly known terms are used, some of the terms developed for Project Human Resource Management appear to be unique to PMI® (in fact, much of the terminology has been used in project management literature for many years, but has not always been widely used). In the area of project organization structures, for example, some experts with years of experience in the field have never encountered terms or concepts such as "Project Expeditor" or "Weak Matrix". Therefore, it is essential to memorize the PMI® definition and classification of the following topics:

Project Organization Structures

Stages of team development

decision-making guidelines

Guidelines for influencing

Negotiation skills

Conflict management concepts

Despite the unfamiliarity of some terms, most examinees do not find the HR questions on the exam difficult.

PMI ® sees Project Human Resource Management in four elements: Plan Human Resource Management, Recruit Project Team, Develop Project Team and Manage Project Team.

Below is a list of the most important topics and key terms in Project Human Resource Management. Use this list to focus your learning efforts on the areas that are likely to appear on the exam.

Topics & Key terms

Forms of organization

Functional

Project expeditor

Project coordinator

Weak matrix

Strong matrix

Balanced matrix

Projectized

Composite

Plan human resource management plan tools and techniques

Organization chart and position descriptions

Hierarchical-type charts

Matrix-based charts

Text-oriented formats

Networking

Organizational theory

Expert judgment

Develop human resource management plan outputs

Human resource management plan

Roles and responsibilities

Staffing management plan

Project organization charts

Acquire project team

Functions

Roles

Negotiation

Project manager roles and responsibilities

Types of power

Acquisition

Multi-criteria decision analysis

Virtual teams

Project staff assignments

Resource calendars

Develop project team objectives

Interpersonal skills

Communication skills

Emotional intelligence

Conflict resolution

Negotiation

Influence

Team building

Group facilitation

Training & Team-building activities

Approaches

Stages of team development

Goals and results of project team building

Symptoms of poor teamwork

Ground rules for project team building

The team-building process

Review Questions, Answers and Explanations (online)

Communications Management

READERS WHO READ THIS chapter are frequently shocked that it does not address communication skills in areas such as project writing styles, persuasion, and presenting strategies. Rather, communications management encompasses all duties associated with the creation, compilation, transmission, storage, distribution, and maintenance of project records. This knowledge domain today consists of just three procedures for determining what to communicate, to whom, how often, and when to reassess the strategy. It entails determining who your stakeholders are and what they need.

Communication management also requires precise reporting on project status, performance, change, and earned value, as well as strict attention to information control to verify that the communication management strategy is performing as planned.

PHILOSOPHY:

There is an old joke in project management circles about "mushroom project management," in which you manage projects by burying everyone in manure, leaving them in the dark, and peeking back regularly to see what sprouts.

The thought given here is pretty unique. It emphasizes on keeping stakeholders up to date throughout the process. Under this paradigm, communication may be official and casual, written and oral, but it is always proactive and complete. It is critical that the project manager distributes correct project information in a timely and appropriate way to the appropriate audience.

IMPORTANCE:

The relevance of communications management in the test is medium to high. You may encounter multiple questions that are directly related to this chapter, so you should familiarize yourself with the methods, words, and ideas provided here.

PREPARATION:

Although the number of content in communications management is less than in most other fields, fundamental ideas must be understood. Be prepared to answer questions on the exam on the inputs, tools and procedures, and outputs for each process. The emphasis is on these areas since they are crucial to the proper running of the procedures and are not obvious to most test-takers.

The communications model and understanding communication pathways are two more critical aspects. You may anticipate questions regarding these topics on the test.

Communications Management Processes

Project communications management is divided into three stages that follow the well-known pattern of plan, execute, and control. These procedures have an impact on three process groups: planning (Plan Communications Management), execution (Manage Communications), and monitoring and control (Monitor Communications).

Process Group	Communications Management Process
Initiating	(none)
Planning	Plan Communications Management
Executing	Manage Communications
Monitoring & Controlling	Monitor Communications (none)
Closing	(none)

The primary outputs associated with the three communications management processes are shown in the table below.

Process	Primary Outputs
Plan Communications Management	Communications Management Plan
Manage Communications	Project Communications
Monitor Communications	(No Key Outputs)

Project Manager's Role in Communications

The capacity to communicate effectively is the most critical skill set for a project manager. It pervades everything he or she does. You may notice questions on your test asking you what the project manager's most significant job or talents are, or how the project manager spends the majority of his or her time. Almost usually, the solution is tied to communication. It is estimated that a competent project manager spends around 90% of his time communicating, with the project team accounting for 50% of that time.

Also, although communications consume the bulk of the project manager's working day, one person cannot and should not attempt to oversee everything that is said on a project. Project managers that request that every e-mail or conversation be routed via them first demonstrate a lack of project management. Instead, the project manager should be in charge of communication. This is accomplished by developing a solid communications management strategy, sticking to it, and routinely evaluating and regulating the outcomes.

PLAN COMMUNICATIONS MANAGEMENT

Plan should be considered for the test. The communications management strategy is the single important outcome of communications management. The communications management plan, as the name suggests, is the strategy that governs communication on the project. It specifies:

How often will messages be provided and updated?

What format will the messages be provided in? (e.g., e-mail, meetings, printed copy, web site, etc.)

What information will the messages contain?

Who will get these messages from the project stakeholders?

WHY IT IS IMPORTANT:

The communications management strategy establishes stakeholder expectations for the project by informing them of what information they will get, when and how they will receive it. Conflict should be reduced if the project manager takes effort in identifying these channels of communication early on. Keep in mind that the formality with which the communications management strategy is defined will vary widely across projects. It may not make sense for the project manager to go to considerable efforts to establish an excessively formal communications management strategy on a short project.

WHEN IT IS PERFORMED:

Plan Communications Management, like many other planning procedures, is normally completed early in the project, before regular project communications begin; however, it may be reviewed as required. It is dependent on the Identify Stakeholders procedure, thus it would be undertaken after that process was finished.

HOW IT WORKS / INPUTS:

Project Management Plan - The stakeholder engagement strategy is a critical component of the project management plan in this case. Communication is usually always the main means of keeping stakeholders involved.

Project Documents - The stakeholder register, which identifies which stakeholders will receive project communications, is the most critical document to include in this process.

HOW IT WORKS / TOOLS:

Communication Requirements Analysis - This one is capable of covering a lot of territory. It is very easy to describe, but may be difficult to execute on a real-world project. The purpose of this approach is to determine which stakeholders should get project communications, what communications they should receive, how these communications should be delivered, and how often they should be sent.

Channels of Communication

Determining the communication channels, or pathways of communication, that exist inside the project is an important component of understanding its communication needs. Expect at least a few of test questions to directly connect to this subject. Because the project manager is responsible for managing and controlling project communications, it is critical to realize that even adding a single person to a project may have a considerable influence on the number of pathways or channels of communication that exist between individuals.

Channels = n (n-1) 2 (where n is the number of persons working on the project)

The algorithm for determining communication channels above should not frighten you. It is a pretty straightforward geometric expansion. Refer to the two images below before learning the formula. The graphic shows that four persons generate six communication channels, which is validated by the formula: 4 (4-1) 2 = 6.

If there were five persons, the formula would be 5 (5-1) 2 = 10.

The notion should be simple to grasp if you understand the images that follow and how individuals interact to build communication channels.

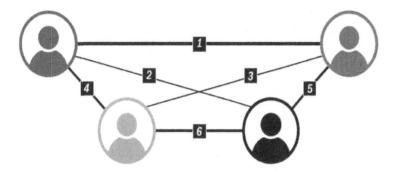

Four people create six communication channels, as illustrated above.

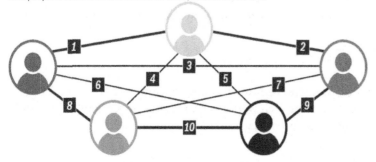

Five people create ten communication channels, or paths, as depicted in the illustration above.

Official Communication Channels

When examining the project's communication needs, the number of communication channels is of particular relevance. If there are several channels of communication on the project, the project manager should attempt to determine which channels are official. It may be important, for example, to identify who may formally interact with the client or critical subcontractors.

Communication Technology - Technology is a tool, and the appropriate instrument for a specific communication requirement should be chosen. While face-to-face meetings may be required for certain projects, others may benefit from a project web site, portal, or e-mail. Technology should be suited to the situation. When selecting the correct technology, it is also important to consider information sensitivity and security.

Communication Models - The communication model is a structured approach to understanding how communications are conveyed and received. This model specifies the roles of the transmitter and the recipient.

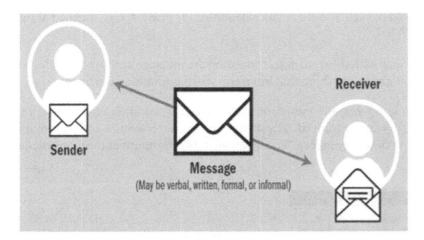

The sender is responsible for:

- Clearly encode the message

- Choose a communication method.

- Send the email

- Confirm that the recipient got and comprehended the message.

The receiver is responsible for:

- Decrypt the message

- Acknowledge (Confirm that the message was received)

- React and provide feedback

It is not always possible to simply broadcast a message and expect it to be correctly received, encoded, and understood. "Noise" may disrupt the transmission of a message. Noise is defined as anything that interferes with the receiver's capacity to interpret a message. Language and cultural challenges, transmission technique, distance, and prejudice, for example, may all introduce noise into the message. Both the transmitter and the receiver must be cognizant of noise and endeavor to keep it from interfering with the message.

Messages may be sent both verbally and nonverbally. The following are some words connected to various modes of communication:

Active listening - Active listening necessitates that the receiver take efforts to confirm that the sender's message was comprehended. It is comparable to effective listening (below).

Effective listening - Effective listening requires the listener's undivided attention and thinking. Being an excellent listener entails monitoring nonverbal and physical messages and providing feedback on whether the message has been fully comprehended.

Feedback - The verbal and nonverbal indicators that a speaker must watch to determine if the listener completely comprehends the information are referred to as feedback. Positive response such as nodding and smiling may suggest that the message has been understood and accepted, however nodding and a blank gaze may indicate that the message needs to be re-coded for better communication. It is also possible to provide feedback by asking questions or repeating the speaker's statements.

Nonverbal - Body language, such as facial emotions, posture, and hand gestures, is used in nonverbal communication. In reality, nonverbal communication is the majority of communication between sender and receiver. As a result, in order to comprehend the information, a skilled listener must pay close attention to nonverbal communication.

Paralingual communication is vocal but not spoken, such as tone of voice, loudness, or pitch. A high-pitched shriek does not use words, yet it conveys well.

Communication Blockers - Anything that interferes with the transmitter encoding the message or the receiver decoding it is considered a communication blocker. It might be anything that interferes with communication lines.

Communication Strategies - You will need to know certain communication methods, and it is critical that you grasp what they are as well as how and when they are employed. The distinction between formal and informal is sometimes perplexing to many individuals the first time they meet it. The following table summarizes the many modes of communication.

Method	Examples	When used
Informal Written	E-mail messages, memorandum	Used frequently on the project to convey information and communicate.
Formal Written	Contracts, legal notices, project documents (the Charter), important project communications	Used infrequently, but essential for prominent documents that go into the project record. The project plan is a formal written document.
Informal Oral	Discussions, phone calls, conversations	Used to communicate information quickly and efficiently.
Formal Oral	Meetings, speeches, mass communications, presentations	Used for public relations, special events, company-wide announcements, sales.
Internal	Emails to the team, Memos or presentations to senior management	Used to communicate within the performing organization.
External	Messages or presentations to customers, regulators, the public, or investors	Used to communicate with stakeholders outside of the performing organization.
Official	Communication to government or regulatory bodies.	Used to communicate with any party that operates in an oversight role for the project.
Unofficial	Anything that is not official, including the majority of project communication to internal or external stakeholders.	Used for most project communications to ensure successful delivery.

Be mindful that the medium, as much as the content, influences whether a type of communication is formal or informal.

Another approach to look about communications is to categorize them into one of three types:

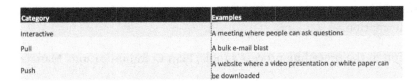

Category	Examples
Interactive	A meeting where people can ask questions
Pull	A bulk e-mail blast
Push	A website where a video presentation or white paper can be downloaded

Interpersonal and Team Skills - This technique appears regularly throughout the book, but it is especially crucial when it comes to communication. Understanding your communication style, as well as being politically and culturally aware, are critical components of interpersonal and team abilities.

Data Representation - The stakeholder engagement assessment matrix is an effective tool for demonstrating how stakeholders interact with the project.

HOW IT WORKS / OUTPUTS:

Communications Management Plan - The project management plan includes the communications management strategy, which outlines the following:

Who should be notified about project communications?

What kind of communication they need and what should be included

Who should transmit the message?

Who should have authority over confidential communications?

How the message will be delivered

How often will it be updated?

Definitions are provided so that everyone is on the same page.

MANAGE COMMUNICATIONS

WHAT IT IS:

It is easy to think of the Manage Communications process as the implementation of the communications management strategy. In other words, the communications management strategy specifies how communications will be handled, and the Manage Communications process does that.

Keep in mind that, although Manage Communications must follow the communications management strategy, it must also be flexible enough to meet unexpected information requirements.

WHY IT IS IMPORTANT:

Manage Communications is the procedure that handles the majority of project communications.

The following four statements summarize the approach to this process:

Always deal with the issue.

Always speak directly; always convey the truth; and always disseminate correct information.

WHEN IT IS PERFORMED:

Manage Communications provides general updates to stakeholders on the project's progress in accordance with the communications management strategy. It may begin early in the project, but it often grows in prominence and activity throughout the building stages.

HOW IT WORKS / INPUTS:

Work Performance Reports - Much of the project communication will be about the project's performance, and the performance reports will be the source of that information.

Communication Technology: See the explanation in the preceding process's tools, Plan Communications Management.

Communication Methods: See the explanation in the preceding process's tools, Plan Communications Management.

Communication Skills - This tool encompasses your ability to craft a message, remain on topic, and how effectively you handle criticism. It also involves how you deliver presentations and develop and manage communication expectations with stakeholders. The same rules that apply to high Emotional Intelligence will apply to the test.

Project reporting resembles labor performance reports in many ways. Project reporting includes any discussions concerning deliverables, but other work performance reports are mainly concerned with how the job is proceeding.

Interpersonal and team skills - The main talents to notice here include active listening, conflict resolution, good meeting management, and political awareness.

HOW IT WORKS / OUTPUTS:

Project Communications - This output is used whenever information is transmitted with stakeholders. As previously stated in this chapter, communications may be professional or casual, oral or written. These emails will contain updates on how the project is developing, how the team is doing, and how the deliverables are coming along.

MONITOR COMMUNICATIONS

WHAT IT IS:

Monitoring and regulating procedures compare what was intended to the work that was completed. That is precisely what Monitor Communications does. It contrasts the preceding process's (Manage Communications) outcomes with the communications management strategy. If there are disagreements, changes are made to the plan or the manner the task is done.

WHY IT IS IMPORTANT:

Communication challenges are to blame for far too many project problems and failures. It is critical to develop a solid strategy and then execute it effectively.

The nature of what this process accomplishes, how it is carried out, and how the Data Representation tool is utilized are the most critical aspects to understand.

WHEN IT IS PERFORMED:

Monitor Communications begins early in the project and continues on a regular basis. It would be a suitable time to complete this approach as long as project communications are ongoing.

HOW IT WORKS / TOOLS:

Data Representation - The concept here is summed up by the phrase "a picture is worth a thousand words." Graphics, photos, charts, and tables may all be utilized to assist individuals in seeing and comprehending data. The stakeholder engagement assessment matrix is one tool used in communications management (covered in the Plan Stakeholder Engagement process chapter). It allows you to arrange and illustrate how stakeholders are involved in the project.

Consider this tool to be a data visualization tool for the test.

Interpersonal and Team Skills - This gadget appears as a key once again. Observation and discourse, often known as MBWA (Manage By Walking Around), are essential in this situation. In other words, remain involved with your team.

Meetings Meetings are a crucial element of communication, and they are usually considered as formal communication, even if they are impromptu. A lessons learned meeting, also known as a post mortem meeting or an after action review, is one form of meeting you should be aware of. These discussions focus on one basic question: "If we were to undertake this action again, what would we do differently knowing what we know now?" The outcomes of these become lessons learnt, which may be applicable to current project and future ones.

THE AGILE VIEW OF COMMUNICATIONS MANAGEMENT

On agile projects, communication is noticeably more open and dynamic. Because teams are often colocated, agile projects rely on "osmotic communication," in which the team learns from and absorbs knowledge from other talks. Furthermore, the product owner is integrated within the team, allowing for effective and efficient communication.

Communication should be quick in this context, and impediments to direct, open communication should be aggressively eliminated. Stand-up meetings and regular reviews are also used in agile projects to promote collaboration. Conversation and involvement are preferred than sticking to a plan.

Information regarding performance, value delivery, and priorities is prominently displayed and freely shared.

Healthy agile teams avoid communication silos and instead focus on the team's common knowledge.

Plan Communications Management

An agile project does not need a communications management strategy, which is part of the project plan. The goal of this plan is valuable, but agile prefers more casual and regular updates, as well as a continual flow of information.

Manage Communications

This is the procedure through which information is exchanged. This would most likely appear different on an agile project than on a predictive project. On agile projects, information is disseminated to the team via daily stand-up meetings and osmotic communication. It might be communicated through the organization's "scrum of scrums" or via more conventional means like as presentations, emails, and meetings. Another method of communicating information would be to use large, conspicuous charts. Burndown charts, burnup charts, Kanban boards, and product backlogs are some examples.

Agile advocates for a transparent approach to keeping stakeholders informed, such that current information, both good and bad, is easily visible and accessible.

Monitor Communications

This procedure compares the plan to the completed outcomes and makes improvements on a predictive project. Because there is less rigorous commitment to following a plan on an agile project, this procedure becomes less critical.

Because agile teams are constantly making changes throughout the project, any changes to what information is given and how it is presented and disseminated would naturally fall under this process.

Review Questions, Answers and Explanations (online)

Risk Management

Assess Risk Quantitatively

Quantitative risk assessment numerically analyzes the likelihood of each risk, its impact on project objectives, and the extent of overall project risk. It can be used separately or together with qualitative assessment.

The process begins with the results of the earlier risk identification step. For each of the identified risks, you must quantify the probability of occurrence by asking, "What is the probability that this risk will occur?" "Ninety percent," the team decides. That means there is a 10 percent probability that the risk will not occur. Clearly, the probability that the risk will occur plus the probability that it will not occur equals 1. The estimate of the probability is nothing more than an estimate based on solid historical information from similar experiences in previous projects or on the opinion of experts.

The next step is to determine the impact of the risk. "What will happen if this risk occurs?" is the question you should ask While the impact can be expressed in almost any unit, from percentage loss of market share to loss of revenue, the real focus here is on estimating the timing or financial magnitude of the risk. For example, if schedule is the most important project objective, the status of the risk event is calculated in terms of time.

Risk event status = risk probability × impact = 90% × 60 days = 54 days

In this example, the potential impact on the schedule for a given risk event has been set at 60 days, with a 90% probability that it will occur at that time. The current status of the risk event is therefore 54 days, which represents the current risk for that event.

When the status is calculated for all risk events, the question naturally arises: which risks are truly vital and deserve attention, and which are insignificant? To answer this question, we will apply principles similar to those used for qualitative severity assessment. First, establish numerical severity intervals that determine whether a risk event should be classified as critical (potential showstopper), near critical (soon to be potential showstopper), or noncritical (insignificant risks). For example, on a smaller project, a risk event that lasted longer than 15 days was critical, a risk event that lasted between 7 and 14 days was near critical, and a risk that lasted less than 7 days was non-critical. Second, respond to the highest ranked risks, up to an agreed level.

Determine Risk Response

Once the risks have been qualitatively or quantitatively assessed, the project manager must determine how to address the risks that may have the greatest impact on the project. This section of the risk management plan explains the response options and actions available to the project team in addressing the risks.

Each appropriate risk response action essentially falls into one of the four broad categories of response strategies: avoidance, transfer, mitigation, and acceptance of the risk. 16 Modifying the project plan or project conditions to eliminate the selected risk event is risk avoidance. For example, if the risk is that an expert is not available to perform a high-quality business process analysis, the risk can be avoided by hiring such an expert. Risk transfer involves shifting the consequences of a risk to a third party who also bears responsibility for the response. For example, if projects within a company have been exposed in the past to the risk that the quality of testing was too slow due to internal capabilities, the risk can be transferred to a third party by hiring a professional company to perform the testing.

Managing Project Risk

The purpose of risk mitigation is to reduce the probability or impact (or both) of an adverse risk event to an acceptable threshold. A relatively common risk on many projects is the potential delay of decisions caused by the busy schedule of the executive sponsor. This risk can be mitigated in a number of ways, such as reducing the number of key milestone decision points or delegating decision-making authority to one of the executive's direct subordinates. The three response strategies - avoidance, transfer, and mitigation - are used when the risks they respond to are among the highest ranked risks. Of course, these actions are included in the project plan.

For those risks that are not among the highest ranked risks, or for risks for which there is no other viable response strategy, a risk acceptance strategy is used. This means that the project managers have decided not to change the project plan or are unable to formulate a viable response to a risk. A typical example of risk acceptance is the establishment of contingency reserves. For an explanation of how reserves are established, see "How Many Reserves and Provisions Should You Plan for?"

How Much Reserves and Allowances to Plan For?

Let us think back to the continuum of total certainty (known) - risk (known unknown) - total uncertainty (unknown unknown). What kind of reserves do we need to respond when one of these categories strikes? First, known risks do not require reserves because of their absolute certainty. How do you account for the risk consequences of the known unknowns? Many companies add them to the base estimate as a separate fund for forward and cost reserves. Others include them in individual activities. While we prefer the first approach, the second - which, by the way, is too risky because activity owners tend to use reserves liberally - seems to be more widely used.

How is the fund formed? Popular methods include the use of standard allowances and percentages based on past experience. We believe that using the risk response plan can be a very appropriate way to calculate the fund. Take a risk from the plan that is not one of the highest ranked risks - let us call it a lower ranked risk. Multiply the risk probability by the risk impact and you get the status of the risk event, which can be expressed in terms of cost or schedule. These numbers are essentially cost and schedule reserves or surcharges for the risk event. If you add up the allowances for all the subordinate risk events in the plan, you get a contingency fund for the project. And what about the reserves for the unknown unknowns? Although they are absolutely unpredictable, such things can happen. That's why some companies build management reserves for the cost, schedule, or both, to be ready for those future situations where cost or schedule goals might be missed. Once the reserves are depleted, the cost basis is changed. The management of management reserves is in the hands of top management, usually the project sponsor.

An essential part of response development is the identification and assignment of risk owners - individuals or parties responsible for each preventive action, trigger point, and contingency. This should recognize that while some risks are independent and their owners have full responsibility for their management, some risks may be interdependent. When this is the case, their preventive actions, trigger points, and contingency actions should be developed and held accountable in a mutually dependent manner.

Risk Monitoring

Most of a project manager's attention to risk management is focused on activities related to risk identification, risk assessment, and risk response planning. Where project managers have historically spent less time and attention is on activities related to risk monitoring. It is not uncommon, therefore, for project managers to be repeatedly surprised when a risk they had previously identified but not monitored suddenly becomes an issue. To guard against this, careful risk monitoring must be part of every project manager's activities, and he or she must have tools in his or her PM toolbox to perform this function effectively.

There are four main elements to risk monitoring: (1) systematically tracking the status of previously identified risks, (2) identifying, documenting, and assessing emerging risks, (3) effectively managing the risk reserve, and (4) capturing lessons learned for future risk identification and assessment activities.

This section of the risk management plan should discuss how project risks will be monitored on an ongoing basis. The key to risk monitoring is to ensure that it is used throughout the project cycle and includes the identification and use of trigger conditions that accurately indicate whether the probability of a risk occurring is increasing or has exceeded.

As mentioned earlier, it is advantageous for the project manager to assign top-level responsible parties to the risks. A key responsibility of the risk owner is to continuously monitor the status of the risks for which he or she is responsible and report on them regularly to the project manager and team.

Because the timing of when risk events can affect a project is limited, not all risks should be addressed in every status meeting. Rather, the project manager should ensure that the responsible risk owner updates the status at the appropriate time as the triggers for a risk event in the project plan approach.

Using the Risk Management Plan

There is no project that cannot benefit from the development and use of a risk management plan because all projects contain an element of uncertainty about the future. Small projects tend to rely more on qualitative assessment of risks and often choose to address only a few of the highest level risk events. Not surprisingly, most risk management planning is informal, as is periodic reassessment of the plan during the project.

Although sometimes too simplistic for large and complex projects, the risk management plan is still commonly used, being more formal and more oriented toward quantitative risk assessment and prioritization. For larger projects that focus on a greater number of the highest priority risk events, more formal periodic reassessments of the plan are also performed.

Although the use of the risk management plan should be institutionalized on a project, the development of the plan can vary widely. On smaller projects, only a few hours may be required to conduct a planning session and develop a plan. This time requirement increases proportionally as projects become larger and more complex. Dozens of hours may be required to develop a quality risk management plan for a team responsible for a large and complex project.

Benefits

The benefits of developing and using a risk management plan are many. The plan helps sift through the myriad of uncertainties and identify and highlight the project areas of highest risk, both before work begins and throughout the project. This gives the project manager the ability to proactively find effective ways to mitigate these risks, rather than being confronted with them only when they become problems.

The risk management plan provides a systematic response. By developing a framework and methodology for risk management, a project manager is able to respond calmly and systematically to risks. This reduces the need to make unplanned decisions and actions.

Projects typically involve a number of stakeholders that span a company or multiple companies. When a project manager has developed a risk management plan and adheres to it, it creates confidence among all stakeholders that their interests are adequately protected from risk. This protects the project from unwanted and unnecessary intervention by stakeholders or individuals who are not part of the project team. Appropriate risk management allows the project manager to have greater control over the project and project decisions.

Finally, a well-documented risk management plan provides a great opportunity to gain important insights for future projects. Many risks are related to the particular environment in which a company operates, as well as the general policies and practices associated with the company itself. These risks typically affect every project within an organization and can be directly addressed and dealt with in a project's risk management plan.

Issues and Risks

What is the difference between problems and risks? Without pretending to deal with the semantics of the difference, let us take a look at how they are used in industry. First of all, the terms are generally used interchangeably. For example, the Project Management Body of Knowledge (PMBOK) Guide states, "Reports commonly used to monitor and control risks include Issues

Logs..." Some project managers believe that risks and issues are different problems and therefore should be classified into different categories that require different management responses. We agree with this view.

A problem is an event that has already occurred. Its time horizon includes the past and the present. For example, the loss of a team member is a problem that has resulted in a delay of one month. In contrast, a risk can be described as what could happen to the detriment of the project. For example, "A possible loss of the project manager could result in a delayed completion of the project." Risks are in the future. So, while we strive to solve a problem, our response as managers is to prevent a risk or its effects from occurring.

Questions like "What are the causes of the deviation?" are about finding out what happened that caused the deviation from the schedule. Answers to questions such as "What new risks may occur in the future and how might they change the tentative completion date?", on the other hand, aim to identify future events that need to be addressed to reduce their impact on the project.

The Risk Identification Checklist

The first step in the risk management process is to identify all events that could affect the success of the project. Although risk identification is the first step in the risk management process, it is not a one-time event. Risk identification is an iterative process that occurs throughout the project cycle. Some project teams start by identifying risk categories, such as technology risk, market risk, business risk, and human risk, and then use brainstorming and other problem identification techniques to identify all potential risk events within each category.

The key element of this step is to try to identify all potential risks. Do not judge whether or not a risk is a real concern in this step; that is the next step in the process. If done well, risk identification can be overwhelming, especially at the beginning of a project when the number of unknowns is highest. Remember, the goal of risk identification is to eliminate as many potential risks as possible so they can be brought to the table and discussed.

The risk identification checklist is a good tool to identify the different risk categories as well as a number of general risks that occur in many projects.

Developing a Risk Identification Checklist

The risk identification checklist is unique to each organization because each organization has its own set of uncertainties associated with the business environment in which it operates, the policies and practices that guide its operations, the constraints that affect its project teams, and its ability to access and use information to inform the team about future events.

Developing a standard set of risk categories and elements is a good practice because it promotes consistency in identifying various risks that may impact project outcomes. The questions included in the checklist can be developed by first understanding the various work activities in the work breakdown structure (WBS), the constraints within which the project must operate, and the information in other guiding project artifacts such as the project business case and project charter (Chapter 3). Additional questions can then be developed by drawing on historical insights through review of risk events and issues that affected previous projects.

Using a Risk Identification Checklist

Effective risk management begins with thorough risk identification. Many claim that risk identification is the cornerstone of good project planning and execution. They base this on the notion that all projects face a variety of uncertainties that will become problems and obstacles if ignored or not managed proactively and with foresight. The ability to deal with uncertainties in advance depends on a project team's ability to predict their possible occurrence. This ability is based on the identification of risks.

The risk identification checklist should be developed in the early stages of the project, or better yet, it should be created as a standard job aid by project team members. Regardless of how it is developed, it must be implemented in the earliest phases of a project.

The checklist serves as a guide for all project stakeholders attempting to predict potential risk events. It is intended to help the project manager ensure that various risk perspectives are considered, such as risks related to project management, environmental risks, risks related to resources and collaboration, risks related to stakeholders, and, where appropriate, certain technological risks.

The checklist should be distributed to all members of the project team as well as key stakeholders tasked with identifying potential risks to the project. Best practices include ongoing use of the checklist throughout the natural project cycle as new uncertainties arise.

To become institutionalized in an organization, the risk identification checklist should be updated regularly to capture common risk events in an organization's projects. An opportune time to update the checklist is during the postmortem review process for each project. In reviewing the issues and risks that have occurred on a project, those issues and risks that have a systemic tendency to impact future projects can be added to the risk identification checklist for future use.

As mentioned earlier, good risk management is based on good risk identification: risks must be identified before they can be actively managed. The risk identification checklist adds value by helping the project team identify risk and ensuring that risk is considered from multiple perspectives. Without prompting, many project teams focus almost exclusively on project risk. The checklist helps broaden the view by asking the team to also consider areas of risk arising from the business environment, resources and collaboration, and stakeholders, to name a few.

If the risk identification checklist is updated regularly, it can also serve as a database for the organization's risk knowledge. Many risks and issues are systemic to any organization. If you document the sources of these systemic risks and issues in the checklist, each project will benefit from lessons learned from previous projects.

The Risk Register

The risk register contains a record of identified risks associated with a project and serves as a central repository for all open and closed risk events. The risk register typically contains a description of each risk event, an identifier of the risk event, the outcome of the risk assessment, a description of the planned response, and a summary of actions taken and current status. Often, risk events are prioritized in the risk register based on the outcome of the risk assessment or a qualitative analysis.

Creating a Risk Register

The risk register is probably the most important tool for managing project risks. A good register contains all the necessary information about project risks, provides a comprehensive catalog of risks, a severity determination, and describes the possible responses to risk events.

The information in the risk register can be presented in a variety of ways, including a database, a paragraph-style document, or a spreadsheet. The spreadsheet is by far the most commonly used format because it contains all of the project risk information without requiring the user to scroll through multiple pages.

There are no standard information components that must be included in a tab. We recommend that you search for different examples of a risk register and then adopt and customize the content for your specific needs. However, we recommend that you keep your register simple. The more complicated a register becomes, the more time you will have to spend managing your document, leaving less time to manage your project. The following elements should be included in a risk register.

Risk Identifier

Each risk event must have a unique identifier for cataloging and monitoring purposes. The most common approach is to assign a chronological number to each identified risk. Another approach is to assign risk events to the WBS element with which they are associated. For example, risks associated with a level 3 WBS element could have identification numbers 3.0.1.1, 3.0.1.2, 3.0.1.3, and so on.

Risk Description

The most important part of the risk register is the risk description, at least as far as the identification of risk events is concerned. We recommend using the "IF /THEN" format for your risk descriptions. This format describes not only the risk, but also the possible consequences: "IF" this will occur (risk event), "THEN" that will be the result (consequences).

Dates

For the purposes of timing, aging, and tracking risks, the risk register must include a date component. The most common and useful dates are the date the risk was identified, the risk trigger date (when the risk is likely to occur), and the closure date.

Severity

To prioritize risk events (remember that you cannot address every identified risk event), a severity component must be included in the risk register. The severity of the risk can be either quantitative (1, 2, 3) or qualitative (high, medium, low), which is an acceptable approach. Specific definitions for the numeric values or the qualitative values must be documented.

Remember to evaluate the severity of a risk from two perspectives: (1) the likelihood that a risk event will occur, and (2) the severity of the impact if it does occur. The overall severity of the risk must consider both the probability and the impact.

Response

For each risk event that a project team decides to manage, a response approach must be defined and documented in the registry for reference and tracking purposes. For low priority risks and others that the team decides not to manage, the default response is acceptance. The risk register must include a field indicating the selected response for each risk event.

Owner

Each risk event, regardless of priority, must be assigned an owner. Therefore, the risk register must contain an owner component. The risk owner is the person responsible for monitoring the risk event and taking action to address the risk, if necessary.

Status

Risk events are inherently dynamic, meaning they can change state over time. To facilitate communication, a risk register should include a risk status field. The most common risk statuses include open, monitoring trigger, response initiated, and closed.

The risk register is a very flexible tool because, as mentioned earlier, it can be built from any number of components. Take the time at the beginning of a project to design the format and components of the risk register to support the risk management methodology described in the risk management plan.

Using the Risk Register

As the central tool for risk management in a project, the risk register has many valuable functions. First, the register serves as a central repository for all risk events. Because it catalogs all project risks, it must be deployed at the earliest stages of a project and used throughout the project lifecycle. Identifying new risks and updating the risk register should be part of an ongoing risk management process.

Since all risk events for a project are included in the register, there is an opportunity to use the tool to prioritize risk events. Since most projects contain more risks than a project has resources to manage, trade-off decisions must be made about which risk events to manage and which to either accept or simply monitor. The risk register provides the necessary data and structure to show the priority of risk events. Typically, one focuses on the three to ten most important risks at a given point in time.

The risk register also promotes risk-related communication with project stakeholders. This can be done either by using the registry itself as a communication tool or by using selected information within the registry as the basis for other project communication tools. In its entirety, the risk register can be used to communicate the entire risk profile for a project. However, this is not our recommended approach, as too much risk information can cause project stakeholders to become anxious. Rather, we recommend selecting information on the key risk events that are active during a given reporting period and including that information in the risk register and the current summary status report.

Because most risk events have consequences, the risk register is also an effective tool to assist project managers in developing budget and schedule risk reserves and incorporating these reserves into the project plan. By effectively using the IF /THEN approach to describing risk events, the assessment of potential exposure to the highest priority risks provides a minimum, most likely, and maximum range of exposure for the project.

Finally, the risk register is used to regularly monitor the status of identified risk events. Project team members must balance many tasks at any given time. Therefore, they need an ongoing process and tool to remind them of their risk management duties. By effectively using dates within the register, the project manager can track the overall risk trend of a project Risk trend charts show the overall risk profil of the project over time. If risk is effectively managed, the severity of project risk should decrease over time, as shown in the figure. If it does not, additional resources may be needed to address specific risk events or an assessment should be considered regarding project termination.

Benefits

The benefits of using the risk register are significant. The register provides the project manager and the organization as a whole with a central repository of knowledge about risks. The knowledge of project uncertainties contained in the risk register can be used not only to manage the risk of a specific project, but also to mitigate systemic risks that affect many projects within an organization.

The register is also useful to project managers as it assists them in resource allocation. Since it is generally not possible to manage all risk events, the prioritization information contained in the register provides valuable insight into where resources should be allocated to prevent the greatest risks to projects.

By using the risk register to estimate the risk reserve, the tool adds value by helping to create more realistic project plans.

However, the greatest benefit is that the risk register helps project managers protect their project and business goals from being compromised by the myriad of uncertainties that surround a project.

The Risk Assessment Matrix

Once you have identified the risks that could impact the project outcome, you need to determine which risks you will spend the project budget, time, and resources to address, because not all risk events require action. The risk assessment step is necessary to sift through all the identified risk events and determine those that pose the greatest threat to the success of the project. The result is a prioritized "short" list of project risks that the team can then manage.

Scenario analysis is one of the most common methods for evaluating risk events. Scenario analysis analyzes each risk event in terms of the outcome of a risk event occurring, the severity of the impact of the outcome, the probability of a risk event occurring, and the understanding of when the risk event might occur.

We recommend that a project team begin with a qualitative approach to risk assessment, at least for the first iteration of the analysis. By this we mean assessing whether the severity of impact and likelihood of occurrence for each of the identified risks is high, medium, or low. This rough analysis will do two important things. First, it quickly prioritizes the risks so that the highest risk can be identified for immediate action. Second, it gives the project manager and team an overview of the overall risk to the project. The risk assessment matrix is an excellent tool for this type of risk assessment.

If additional analysis is required, more quantitative risk assessment methods can be used in the next iteration. For the more sophisticated project, we recommend the Monte Carlo analysis technique for quantitative analysis.

Developing a Risk Assessment Matrix

Good project management decision making includes a comprehensive understanding of the data that represents the status of the project at the time the decision is made. Better project management decision making also includes understanding the critical uncertainties or risks that may affect the outcome of the decision. However, attempting to include all project risks in a decision is an impossible undertaking. Rather, a project manager must have a way to distinguish the critical risks from the non-critical risks. The risk assessment matrix focuses on the severity of the risk, providing a way to differentiate.

The first step in this process is to design a risk assessment matrix that meets the needs of the project manager.

Design the Matrix Format

Risk assessment matrices come in a variety of formats that project managers can search for and use for their purposes. The format shown in Figure 14.3 is, by and large, the most common.

The matrix is simply a 5 × 5 (sometimes 4 × 4) matrix, with risk probability on one axis (in this case, the vertical axis) and risk impact on the other axis.

For each of the cells representing the probability of a risk event occurring, the probability levels (or scale) must be represented. Similarly, the impact that a risk event may have on one or more of the project objectives must be presented in each of the risk impact cells.

When you create the matrix, the cells that intersect the different probability and impact levels are left blank.

Define the Rating Scales

The next step is to define the scales for which risk probability and risk impact are to be assessed. Remember that risk assessment at this stage is qualitative, not quantitative, even though numerical values are used to represent qualitative scales. For this reason, assessment scales must be simple and unambiguous to provide a consistent qualitative assessment for all risk events. For example, try using a five-point scale for probability of occurrence: Almost Certain (NC), Very Likely (HL), Likely (L), Low Probability (LL), and Very Unlikely (VU). However, these qualitative values are not sufficient. A description of the individual values must be determined by the project team.

In the same way, a discrete scale for the impact of the project risk must be defined. This scale must be based on specific details of the project. Based on the highest priority goal, e.g., the project completion date, develop the risk impact scale relative to that goal.

The final scale to define is the risk severity scale. This is usually achieved by using a formula and calculation that incorporates the risk probability and risk impact values. Although nonlinear formulas can also be used, linear formulas such as severity = [probability + (N × impact)] are easier to use. For example, N may be equal to two, meaning that the impact is twice as important as the probability in determining the severity of the risk. In this case, the assessed probability and impact for each risk would be substituted into the formula Severity = [Probability + (2 × Impact)] and the value obtained would be entered into the probability-impact matrix (P-I).

Populate the Risk Assessment Matrix

Using the risk severity formula developed in the previous step, calculate the values for each cell in the matrix. Next, divide the matrix into three severity levels-high, medium, low-based on the organization's threshold for risk severity. The higher the value in a cell of the matrix, the higher the rank and severity of potential impact to the project. For example, a risk with a severity score of 15 is more critical than a risk with a score of 8 and should therefore be prioritized higher.

The severity levels depend on how the severity is calculated and how the project manager divides the numeric values in the matrix.

Now that the risk assessment matrix has been developed and populated with data, it is ready to be used in a project.

Using the Risk Assessment Matrix

The biggest challenge in conducting a qualitative risk assessment is to design the assessment scales appropriately. However, once this is accomplished, the assessment can be used for the life of the project to effectively manage project risk.

When risk identification is done appropriately, a large number of risks are often identified, depending on the nature of the project. The challenge for the project manager is to identify those that will both have the greatest impact on the project and are most likely to occur. This is where the risk assessment matrix is of great use.

Because resources are limited, the project manager must use the matrix to determine which risk events most justify the use of project resources. Some larger projects typically focus on the 10 highest ranked risks. In contrast, some smaller projects decide to manage the top three risks, citing a lack of resources to manage a larger number of risks. Both approaches can be ad hoc. So what is a reasonable approach? The answer lies in the matrix. Respond to the risks ranked highest in the matrix, up to an agreed level. 24 For example, focus on addressing risks up to a risk value of and treat other risks as non-critical. With this approach, you will neither waste resources nor disregard important risks. It should be noted that non-critical does not mean important. Rather, it means that scarce project resources are not needed immediately to address the risk event, but may be needed in the future.

Having appropriately prioritized project risks and selected risk events for action, the project team can now develop strategies and actions to address the risks. Consult the risk management plan to determine which approach to risk management is preferable given the stage of the project and the current project situation. Remember that the project manager's ability to take action to mitigate or avoid a risk event may be limited by where a project is in relation to the project cycle. In particular, as a project nears the end of project execution, it may be too late to effectively mitigate or avoid an emerging risk. In this case, the only response option may be to accept the risk or cancel the project.

Variations

The result of risk analysis is an abbreviated list of critical risk events that can be actively monitored, managed, and communicated to stakeholders. A variant of the risk assessment matrix, called a risk map, is somewhat more effective for monitoring and communicating risks.

The map displays the most critical risks from the two dimensions of probability of occurrence and risk impact. The scales shown on the x and y axes are the scales used to score each risk event. We show numbered scales, but others may prefer to choose more qualitative values such as high, medium, and low.

Typically, a threshold line is drawn to visually delineate the critical risk events from the lower severity events. The line is established based on the description of scale levels discussed earlier. It is important to include risk events that are below but close to the threshold, as these are the risks that are most likely to transition to a critical state.

The final piece of information that can be included in a risk map is the change in probability of occurrence or impact. We recommend that project managers include this information because it reinforces the behavior of ongoing risk monitoring and analysis.

Benefits

The risk assessment matrix helps sift through the myriad of uncertainties to identify and highlight the highest-risk project areas - both before work begins and throughout the life of the project. This provides an opportunity to focus project resources and find effective ways to proactively mitigate risks, rather than confronting them only when they become issues later in the project.

In addition, the matrix provides information for sound contingency planning and effective decision making on the project. It is impossible to predict all possible risk events. Therefore, one of the best practices of organizations is to plan for a timeframe and budget based on a risk analysis. The level of contingencies can be derived from the risk impact information in the risk assessment matrix.

Much of the utility of the tool comes from its visual representation of the extent of risk and its simple design, making it more than suitable for situations where a detailed quantitative risk assessment is not required. This is especially the case in the early stages of the project cycle.

Finally, the risk assessment matrix is useful for increasing the visibility and awareness of top managers within an organization of a project's critical risks. In this way, informed decisions can be made regarding risk in the right context.

With the risk register and risk assessment matrix in a project manager's toolbox, he or she has the means to identify, document, assess, prioritize, and monitor any future event that could prevent a project team from fully achieving project objectives. However, none of these activities meet the true intent of risk management. The real purpose of project risk management is to use the information gained to proactively make adjustments to the project plan to account for the uncertainties that surround any project and to make better risk-based decisions.

The Risk Dashboard

Due to the dynamic nature of project risks, risk monitoring must continue throughout the life of a project. New risks will be identified, many expected risks will disappear, some risks will be mitigated, and some will change in severity due to a change in probability of occurrence or a change in potential impact on a project.

Regularly scheduled risk reviews enforce consistent risk monitoring and enable repeated risk identification, assessment, analysis, and response planning as a project moves through its life cycle. To facilitate risk reviews, a number of tools are required to help project managers navigate the monitoring process in an efficient manner. Efficiency lies in the ability to keep discussions at a high enough level that the team does not get bogged down in risk details. The best tools are the risk identification matrix, the risk assessment matrix, the risk map (all covered in the previous sections), and the risk dashboard.

Developing the Risk Dashboard

The Risk Dashboard is a business intelligence tool that provides key risk statistics about a project. The dashboard helps the project manager and his top management to assess the state of a project as well as potential issues the project is facing.

The risk dashboard needs to be carefully designed. Since it is a project and business intelligence tool, you need to make sure that the most important information is collected, that it is presented effectively, and that it can be interpreted easily and correctly. All effective dashboards start with selecting the right metrics.

Choosing Risk Metrics

An organization, such as a program or project management, needs to develop a risk metrics system to effectively measure and monitor the risk status of each of its projects. However, this is not an easy task.

If selected and used well, risk metrics can improve project and organizational performance over time. However, if poorly managed, they can be counterproductive by reinforcing the wrong behaviors. To avoid this, take time to develop your risk management philosophy before selecting your metrics. This involves what information needs to be tracked and why, what decisions depend on the information, and what behaviors you want to reinforce and which ones you want to change.

The philosophy developed leads to understanding what metrics are needed for a risk dashboard. Just as every company is unique, so are the risk metrics they want to display.

The risk status provides an overview of the total number of open and closed risk events over the life of the project to date. The risks identified per month provide an indication of the level of uncertainty faced by the project team over time. The maximum possible risk shows the potential impact on the project and the business based on the current identified risk events. The status of the risk reserve provides information on how much risk reserve has already been used and what is still available to the project manager.

Outline the Dashboard Layout

Now that the metrics to be displayed in the risk dashboard have been determined, you know what information to display in the dashboard. Now you need to determine how you want to display this information.To do this, take a few minutes to sketch out the structure of the dashboard. This does not have to be a wordy sketch. The point is to logically structure the information and determine how it will be presented.

We chose to present summary and trending information about project risk events on the left side of the dashboard. Summary information about the impact of the risk events is presented on the right side of the dashboard. We chose this layout to show cause and effect on the risk dashboard from left to right. The goal is to design the dashboard so that it is comprehensive in content, appealing to the eye of the recipient, and meaningful in its presentation of the information and messages it conveys.

Create the Dashboard Graphics

The purpose of a dashboard is to present a large amount of important information about a project in a very clear way so that decisions can be made. The risk dashboard should therefore be simple and quick to interpret, with only a few key indicators, much like the dashboard in a car. The best way to achieve this is to display the data graphically.

Once you have selected the key metrics and measures, you need to consider how these metrics should be represented graphically. Trend information is best represented in a line graph, while comparing information (such as the number of active, inactive, or closed risks) is best represented in bar or pie charts.

We recommend using common chart styles and keeping them simple. Remember that the main user of the risk dashboard will be your top management team. You will want to spend your time talking to them about the risk status of your project, not helping them interpret your charts.

Populate the Dashboard

This final step in dashboard development is to collect, summarize, and graphically display current risk information about your project. While all of the previous steps are typically done once at the beginning of a project, this step is done continuously throughout the life of the project.

It is generally accepted that the best risk management practice is one that is performed continuously, or at least regularly, due to the dynamic nature of project risk.

Managing Project Risk

Keeping the information in the risk dashboard up to date is a great feature to ensure that risk is actively monitored and managed.

Using the Risk Dashboard

The risk dashboard is a tool that provides effective project and business information. Its main application is to monitor the state of a project, communicate the current risk status and trends, and support various risk-based decisions.

How well a project team manages the uncertainties associated with a project is generally referred to as project health. A healthy project is one that is on track to achieve its goals and business objectives. This means that the project is actively protected from the potential negative impact of risks created by uncertainties. The risk dashboard is the best indicator of a project's health. It supports effective risk monitoring by collecting important information about risk status and presenting it in a way that conveys the health of the project.

Because the dashboard contains important information about the health of the project, it is also an important communication tool. All project stakeholders have a vested interest in the outcome of a project for a variety of reasons, so they also have a vested interest in knowing the health of the project. The risk dashboard provides project stakeholders with risk status and trend information in summary form. When properly designed, project stakeholders can determine the state of a project within minutes.

The risk dashboard is also a good tool for decision making. Good project decisions are those that are made based on information about the current status of a project. Better decisions are those that also include information about a project's current and future risks. The dashboard contains the important information needed to support key risk-based decisions.

During project planning, the risk dashboard can be used to determine the amount of risk reserve for a project. The risk reserve is the amount of time and resources needed beyond the estimate to mitigate the risk of overruns. Risk events will occur and not all risk events can be predicted. In addition, not all identified risks can be avoided or mitigated. Therefore, a risk reserve is a necessary aspect of any project plan.

As a project moves through its lifecycle, the dashboard is used to determine when a risk reserve is needed to complete an aspect of the project (e.g., completion of a milestone) and to track the amount of reserve remaining.

Benefits

All projects (small or large, simple or complex) will benefit from using the risk dashboard. A dashboard is an effective project delivery tool that focuses on the health of the project. As such, it provides the basis for risk-based project decisions to be made by both the project manager and the organization's top managers. The risk dashboard also adds value by serving as a predictive and forward-looking project and business intelligence tool. This is especially true when the dashboard includes information on potential risk exposure, risk severity trend, and risk reserve consumption.

Finally, the risk dashboard facilitates ongoing risk monitoring and management. Unfortunately, it is an all-too-common practice that project risk management begins and ends with the identification and assessment of risks. The real value comes from the ongoing monitoring and management of risks as new uncertainties arise during the course of a project.

Review Questions, Answers and Explanations (online)

Procurement
Management

PROCUREMENT MANAGEMENT IS THE set of processes that are used to obtain goods, services, or scope from outside the organization.

Even though it is relatively small, procurement management can be a challenging knowledge area on the exam. One reason it can be so difficult is that few project managers have formal procurement training in their backgrounds, and even if they do, it may differ in key ways from what is presented here.

PHILOSOPHY:

This procurement management approach is steeped in formal government procurement practices.

The over arching philosophy of procurement management is that it should be formal. Many people's practical experience may differ from this rigid approach, but it is necessary to understand it and to be able to apply this philosophy on the exam.

IMPORTANCE:

Several questions on the exam will be drawn from the material in this chapter. If formal procurement is new to you, this will be especially important. You will also need to master the concept and formula for Point of Total Assumption (PTA).

PREPARATION:

As mentioned earlier, it would be wise to take special care in this section if you do not have a background in formal procurement activities.

Keep in mind as you approach this material that it was not written to be memorized. It was written to be practiced and applied. For this chapter in particular, understanding is more important than memorizing.

This also applies to key terms, concepts, the processes, and their components.

If formal procurement is a new concept, you would do well to read this chapter carefully and then skim <u>Chapter, Project Procurement Management</u>, in the 6th Edition *PMBOK*® *Guide*.

Procurement Management Processes

There are three processes in procurement management. These processes are displayed in the figure at the beginning of the chapter and summarized in the following tables.

Process Group	Plan Procurement Management
Initiating	(none)
Planning	Plan Procurements Management
Executing	Conduct Procurements
Monitoring & Controlling	Control Procurements
Closing	(none)
Process	**Primary Outputs**
Plan Procurements Management	Procure. Mgt. Plan, Independent Cost Estimates, Make or Buy Decisions, Procure. Strateg, Bid Documents, Procure. S.O.W., Source Selection Criteria
Conduct Procurements	Selected Sellers, Agreements
Control Procurements	Closed Procurements, Work Performance Info

Procurement Roles

In procurement management, there are two primary roles defined, and the project manager could play either of these roles. In fact, it is not uncommon for project managers to play both roles on the same project. The roles are:

Buyer - The organization or party purchasing (procuring) the goods or services from the seller.

Seller - The organization or party providing or delivering the goods or services to the buyer.

Contract Types

When procuring goods or services, the type of contract that governs the deal can make a significant difference in who bears the risk. There are four categories of contracts you must know for the exam. They are listed below with information on each one:

Type of Contract	Who Bears the Risk	Explanation
Fixed Price	Seller	Since the price is fixed, cost overruns may not be passed on to the buyer and must be borne by the seller.
Cost Plus Fixed Fee	Buyer	Since all costs must be reimbursed to the seller, the buyer bears the risk of cost overruns.
Cost Plus Incentive Fee	Buyer and Seller	The buyer bears most of the risk here, but the incentive fee for the seller motivates that seller to keep costs down.
Time and Materials	Buyer	The buyer pays the seller for all time and materials the seller applies to the project. The buyer bears the most risk of cost overruns.

Fixed Price Contracts (AKA Lump Sum Contracts) - Fixed price contracts are the easiest ones to understand. There is generally a single fee, although payment terms may be specified so that the cost is not necessarily a lump sum, payable at the end.

This type of contract is very popular when the scope of work is thoroughly defined and completely known. Three types of fixed price contracts are:

Firm Fixed Price (FFP) - The price is fixed, with no provision for cost or performance overruns. The risk is entirely shifted to the seller.

Fixed Price Incentive Fee (FPIF) - The price is fixed, with an incentive fee for meeting a target specified in the contract (such as finishing the work ahead of schedule). With FPIF contracts, both parties agree to a price ceiling, and all costs above the price ceiling must be covered by the seller.

Fixed Price Economic Price Adjustment (FP-EPA) - This type of contract is popular in cases where fluctuations in the exchange rate or interest rate may impact the project. In this case, an economic stipulation may be included to protect the seller or the buyer. The economic stipulation may be based on the interest rate, the consumer price index, cost of living adjustments, currency exchange rates, or other indices.

Cost Reimbursable Contracts

Another type of contract is cost reimbursable where the buyer agrees to pay the seller for actual costs plus a fee that is actually the seller's profit. There are three common varieties of this type of agreement:

Cost Plus Fixed Fee (CPFF) - The seller passes the cost back to the buyer and receives an additional fixed fee upon completion of the project. The fee is calculated as a percentage of the planned costs.

Cost Plus Incentive Fee (CPIF) - The seller passes the cost back to the buyer and gets an incentive fee for meeting a target (usually tied back to keeping costs low) specified in the contract.

Cost Plus Award Fee (CPAF) - The seller passes the costs back to the buyer, but the seller's profit (award fee) comes from a decision on whether or not to grant it, made subjectively by the buyer based on the seller's performance. The decision may not be appealed by the seller.

Time and Materials Contracts

In a time and materials contract, the seller charges for time plus the cost of any materials needed to complete the work.

Point of Total Assumption

Because there are numerous types of contracts where the risk is shared to one degree or another, it is important to be able to calculate how risk is allocated between the buyer and seller. One consideration, particularly when using Fixed Price Incentive Fee contracts, is the Point of Total Assumption.

The Point of Total Assumption (PTA) is the cost point in the contract where a subcontractor assumes responsibility for all additional costs. This concept can be challenging to understand at first, so to help with this, consider the following situation. Company ABC is subcontracting out the installation of industrial shelving to company XYZ for an estimated $75,000. The selected contract is Fixed Price Incentive Fee, so ABC pushes for a cap (called a price ceiling) to protect them from serious cost overruns. The terms of the contract are that XYZ's target cost is $71,000, the target price to ABC is $75,000 and XYZ's ceiling price to ABC is $84,000; however, for every dollar over the target cost, the share ratio is 3:1. This means that ABC (the buyer) will pay $0.75, while XYZ (the seller) will have to pay $0.25 of every dollar overrun. Knowing this information, it is fairly simple to calculate the PTA.

The formula is: Target cost + (ceiling price – target price) ÷ ABC's % share of cost overrun.

In this case, it would be $71,000 + ($84,000 - $75,000) ÷ .75, which simplifies to $71,000 + $12,000 = $83,000.

In other words, at the point the cost reaches $83,000, the subcontractor (XYZ) would assume the total burden of cost overrun. The ceiling price is still $84,000, but XYZ is bearing 100% of the cost overrun burden above $83,000 in cost (the PTA). The PTA is important, because it helps identify the cost point in the contract where the seller has the most motivation to bring things to completion.

PLAN PROCUREMENT MANAGEMENT

WHAT IT IS:

This process involves looking at the project and determining which components or services of the project will be made or performed internally and which will be "procured" from an external source. After that decision is made, the project manager must determine a strategy for conducting procurements and the appropriate type of contracts to be used on the project.

WHY IT IS IMPORTANT:

This process has a lot of important outputs, and your understanding of them will help you on the exam. Currently, best practices in the field of project management favor buying externally vs. building internally, all other things being equal; however, there are numerous factors that should go into your decision on whether to "make or buy."

Carefully planning what to procure and how to go about the processes of procurement will ensure that the right things are procured in the right way.

WHEN IT IS PERFORMED:

Because a project may have multiple subcontractors, potentially in every phase of the project, any of the procurement processes could be performed repeatedly and at any time throughout the project.

HOW IT WORKS / INPUTS:

Business Documents - The business case and the benefits management plan are key documents that will help the project team plan procurements. Each may influence why project components are being created and how and when the project expects to deliver benefits.

Project Management Plan - The project management plan describes what will be done and how it will be accomplished. This information will be useful to review when considering what components of the scope should be procured (i.e., performed by groups outside of the organization).

Project Documents

Requirements Documentation - Requirements are a key part of the project plan and may carry legal or contractual obligations that need to be considered in procurement.

Enterprise Environmental Factors - There may be factors at work in an organization that have a strong influence on procurement. For instance, an organization may have a strong culture of building internally rather than buying, or they could have a strong culture of buying from a few trusted sellers. All of this should be factored in when making procurement decisions.

HOW IT WORKS / TOOLS:

Data Analysis - Make-or-buy analysis is hard to explain. The study considers risk, cost, disclosing private knowledge, and other considerations that may influence the choice to make or acquire.

This tool requires decision-makers to look beyond the project. If the performing organization wants to learn how to produce that sort of software, the project may benefit from making rather than buying a software component.

Source Selection Analysis - This tool chooses your vendor. Try these:

When quality is not an issue, lowest cost may work. If your project requires an ISO-compliant component, then anything that meets this standard should work.

Qualifications Only - When a product or service is small enough to not need a complex procurement procedure, the buyer may utilize "qualifications only" as the only criteria. In this situation, the buyer shortlists suppliers based on experience, references, etc.

Quality-Based (Technical Score): Most procurements are value-based (quality and cost). If financial terms can be reached, the highest-rated vendor is chosen.

Quality and Cost-Based - Like the previous one, but quality and cost are rated and weighed in the choice.

Sole Source - This uncommon proposal requests just one vendor. That vendor negotiates with the buyer. This environment lacks competition, which reduces the benefits of purchase.

Fixed Budget: The buyer tells the vendor the budget, and they negotiate scope, quality, and timeline. Scope modifications would make this procurement ineffective.

HOW IT WORKS / OUTPUTS:

Procurement Management Plan - Plan Procurement Management produces an essential procurement management plan. It governs all procurement management procedures. This involves determining what will be acquired on the project, how a seller will be chosen, what contracts will be utilized, how risk will be handled, and how sellers will be managed, including how their performance will be monitored.

Procurement Strategy - The procurement strategy defines how the procurements will be organized, how the contracts will be structured, and which procurement phases will be carried out.

Bid Documents - Many organizations have different procurement papers. Do not bother about IFBs and RFPs (RFP). Know that buyers write bid papers and provide them to potential sellers for the test (s). They explain the job.

Procurement Statement of Work - The test requires this document, which many find puzzling. The project scope has been specified, as seen in the project scope statement from the Define Scope step. Define Scope is not a procurement statement of work. Instead, a procurement statement of work details a component of the scope so prospective sellers may determine whether they wish to (or are competent to) pursue the task. Expect test questions on the preceding sentence. The procurement statement of work should also emphasize the result rather than the process to empower sellers to be innovative.

Source Selection Criteria - This output requires source selection criteria before seller selection. This keeps procurement impartial. You may pick the lowest-priced qualified bidder (in which case the qualifications must be stated) or the bidder with the greatest technical competence or lowest risk. Specify criteria before other purchase operations. These source selection criteria may or may not be disclosed with potential sellers.

Make-or-Buy Decisions - The project team did make-or-buy analysis throughout data analysis, and now it is time to act. Decisions and supporting evidence should be recorded.

Independent Cost Estimates - This procurement sanity check ensures expenses are correct. External or internal firms may assess costs.

CONDUCT PROCUREMENTS

WHAT IT IS:

This book's procedures mostly work as advertised. Conduct Procurements accomplishes that. It executes the procurement management strategy, chooses a vendor, and awards the contract.

WHY IT IS IMPORTANT:

This execution starts procurement. You have chosen and prepared the procurement management strategy. Issue the bid package to prospective sellers, convene bidder conferences, review offers, and choose a seller. However, real life is not so easy, and this might be a difficult test topic.

WHEN IT IS PERFORMED:

When you are ready to buy, you do this. After Plan Procurement Management.

Conduct Procurements occurs as required. If there are many contracts, it may be done several times, or not at all if the project is not purchasing anything.

HOW IT WORKS / INPUTS:

Seller Proposals - Prospective sellers submit proposals for the task, including how they will meet the bid request, technical details, price, and conditions. To assess bids on technical quality and price, the price should be separated from the other components.

HOW IT WORKS / TOOLS:

Advertising - Advertise the bid to increase seller replies. Trade magazines, internet sources, and even newspapers may help you acquire more and better bids by reaching a big and focused audience. Advertising may be mandated by law.

Bidder conferences enlighten prospective sellers and level the playing field. The project manager must not hold secret meetings or exclude suppliers.

Seller proposal assessments are a typical data analysis method here. Compare them to the seller assessment matrix and proposal description of work.

Interpersonal and Team Skills - This technique emphasizes negotiating. The project manager negotiates with customers, sellers, teams, and organizations. Organizations and people may negotiate. Negotiating seeks a durable win-win solution.

HOW IT WORKS / OUTPUTS:

Selected Sellers - The RFP was created, the sellers responded with bids, talks took place, and now a seller has been chosen to supply products or services on the project.

Agreements - The agreements that emerge from this process, generally in the form of a contract, are official papers that control the buyer-seller relationship. In general, consider "contract" when you encounter the term "agreement" on the test.

Contracts are legal contracts that use highly specialized and technical terminology and should only be drafted and altered by experts in that industry (e.g., the contracting officer, procurement office, legal counsel). The project manager should not draft, negotiate, or amend the contract on his or her own.

The contract specifies the work to be done and, maybe, how that work will be done (e.g., location, work conditions). It may state who will do the task, when and how the seller will be paid, and the delivery conditions.

In truth, as long as the terms and conditions are lawful and mutually agreed upon both buyer and seller, there is very little that the contract cannot state in some form. Several additional legal elements, depending on the jurisdiction that regulates the contract, legal consideration, and other technical legal problems that are outside the scope of this essay, may come into play.

How disputes (also known as claims) will be settled is a crucial component to mention in the contract. This comprises the conflict settlement procedure, the parties involved, and the location of the dispute resolution.

CONTROL PROCUREMENTS

WHAT IT IS:

Control Procurements, in a nutshell, is the monitoring and controlling process in which the buyer and seller analyze the contract and work outcomes to verify that the results fit the contract. This usually involves a check to see whether the products or services are being delivered.

Are the products or services arriving on time?

Are the correct amounts invoiced or paid?

Are the contract's extra terms being met?

Is the buyer/seller connection being handled and maintained properly?

Control Procurements is a process that is carried out by both the buyer and the seller, and because of the repercussions of any problems here, project managers from both the buyer and seller should utilize whatever resources are required to investigate the possible effects of any choices.

WHY IT IS IMPORTANT:

From a project management standpoint, the contract may be considered as a strategy (albeit a very specialized and binding type of plan). The Control Procurements process guarantees that the project's outcomes match the plan and that all contract requirements are satisfied.

WHEN IT IS PERFORMED:

Control Procurements, like the other procurement management activities, may be carried out at any time throughout the project when products or services are required. It is normally conducted at set intervals for a certain contract, although it may also be performed as requested or required.

HOW IT WORKS / INPUTS:

Agreements - The previous process's agreements (remember to imagine "contracts" when you encounter this term) are brought in here. The agreements represent the purpose and will be contrasted to the outcomes.

Procurement Documentation - This entry contains everything you will need for procurements. It is not necessary to remember the list, but anything that may be beneficial here will be included.

Approved Change Requests are generated as a result of the Perform Integrated Change Control procedure. They must be included in this process since changes to the project's scope, price, schedule, or other factors may have an influence on procurements.

HOW IT WORKS / TOOLS:

Claims Administration Claims are essentially disputes. They might be concerning the scope of the contract, the effect of a modification, or the interpretation of a specific clause. The contract defines the basic (legally binding) aspects of the claims administration procedure, although there may be other components in the procurement management plan.

The most essential aspect of claims administration is to recognize that conflicts must be handled and eventually resolved, and that the mechanism for doing so should be outlined ahead of time.

Contracts are fulfilled when all of the contract's terms, conditions, and claims have been met. This should be objective, and everyone should agree on it; nevertheless, this is not always the case. Mediation or arbitration may be required in certain cases. Both are types of Alternative Dispute Resolution (ADR). Litigation is another alternative, but it is the least ideal way to get a resolution and should only be used as a last resort after all other kinds of ADR have been explored.

Data analysis is done by the buyer to ensure that the seller is performing in accordance with the agreement. To assess how things are going, use methods like performance evaluations, earned value analysis (EVA), and trend analysis.

Inspection focuses on the product itself and its adherence to requirements. Inspections are not intended to assess the seller's performance (i.e., how quickly or cost-effectively they are delivering the results). Instead, the buyer may utilize them to assist the seller in identifying issues with the manner they are providing job outcomes.

Audits - Unlike the preceding instrument of inspection, audits concentrate on the purchase process.

HOW IT WORKS / OUTPUTS:

Closed Procurements - The fundamental outcomes of Control Procurements are closed contracts. The buyer's contract administrator notifies the seller in writing that the contract is finalized.

Work Performance Information (WPI) is the actionable data about the seller's performance that emerges from this procedure.

Updates to Procurement Documentation - As change requests are considered, data is analyzed, inspections are performed, and audits are performed, procurement documentation will most likely be updated.

THE AGILE PERSPECTIVE ON PROCUREMENT MANAGEMENT

Vendor connections are seen as possibilities for cooperation in agile initiatives. In fact, some vendors may end up joining the team. Agile, in general, prioritizes cooperation above negotiations.

Because procurement in certain businesses may be quite formal, agile or adaptive approaches can undertake procurement tasks in a highly flexible manner without modifying the procurement process.

Procurement Management Plan

On an agile project, this process would entail understanding the structure of the organization's procurement rules and mapping out how they would be executed. There is no defined method since agile values innovative, adaptable solutions.

Procurement Procedures

This executing procedure on a predictive project would strive to analyze bids, pick a seller, and issue a contract. On an agile project, the team may choose a seller and, if beneficial and doable, add them to the team.Procurement Control

Agile projects executed under contract, whether with a customer or a seller (vendor), will assess performance on a regular basis to verify that both parties are achieving their contractual responsibilities and taking remedial action as required. Contracts are often needed by businesses and customers, therefore this procedure does come into play on agile projects from time to time.

Stakeholder
Management

PROJECT STAKEHOLDER MANAGEMENT INCLUDES the processes required to identify the individuals, groups, or organizations that may impact or be impacted by the project, analyze stakeholder expectations and their impact on the project, and develop appropriate management strategies to effectively engage stakeholders in project decision-making and execution. Stakeholder management also focuses on ongoing communication with stakeholders to understand their needs and expectations, address issues as they arise, manage conflicts of interest, and promote appropriate stakeholder participation in project decisions and activities. Stakeholder satisfaction should be among the most important project goals.

Identify Stakeholders - The process of identifying the individuals, groups, or organizations that may affect or be affected by a project decision, activity, or outcome, and analyzing and documenting relevant information about their interests, involvement, interdependencies, influence, and potential impact on project success.

Plan Stakeholder Management - The process of developing appropriate management strategies to effectively engage stakeholders throughout the project life cycle, based on analysis of their needs, interests, and potential impact on project success.

Manage Stakeholder Engagement - The process of communicating and collaborating with stakeholders to meet their needs/expectations, address issues that arise, and promote appropriate stakeholder participation in project activities throughout the project life cycle.

Control Stakeholder Engagement - The process of monitoring the project's overall stakeholder relationships and adapting stakeholder engagement strategies and plans.

In any project, there are stakeholders who are affected by the project or can affect it in a positive or negative way. While some stakeholders have limited ability to influence the project, others can have a significant impact on the project and its expected outcomes. The project manager's ability to properly identify and appropriately manage these stakeholders can make the difference between success and failure.

Identify Stakeholders

Stakeholder identification is about identifying the people, groups, or organizations that may influence or be affected by a decision, activity, or project outcome and analyzing and documenting relevant information about their interests, involvement, interdependencies, influence, and potential impact on project success. The main advantage of this process is that it allows the project manager to determine the appropriate focus for each stakeholder or group of stakeholders.

Project stakeholders are individuals, groups, or organizations that are affected or feel affected by a decision, activity, or outcome of a project. They include individuals and organizations such as customers, sponsors, the implementing organization, and the public who are actively involved in the project or whose interests may be positively or negatively affected by the implementation or completion of the project. They may also exert influence on the project and its outcomes. Stakeholders may be located at different levels within the organization and have different levels of authority, or they may work for the project outside the implementing organization.

It is critical to project success to identify stakeholders at the beginning of the project or project phase and analyze their interest, individual expectations, and importance and influence. This initial assessment should be reviewed and updated regularly. In most projects, there are a variety of stakeholders depending on the size, type, and complexity of the project. Since the project manager's time is limited and should be used as efficiently as possible, these stakeholders should be classified according to their interest, influence, and involvement in the project, keeping in mind that a stakeholder's impact or influence may not occur or become apparent until later stages of the project or project phase. This allows the project manager to focus on the relationships that are necessary for the success of the project.

Identify Stakeholders: Inputs

Project charter

The project charter may include information about internal and external parties related to and affected by the outcome or implementation of the project, such as project sponsor(s), customers, team members, groups and departments involved in the project, and other individuals or organizations affected by the project.

Procurement documents

When a project is the result of a procurement action or is based on an existing contract, the parties to that contract are the key project stakeholders. Other relevant parties, such as suppliers, should also be considered as part of the list of project stakeholders.

Enterprise Environmental Factors

Factors in the business environment that may influence the stakeholder identification process include:

• Organizational culture and structure

• Governmental or industry standards (e.g., regulations, product standards)

• Global, regional or local trends, and practices or habits

Organizational Process Assets

The organizational process assets that can influence the Identify Stakeholders process include, but are not limited to:

• Stakeholders register templates,

• Lessons learned from previous projects or phases, and

• Stakeholder registers from previous projects.

Identify Stakeholders: tools and techniques

Stakeholder Analysis

Stakeholder analysis is a technique for systematically collecting and analyzing quantitative and qualitative information to determine whose interests should be considered during the project. It identifies stakeholder interests, expectations, and influence and relates them to the purpose of the project. It also helps identify stakeholder relationships (to the project and to other stakeholders) that can be leveraged to build coalitions and potential partnerships to increase the project's chances of success, as well as stakeholder relationships that need to be influenced differently at different stages of the project or phase.

Stakeholder analysis generally follows the steps described below:

- Identify all potential project stakeholders and relevant information, such as their roles, departments, interests, knowledge, expectations, and influence. Key stakeholders are usually easy to identify. These include anyone with a decision-making or management role who will be affected by the project outcomes, such as the sponsor, project manager, and key customer. Additional stakeholders are usually identified by interviewing the identified stakeholders and expanding the list until all potential stakeholders are included.

- Analyze the potential influence or support each stakeholder could generate and classify them to define an approach strategy. For large stakeholder communities, it is important to prioritize stakeholders to ensure efficient use of efforts to communicate and manage their expectations.

- Assess how key stakeholders are likely to respond in different situations to plan how you can influence them to increase their support and mitigate potential negative impacts.

There are several classification models for stakeholder analysis, such as:

- Power/Interest Grid, which groups stakeholders based on their authority ("power") and interest ("interest") in project outcomes

- Power/influence grid, which groups stakeholders based on their authority ("power") and active involvement ("influence") in the project

- Influence/impact grid, which groups stakeholders based on their active involvement ("influence") in the project and their ability to effect change in project planning or implementation ("impact")

- Salience model that describes classes of stakeholders based on their power (ability to get their way), urgency (need for immediate attention), and legitimacy (their involvement is appropriate).

Expert judgment

To ensure comprehensive stakeholder identification and listing, the judgment and expertise of groups or individuals with specialized training or expertise should be sought, such as:

- Senior Management

- Other entities within the organization

- Identified key stakeholders

- Project managers who have worked on projects in the same area (directly or through experience)

- Subject matter experts (SMEs) in the business or project area

- Industry groups and consultants

- Professional and trade associations, regulatory bodies and non-governmental organizations (NGOs)

Expert judgments may be obtained through individual consultations (face-to-face meetings, interviews, etc.) or through a panel format (focus groups, surveys, etc.).

Meetings

Profile analysis meetings are project meetings designed to develop an understanding of key project stakeholders. They can be used to share and analyze information about each stakeholder's roles, interests, knowledge, and general position toward the project.

Identify Stakeholders: outputs

Stakeholder register

The most important outcome of the stakeholder identification process is the stakeholder register. This contains all the details of the identified stakeholders, including but not limited to:

- Identifying information. Name, organizational position, location, role in the project, contact information

- Assessment information. Key requirements, key expectations, potential impact on project, phase in life cycle of greatest interest

- Stakeholder classification. Internal/external, supporters/neutral/opponents, etc.

The stakeholder register should be consulted and updated regularly, as stakeholders may change - or new ones may be added - during the life cycle of the project.

Plan Stakeholder Management

Plan Stakeholder Management is the process of developing appropriate management strategies to effectively engage stakeholders throughout the project life cycle, based on analysis of their needs, interests, and potential impact on project success. The main benefit of this process is that it provides a clear, actionable plan for interacting with project stakeholders to support the interests of the project.

The Stakeholder Management plan identifies how the project will impact stakeholders. This allows the project manager to develop various ways to effectively engage stakeholders in the project, manage their expectations, and ultimately achieve the project goals. Stakeholder management is more than improving communication and requires more than managing a team. Stakeholder management is about building and maintaining relationships between the project team and stakeholders with the goal of meeting their respective needs and requirements within the project boundaries.

This process results in the stakeholder management plan, which contains detailed plans on how to implement effective stakeholder management. As the project progresses, the composition of the stakeholder community and the level of engagement required may change. Therefore, stakeholder management planning is an iterative process that is regularly reviewed by the project manager.

Plan Stakeholder Management: Inputs

Project Management Plan

The information used for the development of the stakeholder management plan includes, but is not limited to:

- Life cycle selected for the project and the processes that will be applied to each phase;

- Description of how work will be executed to accomplish the project objectives;

- Description of how human resources requirements will be met and how roles and responsibilities, reporting relationships, and staffing management will be addressed and structured for the project;

- Change management plan that documents how changes will be monitored and controlled; and

- Need and techniques for communication among stakeholders.

Stakeholder register

The stakeholder register provides the information needed to plan appropriate ways to engage project stakeholders.

Enterprise Environmental Factors

All factors of the corporate environment are used as inputs to this process, as stakeholder management should be adapted to the project environment. Of these factors, organizational culture, structure, and political climate are of particular importance as they help determine the best options to support a better stakeholder management adaptation process.

Organizational Process Assets

All organizational process assets are used as inputs to the Plan Stakeholder Management process. Of these, the accumulated experience database and historical information are of particular importance as they provide insight into previous stakeholder management plans and their effectiveness. These can be used to plan stakeholder management activities for the current project.

Plan Stakeholder Management: tools and techniques

Expert Judgment

Based on the project objectives, the project manager should apply expert judgment to decide upon the level of engagement required at each stage of the project from each stakeholder. For example, at the beginning of a project, it may be necessary for senior stakeholders to be highly engaged to clear away any obstacles to success. Once these have been successfully removed, it may be sufficient for senior stakeholders to change their level of engagement from leading to supportive, and other stakeholders, such as end users, may become more important.

To create the stakeholder management plan, judgment and expertise should be sought from groups or individuals with specialized training or subject matter expertise or insight into the relationships within the organization, such as:

• Senior management

• Project team members

• Other units or individuals within the organization

• Identified key stakeholders

• Project managers who have worked on projects in the same area (directly or through lessons learned)

• Subject matter experts in business or project area

• Industry groups and consultants

• Professional and technical associations, regulatory bodies, and nongovernmental organizations (NGOs).

Expert judgments can be obtained through individual consultations (one-on-one, interviews, etc.) or through a panel format (focus groups, surveys, etc.).

Meetings

Meetings should be held with experts and the project team to define the level of commitment required from all stakeholders. This information can be used to prepare the stakeholder management plan.

Analytical techniques

The current level of engagement of all stakeholders must be compared to the planned level of engagement required for successful project completion. Stakeholder engagement throughout the project lifecycle is critical to project success.

The level of stakeholder engagement can be classified as follows:

• unknown. Unaware of the project and its potential impact.

• resistant. Is aware of the project and potential impacts and resists change.

• neutral. Is aware of the project but neither supportive nor opposed.

• Supportive. Is aware of the project and its potential impact and is supportive of change.

• Leading. Is aware of the project and potential impact and actively advocates for the project to be a success.

Current engagement can be documented using the Stakeholder Engagement Assessment Matrix, where C indicates current engagement and D indicates desired engagement. The project team must determine the desired level of engagement for the current phase of the project based on available information.

Plan Stakeholder Management: output

Stakeholder Management Plan

The stakeholder management plan is a component of the project management plan and establishes the management strategies needed to effectively engage stakeholders. The stakeholder management plan can be formal or informal, very detailed or broad, depending on the needs of the project.

In addition to the data collected in the stakeholder register, the stakeholder management plan often includes other information:

- Desired and current level of involvement of key stakeholders

- The scope and impact of the changes on stakeholders

- Identified interrelationships and potential overlap among stakeholders

- Requirements for communication with stakeholders in the current project phase

- Information to be distributed to stakeholders, including language, format, content, and level of detail

- Reason for distributing this information and the expected impact on stakeholder engagement

- Timeframe and frequency for distributing the required information to stakeholders

- Method for updating and refining the stakeholder management plan as the project progresses and develops.

Project managers should be aware of the sensitive nature of the stakeholder management plan and take appropriate precautions. For example, information about stakeholders who oppose the project can be potentially damaging, and dissemination of such information should be well considered. When updating the stakeholder management plan, the underlying assumptions should be reviewed for validity to ensure that they remain accurate and relevant.

Project documents updates

Project documents that may be updated include:

• Project schedule

• Stakeholder register

Manage Stakeholder Engagement

Manage Stakeholder Engagement is the process of communicating and working with stakeholders to meet their needs/expectations, address issues that arise, and promote appropriate stakeholder participation in project activities throughout the project lifecycle. The main benefit of this process is that it enables the project manager to increase stakeholder support and minimize their resistance, thereby significantly increasing the chances of project success.

Managing stakeholder engagement includes activities such as:

- Engaging stakeholders at appropriate stages of the project to maintain or confirm their ongoing commitment to the success of the project

- Managing stakeholder expectations through negotiation and communication to ensure that project objectives are met

- Addressing potential concerns that have not yet become issues and anticipating future issues that may be raised by stakeholders. Such concerns must be identified and discussed as soon as possible to assess the associated project risks

- Clarify and resolve issues that have been identified.

Stakeholder engagement helps increase the likelihood of project success by ensuring that stakeholders clearly understand the project objectives, benefits, and risks. This allows them to actively support the project and guide activities and project decisions. By anticipating people's reactions to the project, you can take proactive measures to gain support or minimize negative impacts.

The ability of stakeholders to influence the project is usually greatest in the early stages and decreases as the project progresses. The project manager is responsible for engaging and managing the various stakeholders in a project and may call on the project sponsor for assistance as needed. Actively managing stakeholder engagement reduces the risk that the project will not achieve its goals.

Manage Stakeholder Engagement: Inputs

Stakeholder Management Plan

The stakeholder management plan provides guidance on how best to involve the various stakeholders in the project. The stakeholder management plan describes the methods and technologies that will be used to communicate with stakeholders.

This plan is used to determine the level of interaction between the various stakeholders and, along with other documents, to establish a strategy for identifying and managing stakeholders throughout the project life cycle.

Communications Management Plan

The Communications Management Plan provides guidance and information on managing stakeholder expectations. Information used includes, but is not limited to:

- Stakeholder communication requirements

- Information to be communicated, including language, format, content, and level of detail

- Reason for disseminating the information

- Person or groups to receive the information

- Escalation process

Change Log

A change log is used to document changes that occur during a project. These changes - and their impact on the project in terms of time, cost, and risk - are communicated to the appropriate stakeholders.

Organizational Process Assets

Organizational process assets that can influence the Manage Stakeholder Engagement process include:

- Organizational communication requirements

- Issue management procedures

- Change control procedures

- Historical information about previous projects

Manage Stakeholder Engagement: tools and techniques

Communication Methods

The communication methods identified in the communication management plan for each stakeholder are used in stakeholder engagement management. Based on the stakeholder communication requirements, the project manager decides how, when, and which of these communication methods to use in the project.

Interpersonal Skills

The project manager uses his or her interpersonal skills to meet stakeholder expectations. For example:

- Building trust,

- Resolving conflicts,

- Active listening, and

- Overcoming resistance to change.

Management Skills

The project manager uses his or her management skills to coordinate and harmonize the group to achieve project goals. For example:

- Facilitate consensus on project objectives

- Influence individuals to support the project

- Negotiate agreements to meet project requirements

- Change organizational behavior to accept project deliverables

Manage Stakeholder Engagement: outputs

Issue Log

Managing stakeholder engagement can lead to the creation of an issue report. This log is updated as new issues arise and current issues are resolved.

Change requests

Dealing with stakeholders may result in a change request for the product or project. It may also involve corrective or preventive action for the project itself or for interactions with affected stakeholders, whichever is appropriate

Project Management Plan updates

Among the elements of the project management plan that may be updated is the stakeholder management plan. This plan is updated when new or changed stakeholder requirements are identified. For example, some communication activities may no longer be necessary, an ineffective communication method may be replaced with another, or new communication needs may be identified. The plan is also updated to address concerns and resolve issues. For example, it may be determined that a stakeholder has additional information needs.

Project documents updates

Project documents that can be updated include the stakeholder register. This is updated when stakeholder information changes, when new stakeholders are identified, or when registered stakeholders are no longer involved in or affected by the project, or when other updates are required for specific stakeholders.

Organizational Process Assets updates

Organizational process assets that can be updated include:

- Stakeholder notifications. You can notify stakeholders of resolved issues, approved changes, and overall project status.

- Project reports. Formal and unofficial project reports describe project status and include lessons learned, issue logs, project completion reports, and results from other knowledge areas

- Project presentations. Information provided formally or informally by the project team to all project stakeholders.

- Project records. Project records include correspondence, memos, meeting minutes, and other documents describing the project.

- Stakeholder feedback. Information received from project stakeholders about project operations can be shared and used to modify or improve future project performance.

- Documentation of lessons learned. Documentation includes root cause analysis of issues encountered, rationale for corrective actions selected, and other types of lessons learned from stakeholder management. Lessons learned are documented and shared and become part of the historical database for both the project and the implementing organization.

Control Stakeholder Engagement

Stakeholder engagement oversight is about monitoring the project's overall stakeholder relationships and adjusting stakeholder engagement strategies and plans. The main benefit of this process is that it maintains or increases the efficiency and effectiveness of stakeholder engagement activities as the project evolves and its environment changes.

Control Stakeholder Engagement: Inputs

Project Management Plan

The project management plan is used to develop the stakeholder management plan. Information used to guide stakeholder engagement includes:

- The life cycle selected for the project and the processes that will be used at each stage

- How the work will be performed to achieve the project objectives

- How personnel requirements are met, how roles and responsibilities, reporting relationships, and personnel management are handled and structured for the project

- A change management plan that documents how changes will be monitored and controlled

- Requirements and techniques for communication between stakeholders

Issue Log

The problem log is updated as new problems are identified and current problems are resolved.

Work Performance data

The work performance data are the primary observations and measurements made during the activities to perform the project work. Various measurements of project activities and outcomes are collected during the various controlling processes. Data is often considered the lowest level of abstraction from which information is derived by other processes.

Examples of work performance data include reported percentage of work completed, technical performance metrics, start and end dates of scheduling activities, number of change requests, number of defects, actual cost, actual duration, etc.

Project documents

Several project documents that originate from initiation, planning, execution, or control processes can be used as supporting inputs for managing stakeholder engagement. These include, but are not limited to:

- Project schedule

- Stakeholder register

- Event log

- Change log

- Project communication

Control Stakeholder Engagement: tools and techniques

Information Management Systems

An information management system provides the project manager with a standard tool to capture, store, and share information with stakeholders about the project's cost, schedule, and performance. It also allows the project manager to consolidate reports from different systems and facilitate the distribution of reports to project stakeholders. Examples of distribution formats include spreadsheet reports, spreadsheets, and presentations. Graphical features allow you to create visual representations of project performance information.

Expert Judgment

To ensure comprehensive identification and listing of new stakeholders, a reassessment of current stakeholders can be made. You should solicit input from groups or individuals with specialized training or expertise, such as:

- Senior management

- Other departments or individuals within the organization

- Identified key stakeholders

- Project managers who have worked on projects in the same area (directly or through experience)

- Subject matter experts in the business or project area

- Industry groups and consultants

- Professional and trade associations, regulatory agencies, and nongovernmental organizations

Expert judgments may be obtained through individual consultations (e.g., face-to-face meetings or interviews) or through a panel format (e.g., focus groups or surveys).

Meetings

Status review meetings are used to exchange and analyze information about stakeholder engagement.

Control Stakeholder Engagement: outputs

Work Performance Information

Work performance information is performance data collected from various controlling processes, analyzed in context, and integrated based on cross-divisional relationships. In this way, work performance data has been transformed into work performance information. Data per se is not used in the decision-making process because its meaning could be misinterpreted. However, the information is correlated and contextualized, providing a solid basis for project decisions.

Work performance information is communicated through communication processes. Examples of performance information include status of deliverables, implementation status of change requests, and estimated completion.

Change requests

Analysis of project performance and stakeholder interaction often results in change requests. These change requests are handled by the Perform Integrated Change Control process as follows:

- Recommended corrective actions include changes that bring the expected future performance of the project in line with the project management plan

- Recommended preventive actions can reduce the likelihood of future negative project performance

Project Management Plan updates

As stakeholders engage with the project, the overall effectiveness of the stakeholder management strategy can be evaluated. If necessary changes in approach or strategy are identified, the affected sections of the project management plan may need to be updated to reflect those changes. Elements of the project management plan that may be updated include, but are not limited to, the following:

- Change Management Plan

- Communication management plan

- Cost management plan

- Human resources management plan

- Plan for procurement management

- Quality management plan

- Requirements management plan

- Risk management plan

- Schedule management plan

- Scope management plan

- Stakeholder management plan

Project documents updates

Project documents that may be updated include:

- Stakeholder Register. This is updated when stakeholder information changes, when new stakeholders are identified, when registered stakeholders are no longer involved in or affected by the project, or when other updates are required for specific stakeholders.

- Issue Log. This is updated as new issues are identified and existing issues are resolved.

Organizational Process Assets updates

Organizational process assets that can be updated include:

- Notifications for stakeholders. Information for stakeholders on resolved issues, approved changes, and overall project status can be provided

- Project reports. Formal and informal project reports describe project status and include lessons learned, issue logs, project completion reports, and results from other knowledge areas

- Project presentations. Information provided formally or informally by the project team to all project stakeholders

- Project records. Project records include correspondence, memos, meeting minutes, and other documents that describe the project

- Stakeholder feedback. Information received from stakeholders about project operations may be shared and used to modify or improve future performance of the project

- Documentation of lessons learned. Documentation includes root cause analysis of problems encountered, reasons for remedies selected, and other types of lessons learned from stakeholder management. Lessons learned are documented and shared so that they become part of the historical database for both the project and the implementing organization.

Agile Project Execution

AGILE PROJECT DELIVERY IS a type of adaptive project delivery that is frequently used in software development as an alternative to traditional approaches that focus on a sequential or linear process that begins with requirements gathering, planning, design, writing software code, testing, and implementation. Agile approaches, as opposed to sequential processes, stress iterative workflow and the gradual delivery of project outputs in short iterations (see "Value proposition of agile methods"). Extreme Programming (XP), Dynamic Systems Development Method (DSDM), Feature-Driven Development (FDD), Crystal, Lean Software Development, Agile Unified Process (AUP), and Scrum are some popular agile approaches.

Extreme Programming, for example, was created to successfully handle projects with changing requirements. XP depends on continuous integration rather than constructing huge, individually designed pieces. Iterations of one to three weeks are used in XP projects to create a fully tested project deliverable (usually in the form of a software release). These iterations encompass the creation, integration, and testing of a modest number of new features. A planning meeting is conducted at the start of each iteration to decide the topic of the iteration and to ease the inclusion of changing needs.

Communication, simplicity, feedback, and bravery are the four ideals that govern XP. These four beliefs serve as the foundation for 12 practices that instruct programmers on how to do their everyday tasks. Employing user stories in the planning phase, working on modest releases, introducing test-driven development, concentrating on simple design, using pair programming, assuming collective ownership for code, and guaranteeing continuous integration are some of the approaches.

DSDM, like XP, has critical elements such as user participation, iterative and incremental development, higher delivery frequency, integrated delivery frequency, integrated testing at every step, and requirements satisfaction.

FDD is also a feature-focused iterative and incremental software development approach (functions valued by the customer).

Scrum is another agile approach that is extensively utilized for project management. This chapter focuses on the Scrum framework's tools and procedures.

Value Proposition of Agile Methodologies

Many practitioners have unrealistic expectations about agile approaches, which may lead to conflict among stakeholders. It is incorrect to link agile methodologies with "faster and cheaper," since this leads to misunderstandings. Many clients believe that since they are utilizing an agile approach, they can request anything and the project team will provide it within two to four weeks; however, this is not totally accurate. Customers also seem to believe that their projects should be finished quicker and sooner than they would have been using a waterfall process, which is not always the case.

Agile approaches provide value by not being "faster." Delivering useable functionality to the client early in the project lifecycle adds genuine value. Any agile approach focuses on shorter work effort iterations to achieve project results that:

Allow for the achievement of business value sooner in the project lifecycle than traditional waterfall methodologies. Customers may be able to monetize projects sooner as a result of this.

Allowing clients to prioritize their tasks. There have been several instances when an agile project is 80 or 90 percent complete and clients determine that the product is enough as is and eliminate the last 10% of the criteria. Customers may still desire the last 10% of the criteria, but they may opt to postpone completing the original scope of work until later because there are other higher priority projects.

Allow clients to adjust requirements with minimal effect on cost and time in specific circumstances.

Reduce project risks by enabling clients to observe particular project progress. Customers will be able to completely grasp what is being supplied and be certain that what is being created meets their requirements.

Scrum Basics

The Scrum framework offers a structure for project teams to utilize throughout software development, including roles, meetings, rules, and artifacts. A project is split into self-organizing teams (scrums) of six to nine persons within this structure. Each team focuses on a certain area of work. A product backlog is a list of client desires and requirements that is used to build software. Scrum employs sprints, which are fixed-length iterations that generally span two to four weeks. Scrum teams are responsible for taking a collection of items from the backlog and generating a deployable set of features that has been thoroughly tested over a sprint. The team is given total autonomy to execute the sprint effectively. A daily Scrum meeting of around 15 minutes is planned each day to review the Sprint's progress, report on problems, and define next tasks. A customer demonstration is held at the conclusion of each sprint. The remaining features and new tasks are gathered, a new backlog is established, and a new sprint starts.

Scrum is an iterative technique that enables teams to produce a subset of high-value features as early as feasible in order to get early input from consumers. It is an alternative to conventional project approaches. The Scrum framework, in essence, promotes empirical feedback, team self-management, and an endeavor to create well-tested product increments in short iterations. Participants in the Scrum management system play various important responsibilities. These include the Product Owner, the Scrum Team, and the Scrum Master, among others.

The Product Owner represents the project's consumer. The product owner provides the team with customer-facing aspects (user stories) based on the product requirements, prioritizes the elements, and adds extra items to the product backlog. The Product Owner is in charge of assuring the commercial value of the project output. New products are not placed into production until the Product Owner has approved the Scrum team's output after the Sprint Demonstration.

Scrum teams are often comprised of six to nine individuals from various specialties.

At the conclusion of each sprint, these personnel are in charge of the analysis, design, development, testing, communication, and documentation of product increments. The team is normally self-organized, although for project reporting, there is some communication with project management.

A Scrum Master is in charge of eliminating roadblocks so that the team may complete the project deliverable. He or she is not in charge of the team. A Scrum Master enforces the rules to ensure that the Scrum process is followed correctly.

The sections that follow provide six tools and strategies for use in a project management toolbox that are often utilized in a Scrum management framework. The Product Backlog and Sprint Backlog, Release Planning, the Daily Scrum Meeting, the Sprint Task Board, the Sprint Burn Down Chart, and the Sprint Retrospective Meeting are all part of the Scrum process.

PRODUCT BACKLOG AND SPRINT BACKLOG

The Product Backlog and the Sprint Backlog are the two most popular forms of backlogs used in Scrum management. The Product Backlog is a prioritized list of all the components that may be created in the future. These things indicate the clients' needs. There is no timetable for assigning these tasks to a team to work on. Additionally, there is no certainty that these projects will ever be allocated to a team.

A Sprint Backlog is a collection of things from the Product Backlog that a Scrum team has committed to developing in the upcoming Sprint.

Information on the Backlogs

Every stakeholder has access to the Product Backlog, which is comprised of customer-facing features - descriptions of the desired product from the perspective of the customer or user. This may be accomplished via the use of user stories or use cases. These characteristics are also prioritized, resulting in an ordered list of essential competencies. The sequence of events, however, may change over time. There are no jobs in the Product Backlog.

A Sprint Backlog contains the tasks that will be accomplished during a Sprint, as well as the customer-facing functionality from the Product Backlog that is linked to those tasks. The tasks in the Sprint Backlog do not need to be prioritized since they have already been set for a certain Sprint version.

The Sprint Backlog is available to the project team and may be consulted during daily Scrum meetings.

Populating Backlogs

Any team member, regardless of job, has the ability to add things to the product backlog. The product backlog, on the other hand, is controlled by the product owner, who may assign priority to items or delete them from the backlog. As previously stated, the product backlog item (PBI) is often written in the form of a user narrative, with a focus on the "what" rather than the "how" of a customer-centric feature. For example, a narrative for a team working on a travel booking website may be: "As a user, I would want to sort flights by price so that I can view the cheapest ones first." The product owner assigns priorities to items in the product backlog. Well-written user stories will often adhere to the following standard structure.: As a <who>, I want to <what>, so that <why>.

The example given provides the 'who', 'what', and why of the story: As a user, I want to sort flights by price so that I can see the cheapest ones first.

It is critical that PBIs go through a refinement process, since some PBIs may be overly vast and poorly defined. To that aim, the team schedules a backlog refinement meeting, which may be used to separate and explain big PBIs, estimate the work required to finish the PBIs, and offer the technical knowledge needed to assist the product owner prioritize the PBIs. It is critical that each item in the backlog be given a priority, and that each priority be different. Priority should not be granted to two things at the same time. Each PBI may be connected with the team's expected effort to finish the item.

Sprint backlogs, on the other hand, must be finished at the sprint planning meeting, which will be described later. Teams look at the product backlog to discover issues to work on while generating a sprint backlog. The items with the greatest priority in the product backlog are added to the sprint backlog first. In certain circumstances, restrictions preclude a high-priority product from being included in the Sprint Backlog. These limitations might, for example, contain certain dependencies that must be satisfied before work can begin. As a result, the most important activities are not always included in the next Sprint Backlog. It is crucial to note, however, that the Sprint Backlog often comprises the highest priority items from the Product Backlog.

During Sprint planning sessions, the Sprint Backlog is produced. Everyone in the team, including the Product Owner and the Scrum Master, decides what will be worked on in the next Sprint. The team analyzes its capacity, development limits, and the importance of the items while generating the backlog.

Benefits

The Product Backlog ensures that project teams are working on the most critical things for providing business value, and that the business sees the most important items for delivering business value. The capacity to identify everything requested, as well as prioritize and reprioritize tasks as required, provides the firm with more strategic flexibility to solve the difficulties at hand.

Developing the sprint backlog requires commitment and participation from the business and project teams. As a consequence, all stakeholders have a common understanding of what the team must produce.

Both backlogs are straightforward to build and simple to read and comprehend for all stakeholders, but utilizing them might provide some early obstacles (see "Overcoming Initial Challenges"). When utilized effectively, backlogs, on the other hand, give a roadmap for how the team should achieve its overall project objectives.

Overcoming Initial Challenges

Challenge 1: The knowledge gap. Product owners may find it difficult to fully define the work, and they need the expertise of team members to define technical requirements, for example.

Challenge 2: Initial difficulty setting priorities. Product owners may initially find it difficult to prioritize the product backlog. However, once the product backlog is created, they find it easier to add new stories and adjust priorities accordingly.

RELEASE PLANNING

A release is a collection of sprints. Multiple Scrum teams are necessary for implementing complicated and big (business) systems. To make planning easier, teams often organize sprints into releases. The number of sprints in a release is set by the project organization, however it is normally between six and eight.

When numerous teams work together to build systems with interdependencies, release planning becomes a helpful strategy. When designing big systems, release planning provides project managers and other stakeholders with a clearer understanding of when future milestones are anticipated to be completed. Furthermore, release planning allows for cooperation across project teams, application teams, and other corporate stakeholders.

The Release-Planning Event

As is customary for major system development, release planning includes a wide range of stakeholders. All members of the concerned sprint teams, as well as project management and senior management, are often present. The tournament is generally held over two days. For the initial release, the release planning event occurs at the start of the release. The event takes occur at the conclusion of each succeeding release.

Before communication between dates can begin, each Scrum team must collaborate to generate a first draft of the release plan. This involves allocating items from the product backlog to sprints included in the release. For example, if a team is working on a five-sprint release, it would plan which Product Backlog pieces it would build in each of the following four sprints, taking dependencies and capacity into mind. The strategy would then be posted for everyone to view by the team (Figure 11.6). The last sprint is designated as HIP (hardening, innovation, and planning). During release planning, no Product Backlog items were anticipated for this sprint. HIP Sprints are discussed farther down in this section.

Attempting to schedule many sprints in advance has certain dangers. Priorities and objectives may change, and the work needed to develop solutions may be larger than anticipated. The release strategy includes time for contingencies to address these risks. This is accomplished by progressively lowering the scope of the release's scope for each sprint. The following is a popular approach for doing this. The number of Product Backlog items allotted to the first sprint in a six-week sprint is equivalent to 100 percent of the team's capability. The second sprint is given Product Backlog items that should use 80% of the team's capacity. The third sprint is given 60% of its capacity, while the fourth and fifth sprints are given 40% and 20%, respectively. As a consequence, the team is able to address certain longer-term business requirements while being adaptable to changes in scope and direction.

Final Release Plans

After all Scrum teams have completed their draft release plans, the plans are displayed either physically or online so that each Scrum team may see the release plans of the other teams. Teams are given time to go through each other's ideas. Teams discuss ideas and are encouraged to ask questions at this session to acquire a comprehensive grasp of what each team would want to focus on in the upcoming release. Each team member strives to discover interconnections between the scheduled tasks of the team during these conversations. Once the teams' dependencies are identified, the teams debate how to coordinate their actions. The draft release plans are then revised to reflect any modifications that are necessary.

After the clubs have updated their drafts, they are given time to go through the release plans again. The review and updating process will continue until all plans are judged to be appropriately integrated. Each member of each Scrum team is requested to commit to the plan before the release plans can be completed. If someone disagrees with one of the release plans for whatever reason, that person expresses their concerns, and the whole group considers whether or not adjustments should be made. The release strategy is not complete unless all stakeholders agree on it.

HIP Sprint

The last sprint of any release is the HIP sprint. This sprint allows teams to verify they are on stable ground for the next release. Hardening (H) refers to actions that decrease technical debt, such as system-wide performance testing, infrastructure upgrades, code alignment with architectural rules, and documentation updates. During the HIP sprint, innovation (I) is encouraged. This time may be used by agile teams to explore ideas that might help the system. The HIP sprint is also the time to start thinking about the next release (P). During this sprint, the release planning event for the next version takes place.

Release Planning versus Sprint Planning

It is critical to understand that release planning is not the same as sprint planning. The product owner and team have a sprint planning meeting at the start of each sprint to discuss and choose the product backlog items that the team will build to produce a functioning capability during the sprint. 14 Traditionally, two artifacts emerge from a Sprint Planning Meeting. The sprint objectives, which are defined by the team and reflect what the team hopes to achieve during the sprint, are the first artifact. The Sprint Backlog, which is the product of the Sprint Planning Meeting, is the second artifact.

As previously said, the product owner is in charge of describing the things that are most essential to consumers, while the team is in charge of determining the scope of work that they may perform. The team breaks down the chosen items into a first list of sprint tasks at the conclusion of the sprint planning meeting and makes the final commitment to complete the job.

While sprint planning is concerned with individual sprints, release planning is concerned with the entire release, which is made up of numerous sprints. Because the team has the ability to do so, it may elect to transfer portions of the product backlog to earlier releases for certain releases. It may also opt to rearrange the components or even reduce their importance and drop them. After identifying the dependencies during release planning, the team may communicate the modifications to the other teams.

Benefits

Scrum teams may plan certain longer-term tasks thanks to release planning. Release planning promotes team cooperation by allowing interdependence between teams to be detected early and accounted for in plans.

Successful release planning may help to integrate general corporate objectives with individual team goals.

Release planning is also useful for detecting cross-team dependencies that may stymie or delay execution progress. The possibility of unplanned delays during development is lowered by identifying dependencies early and taking them into account during release preparation.

THE DAILY SCRUM MEETING

A daily Scrum meeting is a brief meeting that begins immediately after the Sprint Planning meeting is concluded and agreed upon by the whole team (see Figure 11.7). A daily Scrum meeting's major goal is to address the following three questions:

1- What did you finish yesterday?

2- What barriers did I face that hindered me from becoming effective?

3- Finally, what plans do you have for today or before the next Scrum meeting?

By answering these questions, the team now gets a clear view of what is going on, how far the sprint has moved toward its objectives, and what modifications need to be made to the following day's work.

The Scrum team will utilize a sort of task board to discuss the Sprint's progress at the daily Scrum meeting. A task board is an excellent tool for displaying the current state of the sprint backlog across time.

Organizing a Daily Scrum Meeting

A daily Scrum meeting is often conducted at the same location and time each day. The meeting is most effective in the morning since it helps create objectives for the day ahead. During the meeting, each team member informs the team on what was achieved yesterday, what hurdles were faced, and what they intend to do today. The Scrum Master often begins the meeting with the person on his left and goes clockwise around the room until everyone has delivered their status report. Team members should concentrate on answering the three questions above in a clear way and avoid off-topic comments. It is normal for all team members to stand throughout the meeting since sitting tends to lengthen the meeting.

Participants

The whole Scrum team, as well as the Scrum Master, attend a daily Scrum meeting. The product owner is optional and does not have to attend every Scrum meeting. To have an effective daily Scrum meeting, all "participating" Scrum team members must be well prepared to immediately address the task they are responsible for accomplishing.

To prevent diversions from the agenda, it is critical that the Scrum Master conducts the meeting on time. Meetings that deviate from the agenda will most likely go over time, divert team members' attention away from answering their three questions, and even divert the group into side talks about critical concerns. When such distractions arise, the Scrum Master must bring the meeting back on course as soon as feasible.

Benefits

The key advantage of a daily Scrum meeting is that it allows each member of the Scrum team to communicate the status of their Sprint Backlog items while keeping the rest of the team updated on how things are going. Furthermore, a daily meeting allows the team to make minor course changes within each sprint as required.

A daily scrum is a proactive practice that assists self-organizing teams in improving over time by fostering trust among team members. Each meeting, like the sprint postmortem (covered later in the chapter), is built on the ideals of teamwork, empowerment, and cooperation through open discussion and transparency.

A daily Scrum meeting is another effective method for conveying information inside a team. The ability to grasp the large picture while limiting downstream risks is enabled by insight into each team member's scope of work.

Requirements for Effective Daily Scrum Meetings

1. Resources. A daily Scrum meeting necessitates the attendance of the whole Scrum team. If too many resources are spent to a daily meeting, the overall pace of a project might suffer if not handled effectively.

2. Preparation and concentration. Inadequate preparation for the daily Scrum meeting may have a substantial influence on the meeting's overall value. Team members should be prepared to answer the three most critical questions, and they should spend the time required after each meeting to resolve any gaps or concerns:

- What tasks were accomplished the day before?

- What work is being planned for today?

- Is the team experiencing any difficulties or obstacles?

- Time. A daily Scrum meeting must stay on schedule (15 minutes or less). If meetings are consistently running late, the Scrum Master should step in and ensure that each team member adheres to the agenda. This may be accomplished via talks after the Scrum meeting to resolve any issues that are causing the meeting to go beyond its authorized time.

SPRINT TASK BOARD

A Sprint Task Board is used in a Scrum team to classify tasks based on their degree of completion. Sticky notes with tasks are often used to graphically depict the work and progress in accomplishing the assignments. The task board is also known as the "Kanban board."

A task board could include four columns labeled "User Story," "Tasks to Complete," "Tasks in Progress," and "Tasks Completed." All tasks would be in the "Tasks To Do" column at the start of a sprint. When a team member begins working on a task, the task's sticky note is moved to the "Tasks In Progress" column. The sticky note gets moved to the "Tasks Performed" column after the job is completed. All tasks should be in the "Tasks Completed" column at the conclusion of a sprint.

Using the Sprint Task Board

Sprint Task Boards may have more than four columns. More significant columns may provide Sprint teams with a more accurate visual status. A task board may additionally contain columns labeled "Tasks to Complete," "In Design," "In Coding," and "In Test," as well as any other combination of columns indicating how tasks progress through the sprint lifecycle.

It is also a good idea to label sticky notes with task dependencies and the name of the team member working on the job when it is moved to a new column. When necessary, this enables communication and cooperation. The job "Display the prices on the screen in descending order from least to most costly" is a forerunner of "Query the price information from the temporary database, sorted by price." When the work started, Jeffrey Leach, who was in charge of the design, appended his name to it. When the design was finished, James Henry, the coder, appended his name to the assignment and crossed out the designer's name.

Benefits

The use of task boards makes the progress of the team obvious to everybody. It also helps with team collaboration, which may be difficult while working on a sequence of assignments. If the Sprint Job Board is utilized correctly, everyone should know who is assigned to each task, relationships between tasks should be properly accounted for, and no duplicate Effort should exist.

Furthermore, a Sprint Task Board is a plain and easy approach to manage the flow of work and information throughout a Sprint. It graphically depicts each team member's effort and progress throughout the course of a Sprint. Team members may now see what other team members are working on since the task board is now open to them.

THE SPRINT BURN DOWN CHART

In general, a sprint burn-down chart depicts the overall amount of work or tasks to be accomplished in relation to the time given to finish a sprint (or an entire release consisting of multiple sprints). The chart is a basic and easy-to-use tool that offers somewhat accurate estimations of a sprint's or release's overall progress. 18

The tasks must be broken down to the smallest detail before constructing a burndown chart. This is often done during the sprint planning phase, when each job is anticipated based on the number of hours required to finish the work. During the planning meeting, the full team normally determines these estimates.

Developing a Sprint Burn Down Chart

The Sprint Burn Down chart is simple, yet it is very useful to the team when utilized on a regular basis.

The x-axis in the figure reflects the time the team has allotted for the sprint (20 days in this example). The y-axis shows how long it will take the team (in hours or days) to finish all tasks for this sprint (120 hours in this example). The graph's main tendency is to reach a point where there are no more tasks as the number of activities to be accomplished diminishes over time. A trend line may be generated and drawn to show the potential results, i.e., when the task could be finished.

Using a Sprint Burn Down Chart

Each task manager updates a sprint burndown table on a daily basis. A number of ways may be used to collect and convey this information. A basic table contains tasks allocated to a user narrative, as well as their status, owner, projected hours, and remaining hours. In this scenario, after a full day of work on Job B, the business analyst (BA) has concluded that the task would take an extra five hours of labor to accomplish. BA then changes this information in the table's "Hours Remaining" column.

Following the completion of each job, the data for that day is compiled and presented to decide whether or not the sprint went as intended. If the "Actual Tasks Remaining" line is higher than the "Remaining Tasks Trend Line," the sprint is moving slower than predicted and may not complete the defined scope of work. If the "Actual Tasks Remaining" line is lower than the "Remaining Tasks Trend Line," the sprint is proceeding quicker than expected and may be finished ahead of time.

Benefits

The Sprint Burn Down Chart shows each team member the projected total time for all tasks to be done (hours or days) vs the time available to finish a sprint or release. This enables team members to actively estimate the amount of time required to perform each of their duties. The data is then consolidated so that team members can assess if they are accomplishing too little or too much throughout the sprint or release.

The graphic also offers value by informing the whole team of the sprint or release's overall progress. If the project starts to stray favorably or adversely from the trend line, the team will be able to use this knowledge to mitigate future risks. The chart promotes effective communication throughout the team in a transparent manner for all team members during this process.

Finally, a sprint burn down chart enables team members to make informed choices based on correct facts.

THE SPRINT RETROSPECTIVE MEETING

A Sprint Retrospective Meeting is normally held after the Sprint Review Meeting and is the last phase in the Sprint Life Cycle. Following the completion of the Sprint Retrospective Meeting, a new Sprint is formed, beginning with a Sprint Planning Meeting, followed by daily Scrums, a Sprint Review Meeting, and another Sprint Retrospective Meeting. The primary purpose of a Sprint Retrospective Meeting is to facilitate a dialogue that enables the Scrum team to assess and discuss the whole Sprint lifecycle in order to enhance the overall process. The gathering is built on the idea of continuous development. A retrospective meeting is performed at the conclusion of each sprint to assess and discuss everything that went well, as well as everything that did not go so well.

The Scrum team might review current procedures, technology, cooperation, communication tactics, and so on during this meeting. Following the completion of the sprint retrospective, the Scrum team carefully identifies the areas of interest for process improvement and schedules them for the following sprint.

Organizing a Sprint Retrospective Meeting

At the conclusion of each sprint cycle, an effective sprint retrospective meeting takes the time needed to properly discuss and record the sprint retrospective agenda. A sprint retrospective meeting typically lasts approximately an hour and a half, however it may take longer in many circumstances depending on the duration of the sprint, the complexity of the project, the size of the team, or the team's general expertise with Scrum methodologies.

Participants

All members of the Scrum team, including the Scrum Master, are normally present during a sprint retrospective. It is vital for an effective meeting that all team members engaged feel at ease and secure in their surroundings while giving comments and proposals to enhance the process. Because of their possible decision-making authority (or influence) over the other team members, the product owner is usually the sole person who does not participate in the sprint retrospective, preventing the team from being honest and transparent. Inadequacies in the process may continue to effect subsequent Sprints as a consequence of a lack of open and honest dialogue.

Using a Sprint Retrospective Meeting

The purpose of a sprint retrospective, as previously said, is to assess what went well and what may be improved. This process of acquiring information may be carried out in a variety of ways. Visual learning is an excellent tool for assisting the Scrum Master in facilitating team communication. A basic whiteboard, for example, may be separated into three sections: good, terrible, and new. Items that are good would suggest regions that performed well throughout the sprint and do not need modifications. Limiting daily sprint standup meetings to 15 minutes or continuing to utilize bespoke client-side queries are examples of this. Bad points, on the other hand, are places that do not function well and contribute to process flaws. Clarifying the phrase "finished" or "done" so that team members understand it, dividing the product backlog into smaller components during the refinement phase, or shifting the daily scrum meeting from 9:00 a.m. to 8:30 a.m. are some examples.

Finally, the new items would concentrate on areas that had yet to be specified or were absent from the overall process. Setting up a knowledge management system to inventory agenda items that do not fit under the daily Scrum meeting, for example, or installing a video conferencing solution in the Scrum room for external team members to boost cooperation and communication are two examples.

When acquiring and classifying information, a Scrum team might use a variety of strategies. For example, each team member may be given sticky notes with a color scheme (green = good, red = terrible, and yellow = new). Each team member would then fill up as many sticky notes as they needed to explain their ideas. When finished, each team member puts their sticky notes in a box, which the Scrum Master places on the whiteboard in the relevant columns. Using a box guarantees that all suggestions are anonymous and free of judgment, allowing team members to make recommendations in a secure setting.

Selecting Improvement Areas

The team must now use a whiteboard to identify which areas of improvement they wish to include in the forthcoming sprint. Giving each team member a few stars (3 to 5) to put on the things they believe will have the biggest influence on the project is a common strategy. If a team member is passionate about a certain topic, they may focus all of their stars on that topic or distribute their stars over numerous topics. After collecting all of the votes, the team would tally the results to determine which things garnered the most votes. The meeting's outcomes are then queued for the Product Backlog meeting, during which the Scrum Master, Scrum Team, and Product Owner decide which issues are most critical and should be handled in the next Sprint.

Benefits

The key advantage of a sprint retrospective is that it gives the Scrum team a specified time after each sprint to offer input on areas they feel may be improved. Throughout the project lifetime, continuous improvement is vital to the overall integrity and foundation of the project. Neglecting continual process improvement will allow projects to repeat previous errors, reducing total project efficiency significantly.

Furthermore, a Sprint Retrospective Meeting is founded on the ideals of cooperation, empowerment, and collaboration via open discussion and transparency. As a result of their opinions and ideas being heard and considered throughout the project, every team member might be won over to the project.

Things to Avoid

1- Inadequate planning. Poor preparation for a sprint retrospective will almost probably reduce the meeting's total usefulness. This includes a non-structured agenda, a paucity of supplies (post-its, pencils, whiteboard), and even technology challenges that were not anticipated in the sprint retrospective environment.

2- Complicatedness. As previously said, a sprint retrospective may be fairly straightforward at times; but, when certain dynamics get too complicated, the utility of a sprint retrospective can soon disappear. Examples include the number of meeting attendees and the requirement to manage the importance of proposals from previous sessions (the backlog). Due to the political realities of a project, determining the backlog items with the greatest value to the project and the team may be challenging at times.

Bonuses DOWNLOAD Link- https://payhip.com/b/3zEYJ

Should you have any trouble or for any inquiries you can contact me here ytcreativemarket@gmail.com

All the best Alex

Made in the USA
Las Vegas, NV
14 November 2023

80771342R00105